Perspectives on American Labor History

Perspectives on

American
LABOR
History
The Problems of Synthesis

Edited by

J. Carroll Moody and Alice Kessler-Harris

Northern Illinois University Press
DeKalb, 1990

© 1990 by Northern Illinois University Press
Published by the Northern Illinois University Press, DeKalb, Illinois 60115
Manufactured in the United States of America
Design by Julia Fauci

Library of Congress Cataloging-in-Publication Data
Perspectives on American labor history : the problems of synthesis /
edited by J. Carroll Moody and Alice Kessler-Harris.
p.   cm.
Based on papers from a conference held at Northern Illinois
University in the fall of 1984.
Bibliography: p.
Includes index.
ISBN 0-87580-551-5 (pbk.)
1. Working class—United States—Historiography—Congresses.
I. Moody, J. Carroll, 1934–   . II. Kessler-Harris, Alice.
HD8066.P48   1989
305.5'62'0973—dc20   89–3443
CIP

For Herbert G. Gutman
in Appreciation

Contents

· J. CARROLL MOODY ·

Introduction

The essays in this volume are intended to be contributions toward a new synthesis of American working class history. They stem from a conference held at Northern Illinois University in the fall of 1984, which attracted some seventy scholars from the United States and abroad. The conference bore the ambitious, perhaps idealistic, title, "The Future of American Labor History: Toward A Synthesis," a theme that reflected at least three interrelated concerns increasingly expressed by scholars.

First, during the preceding two decades, the quantity and direction of scholarship dealing with myriad aspects of working peoples' lives expanded greatly. The historiographical dimensions of what many call the "new labor history" are well-known.[1] Often explicitly, usually implicitly, the first generation of new "labor" historians rejected the economism and institutional framework that dominated the writing of labor history since the turn of the century.[2] Instead, they sought to re-create the experiences of working people in their private lives, workplaces, and communities. Along with colleagues in other areas of social history, labor historians brought to center stage the history of the "inarticulate," the "subordinate," or "ordinary people," by doing history "from the bottom up."[3] Some employed quantitative methods of research and analysis, others borrowed anthropological and sociological theories, and many were inspired by the sophisticated Marxist scholarship of British historians such as Edward P. Thompson and Eric Hobsbawm. "To a significant extent," writes Leon Fink, "labor history has thus become one of the mainsprings within the larger field of social history; indeed, some practitioners now prefer to identify themselves as 'working-class social historians'."[4] The pioneer works prefiguring these developments prompted the notable Anglo-American labor history conference at Rutgers University in 1973. That gathering of scholars marked, according to Eric Foner, the emergence of labor history "from the history of organized labor to the history of the working class."[5] Thus, over a decade later, there appeared ample reason to take stock of what we had, or had not, learned and what we ought to be trying to find out.

Beyond these largely empirical concerns, a second objective of the conference was to assess the methodological and theoretical approaches that underlay recent working-class history. Clearly the works of Herbert Gutman, David Brody, and David Montgomery, especially if measured by acknowledgments in dissertations, articles, and books, provided a new generation of historians with inspiration and examples of new and fruitful ways in which to investigate the role of the working class in American history. These three creative scholars formed, in the words of Leon Fink, "a kind of informal triumvirate giving coherence and direction to the discipline."[6] Gutman's early articles, based upon his doctoral thesis, explored the community-based actions of workers during strikes and their support by other classes in smaller industrial towns. As significant as his demonstration of interclass attitudes toward industrial capitalism's disruption of more traditional local social values, Gutman's focus on the *community* as the real arena for investigating working-class values, activities, and class relations prompted many other scholars to provide studies of structure and change from Newburyport and Lynn to Omaha and Birmingham. Although some were preoccupied with the issue of working-class occupational and "property" mobility, the best of the studies explore changing social relations in communities where developing capitalist industrialization was altering traditional ways of life. Workers' experiences on the job, as well as in their families, leisure activities, and social and religious organizations added new and important dimensions to American history.

Gutman's greatest impact on a whole generation of labor historians, however, lay in his investigation of a working-class culture that rejected bourgeois society's ideology of possessive individualism and provided a "moral" basis for resistance to the "modernizing" efforts of employers and their allies to impose industrial discipline in the workplace and the community. His most extended discussion of this "culturalist" approach appeared in 1973 as "Work, Culture and Society in Industrializing America," in which Gutman acknowledged the influence of such British historians as E. P. Thompson, Eric Hobsbawm, and Sidney Pollard, and anthropologists Clifford Geertz, Sidney Mintz, and Eric Wolf.[7] In particular, Gutman followed Thompson's model employed in *The Making of the English Working*

Class by investigating the "preindustrial" customs, traditions, and values that people brought to a society as it industrialized. Instructive as the British experience was, however, America was different. Unlike England, with its relatively homogeneous population, where the social transformation that "made" the working class occurred during a protracted yet finite period, in the United States recurrent waves of migration and immigration brought "preindustrial cultural values" into a society while it was industrializing and after it had become industrialized. This "recurrence in different periods of time indicates why there has been so much discontinuity in American labor and social history," Gutman concluded, although "the changing composition of the working population, the continued entry into the United States of nonindustrial people with distinctive cultures, and the changing structure of American society have combined together to produce common modes of thought and patterns of behavior." Thus, Gutman posited an American class consciousness based upon political republicanism, evangelical religion, a mechanic-producer ideology, and ethnic subcultural ideas of a community in which traditional notions of work, cooperation, and reciprocity clashed with "modernizing" norms of atomized *homo economicus*, adrift in the labor market and subject to industrial discipline at work and in their communities. This working-class culture, as Gutman called it, caused the preindustrial native-born mechanics and farm folk, as well as successive groups of immigrants, to resist authority through workplace actions, demonstrations, boycotts, and strikes.[8]

The tremendous influence of Gutman on many scholars, however, did not produce a uniformity of method or approach in labor history. David Brody's *Steelworkers in America: The Nonunion Era*, published in 1960, indicated one of the directions labor history would take in succeeding years.[9] Brody prefaced his exemplary study by stating that although he was writing "labor history," his approach was "somewhat out of the ordinary. The steelworkers themselves have been the focus, not one or another of the institutions or events of which they were a part. My aim has been to study the process by which their working lives in America's steel mills were shaped in the nonunion era of the industry." Brody expanded the traditional boundaries of labor history by examining the dialectical relationship between labor policies of corporations, under both competitive and monopoly capitalism, and workers in the steel mills. Although he gave full attention to the topics most characteristic of traditional labor history—organizing drives, unions, strikes—he presaged later historians' preoccupation with the roles of the largely native-born skilled workers and the immigrant unskilled workers and their communities. Brody's essays later collected in *Workers in Industrial America* set an interpretive standard for historians investigating twentieth century labor history.[10] Unlike the many historians who studied class formation through a culturalist approach, Brody focuses on class development through the prism of economic structure, managerial policy, trade union practices, and the role of the state.

David Montgomery's early essays showed the strong influence of E. P. Thompson, but in his seminal work, *Beyond Equality: Labor and the Radical Republicans, 1862–1872,* he placed workers and their organizations firmly within the great national political debate over the nature and future of American society.[11] Montgomery demonstrates that the bourgeois republicanism of the Radicals, which posited legal and political equality for all citizens within a socially harmonious developing industrial capitalism, clashed head-on with working-class notions of republican equality. Trade unions, reform associations, labor parties, and the International Workingmen's Association combined "to improve the social and economic plight of the working classes" through organization, strikes, and legislative efforts to secure shorter hours and monetary reform. As important a revision of political and labor history as *Beyond Equality* proved to be, the hallmark of Montgomery's scholarship was his focus on the shop floor as the arena for investigating class development and conflict.[12] Montgomery emphasized the role of skilled workers in the struggle to control the workplace in the face of "illegitimate" impositions of technological and managerial work rules from above. Stemming from their position as autonomous craftsmen, as managerial control tightened, skilled workers maintained their solidarity by transferring traditional practices to union work rules and later by engaging in sympathy strikes to maintain or recapture their control of the shop floor.

A focus on the work of Herbert Gutman, David Brody, and David Montgomery, of course, does not do justice either to those who have been influenced by their approaches or those who have followed very different paths in their scholarship. Moreover, fine studies of twentieth century union organizations and struggles more in the tradition of the Commons school have greatly enriched our knowledge of the experiences of the American working class, to say nothing of the diverse works in social history that have illuminated aspects of working-class experience. What is clear is that despite criticisms that some sort of Thompsonian orthodoxy had replaced the old Commons school approach, labor history from the late 1960s into the 1980s was characterized by the diversity of its subjects, approaches, and conclusions.[13]

Indeed, this very diversity led to the third objective of the conference, which proposed to address a growing concern to move toward a synthesis of American history as a whole, incorporating the accomplishments of working-class and other social historians. At the beginning of the decade, Herbert Gutman wrote that "We know more about the American past as we enter the 1980s than we did when we entered the 1960s." At the same time, however, Gutman lamented the failure of scholars to integrate the rich scholarship in social history into a new synthesis of American history. "At its best," he wrote, "this new history revised important segments of the national experience."[14] Eric Foner echoed Gutman's concern when he wrote that "what is disturbing is that, despite the wealth of recent material, no new synthesis has emerged to fill the void" left by the shattering of older interpretations of the American past.[15]

It became apparent, however, that a new synthetic national history encompassing the experiences and the role of the working class and other subordinate groups would benefit from, if not require, new syntheses in the several subfields of social history, perhaps a new synthetic social history as a whole. During the 1970s the preoccupation of younger historians with those Americans typically neglected by historians seemed to portend progress toward meeting Eric Hobsbawm's challenge to move "from social history to the history of society."[16] Indeed, as Michael Kammen noted, "what is called 'the new social history' may very well qualify as the cynosure of historical scholarship in the United States during the 1970s." Yet, no new "history of society" emerged from the prolific output of those scholars who added tremendously to knowledge about the lives of blacks, immigrants, and women in their families, workplaces, and communities.[17] Instead, as James Henretta observed, "The 'new social history' in the United States does not resemble a coherent subdiscipline but rather a congeries of groups—cliometricians, interdisciplinary social theorists, and critically minded social democrats—with the complementary and sometimes contradictory approaches to historical scholarship." Henretta proposed an "'action model' designed to discover and depict history as it was lived by men and women in the past." He would have social historians utilize the "quantitative techniques and structural approaches of *Annalistes*, Marxists, and social scientific historians . . . to delineate the objective character of the society and to determine its hierarchical systems," and place their work within "a narrative, chronological framework of organization [which would facilitate] the presentation of the world-views of the actors themselves."[18]

With much less dispassion, Eugene Genovese and Elizabeth Fox-Genovese wrote a polemical attack on much of the methods and assumptions of contemporary American social history. "To speak bluntly," they wrote, "as admirable as much of the recent social history has been and as valuable as much of the description of the life of the lower classes may eventually prove, the subject as a whole is steadily sinking into a neoantiquarian swamp." They sharply criticized the use to which many social historians put anthropology, sociology, ethnography, and quantification. They found that concentration by social historians on the private spheres in the lives of the lower classes—their culture and customs—too often leads to the conclusion that those classes enjoyed an "autonomous culture," which allowed them to "resist successfully and totally the values and aspirations of the bourgeoisie." Such a conclusion, argued the Genoveses, neglects "a reciprocal influence with their oppressors," "the possibility for appreciating their tragic complicity in their own oppression—a complicity that may be judged tragic precisely because they are led to it by worthy motives within a complex social system that successfully directs their anger and resistance into safe channels." Thus, much of the new social history was "history with the politics left out." In short, they argued, "History, when it transcends chronicle, romance, and ideology—including 'left-wing' versions—is primarily the story of who rides whom and how."[19]

Such criticism of some social history (which included working-class history) obviously affected the discussion at the conference. If a new history of society were to be written, class relations must be central, one line of argument ran. How, then, could the "new labor history," itself fragmented by assumptions, approach, methods, and geographical focus be integrated into a new national history? Several historians of the working class had earlier called for a new synthesis of American labor history. As early as 1978, David Brody raised the question, "As all this research accumulates, we are going to have to start asking ourselves: what does it add up to?" Adherents of the Commons school had little problem with how their research fit into a general synthesis, since the trade union *was* the institutional embodiment of working-class interests, if not ideology. Brody observed that current work in labor history posed great problems in constructing a new synthesis: first, the narrow and local focus of research; and second, the "acute sense of the complexity and variety of working-class experience, in which all lines of inquiry—family, ethnicity, mobility, technology and so on—converge into an intricate web of connections." Although the new generation of American labor historians, in their enthusiasm for Edward Thompson's *The Making of the English Working Class*, believed they had a model for achieving a similar result for the American working class, Brody argued, in effect, that England was not America. Similarly, he rejected Gutman's application of "a Thompsonian perspective" as a synthesizing model because his cultural emphasis focused on "a narrow band of working-class experience," in which class is "wholly jettisoned." The requirements for a new synthesis of American labor history, Brody asserted, were "first, defining the common ground applying to all American workers; second, providing an element of continuity running from the opening chapter to the present; and third, encompassing the dynamic forces shaping the experience of American workers." He concluded that "those requirements can best be met by an economic approach, one that takes as its starting point, not culture, but work and the job, and broadens out from there."[20]

David Montgomery, who like Brody had expanded the frontiers of knowledge about the American working class through his own research, made a major contribution toward an analytical framework for any new synthesis of American labor history, if not for American history generally. In an essay, "To Study the People," he assessed the state of scholarship in labor history within the context of "three subjects of critical importance for anyone who wishes to understand American social and political development during the last 150 years, and on which some light has been shed by historians of this country's working class." According to Montgomery, those subjects are "1) the social relations peculiar to industrial production, 2) the changing and conflicting forms of social consciousness created by people in their efforts to cope with those relationships, and 3) the impact of workers' consciousness and activities on the rest of society." Any synthesis of American labor history, likewise, must employ and integrate knowledge about each of those subjects "through a conception of social change, which enables us to identify the basic characteristics which have distinguished one epoch in the workers' experience from another." Montgomery concluded that "The time is now ripe to address ourselves to that task."[21]

These were the issues and challenges that brought together in DeKalb labor, social, and political historians, sociologists, and economists from fifty-three institutions in the United States, Canada, England, Australia, Germany, and Italy. In order to provide a focused basis for the three days of discussion, conference organizers commissioned six papers. Three dealt with the social categories of race, gender, and class that are crucial to the work of labor and social historians and should be of major concern to historians generally. William Harris, Mari Jo Buhle, and Michael Reich agreed to prepare interpretative, theoretical essays that raised for historians the important questions that flowed from recent scholarship in each of these fields and that should inform future scholarship in labor history. Three other scholars produced interpretive essays suggesting how a synthesis of American working-class history might be approached for particular periods. Sean Wilentz outlined elements of the formation of the American working class in the late eighteenth and early nineteenth centuries; Leon Fink discussed the issues of class, culture, and ideology in the late nineteenth century; and Alan Dawley addressed labor, capital, and the state in the twentieth century. Finally, the organizers selected six from among seventy proposals submitted by historians to provide examples of "new scholarship" attempting to integrate labor history with other fields.

Discussion of these papers and the broader issues they raised was spirited and wide ranging. Early on, however, those discussions revealed that there was little likelihood that participants could reach any consensus about how the goal of synthesis could be obtained, primarily because there were such differences over *what* a synthesis would encompass. Instead of continuing to pursue that apparently elusive goal, the conference settled on attempting to establish a new agenda for labor history. Participants who specialize in black, women's, and ethnic history emphasized the need to integrate their findings into labor history, but specifically how that should be done remained a subject of controversy. Scholars whose research focused on the South criticized the preoccupation of most historians with the experiences of northern workers. Others emphasized that labor historians must examine the relationship of workers to the middle class and farmers, and to the development of capitalist society as a whole. Some participants expressed concern, however, that if every aspect of the American past became the subject of labor history, the discipline would lose its unique identity. Finally, implicit in most of the discussion was the question of whether the cultural approach to working-class history had run its course and, if so, should renewed emphasis be placed on shop floor experiences, the social relations of production, and economic and political organization. Although many participants denied that a new approach was needed, particularly if it meant a return to the early emphasis of the Commons school, it appeared that many others, if not most, believed that labor history, for all its recent accomplishments, was a discipline in transition. With such divergent views, it remained unclear where labor history was or should be going.[22]

The initial announcements about the DeKalb conference resulted in requests to participate that greatly exceeded expectations. Since the conference had been planned and supported by the National Endowment for the Humanities as a "research conference," the organizers believed that the number of participants should be limited in order to allow full and vigorous discussion in plenary sessions without the kind of restraints often necessary when larger gatherings of scholars are held. Many persons who could have contributed to or benefited from the conference, therefore, could not be accommodated, and many others expressed the hope that some or all the papers would be published in the future. We hope that this volume of essays meets those expectations and reaches the broader scholarly community as well.

This volume includes only the conference essays that dealt with the themes of synthesis. Of these, one, that by William Harris, was not available. The five remaining essays have been revised, some very extensively, by the authors in light of discussions at the conference and subsequent commentary by other scholars. Together these essays speculate about the possible ways of integrating class relations, the state, and a shifting economic structure into labor history. And they suggest some intriguing forms of analysis that should open paths toward the project of rethinking the American past.

Two essays reflecting on the themes of the conference complete this volume. David Brody provides some thoughts about the problems involved in effecting a synthesis in American labor history and assesses the contributions of the other essays toward their solution. Alice Kessler-Harris offers her reflections on the conference, the field of labor history as a whole, and suggests "what some of the difficulties of achieving a synthesis, or an interpretive framework, might be." She then proposes "a way of thinking about the past, through gender, that might cast some new light on conceiving American history as a whole."

We have incurred a number of debts to the many persons who contributed to the conference and, through it, to this volume. Alfred Young served with me as codirector of the conference, and he continued thereafter to shape this volume of essays. David Brody, Herbert Gutman, Alice Kessler-Harris, and David Montgomery provided immeasurable insights and suggestions to the conference directors from the earliest stages of planning through the conference itself.[23]

The scholars who attended the conference were active and vigorous participants in discussions of the papers and the broader issues they raised. Their contributions are acknowledged by listing their names at the end of this volume. Some participants deserve particular recognition and gratitude for their extraordinary contributions. Thomas Dublin, Jacquelyn Hall, Dirk Hoerder, Steven Meyer, Shelton Stromquist, and Barbara Tucker presented the "new research" papers. Melvyn Dubofsky, Eric Foner, David Montgomery, and Gary Nash served, along with Alice Kessler-Harris, as moderators of the rather free-wheeling discussions. Eric Hobsbawm in his own inimitable way concluded the proceedings with his reflections on our discussions. Finally, we are also grateful to those who provided the funds to bring together such a superb group of scholars from across the country and overseas. The Department of History, the College of Liberal Arts and Sciences, the College of Continuing Education, the Graduate School, and the president of Northern Illinois University provided funds and other support. The conference would not have been possible without a grant from the National Endowment for the Humanities. We are grateful to all who played any part in the success of this endeavor.

NOTES

1. Early discussions of the new directions in American labor history can be found in Paul Faler, "Working Class Historiography," *Radical America* 3 (1969): 57–68; Thomas A. Krueger, "American Labor Historiography, Old and New: A Review Essay," *Journal of Social History* 4 (1971): 277–85; and Robert Zieger, "Workers and Scholars: Recent Trends in American Labor Historiography," *Labor History* 13 (1972): 245–66. For more recent accounts, see David Brody, "The Old Labor History and the New," *Labor History* 20 (1979): 111–26; David Montgomery, "To Study the People: The American Working Class," *Labor History* 21 (1980): 485–512; Leon Fink, "Industrial America's Rank and File: Recent Trends in American Labor History," in Matthew T. Downey, ed., *Teaching American History: New*

Directions, Sponsored by the Special Interest Group for History Teachers, National Council for the Social Studies, Bulletin No. 67 (Washington, DC, 1982), pp. 73–82; and Ronald W. Schatz, "Labor Historians, Labor Economics, and the Question of Synthesis," *Journal of American History* 71 (June 1984): 93–100.

2. For an assessment of the first generation approach to labor history, see Paul J. McNulty, "Labor Problems and Labor Economics: The Roots of an Academic Discipline," *Labor History* 9 (1968): 239–61. See also John H. M. Laslett, "The American Tradition of Labor Theory and Its Relevance to the Contemporary Working Class," in Irving Louis Horowitz et al., eds., *The American Working Class: Prospects for the 1980s*, pp. 3–30 (New Brunswick, NJ, 1979); and Walter Licht, "Labor Economics and the Labor Historian," *International Labor and Working Class History* 21 (Spring 1982): 52–62.

3. For example, see Jesse Lemisch, "The American Revolution Seen from the Bottom Up," in Barton J. Bernstein, ed., *Towards a New Past: Dissenting Essays in American History* (New York, 1968).

4. "Industrial America's Rank and File," p. 73.

5. "Labor Historians Seek Useful Past," *In These Times* (December 12–18, 1984), p. 11.

6. "Industrial America's Rank and File," p. 77.

7. *The American Historical Review* 78 (June 1973): 531–88. This essay is also reprinted in a volume with the same title that contains several of Gutman's previous essays.

8. For a sympathetic, yet critical, assessment of Gutman's contributions to working-class history, see David Montgomery, "Gutman's Nineteenth-Century America," *Labor History* 19 (1978): 416–29. An assessment of Gutman's intellectual odyssey is provided by Ira Berlin's sensitive introduction, "Herbert G. Gutman and the American Working Class," to *Power and Culture: Essays on the American Working Class* (New York, 1987). This collection of Gutman's essays, published after his death and edited by Berlin, contains both previously published and unpublished works. Readers unfamiliar with Gutman's thought and work may be particularly interested in the lengthy interview with him, previously published by MARHO in *Visions of History* (New York, 1976), and a complete bibliography of his published works.

9. Cambridge, MA, 1960.

10. New York, 1980.

11. New York, 1967. See also "The Working Classes of the Pre-Industrial American City, 1780–1830," *Labor History* 9 (Winter 1968): 2–23; and "The Shuttle and the Cross: Weavers and Artisans in the Kensington Riots of 1844," *Journal of Social History* 5 (Summer 1972): 411–46.

12. See especially his *Workers' Control in America: Studies in the History of Work, Technology, and Labor Struggles* (New York, 1979).

13. The number of books and articles in the field published since the late 1960s is remarkable. A mere selective listing of representative works not only would consume many pages but also slight many important contributions. Readers unfamiliar with works in labor history are referred to the review essays listed in note 1, as well as the journals *Labor History* and *International Labor and Working Class History*. A good survey of the findings of labor historians dealing with one period

and with his own evaluations of those works is Melvyn Dubofsky's *Industrialism and the American Worker, 1865–1920* (Arlington Heights, IL, 1985).

14. "Whatever Happened to History?" *The Nation* 233 (November 21, 1981), pp. 522–54.

15. "History in Crisis," *Commonweal* (December 18, 1981), p. 724.

16. *Daedalus* 100 (1971), pp. 20–45.

17. *The Past before Us: Contemporary Historical Writing in the United States* (Ithaca, NY, 1980), p. 34.

18. "Social History as Lived and Written," *American Historical Review* 84 (December 1979): 1295, 1321–22. Also see the comments in the same edition by Darrett B. Rutman and Robert F. Berkhofer, Jr., with Henretta's reply (pp. 1323–33).

19. "The Political Crisis of Social History: A Marxian Perspective," *Journal of Social History* 10 (Winter 1976): 205–20. A slightly revised version is included in their *Fruits of Merchant Capitalism: Slavery and Bourgeois Property in the Rise and Expansion of Capitalism* (New York, 1983). Equally polemical is Lawrence T. McDonnell, "'You Are Too Sentimental': Problems and Suggestions for a New Labor History," *Journal of Social History* 17 (Summer 1984): 629–54.

20. "The Old Labor History and the New: In Search of an American Working Class," *Labor History* 20 (Winter 1979): 111–26; reprinted in Daniel J. Leab, *The Labor History Reader* (Urbana, IL, 1985), pp. 1–16. See also the critical comment of James O. Morris, ibid., pp. 17–26, and Brody's response, pp. 26–27.

21. *Labor History* 21 (Fall 1980): 485. See the response by Robert Ozanne, "Trends in American Labor History," ibid., pp. 513–21. Montgomery has recently accepted his own challenge in his marvelous new book, *The Fall of the House of Labor: The Workplace, the State, and American Labor Activism, 1865–1925* (Cambridge, 1987). For an assessment of his accomplishment, see the discussions by Ruth Milkman, Staughton Lynd, and Alan Dawley in "David Montgomery's *The Fall of the House of Labor:* A Roundtable Symposium" in *Radical History Review* 40 (Winter 1988): 89–114.

22. Published assessments of the conference include Eric Foner, "Labor Historians Seek Useful Past," *In These Times* (December 12–18, 1984), p. 11; Michael Frisch, "Sixty Characters in Search of Authority," *International Labor and Working Class History* 27 (Spring 1985): 100–103; Mari Jo Buhle, "The Future of American Labor History: Toward a Synthesis?" *Radical Historians Newsletter* 44 (November 1984): 1–2; and Barbara J. Fields to the Editors, in ibid. 45 (February 1985): 1 and back page. To be sure, the conference did not end the discussions about approaches to labor history. An interesting recent exchange can be found in Leon Fink's "The New Labor History and the Powers of Historical Pessimism: Consensus, Hegemony, and the Case of the Knights of Labor," with comments from Jackson Lears, John P. Diggins, George Lipsitz, Mari Jo Buhle, and Paul Buhle, and a response by Fink, in *Journal of American History* 75 (June 1988): 115–61.

23. Unfortunately both Herbert Gutman and David Brody were abroad in the fall of 1984 and were unable to attend the conference. They did participate fully along with David Montgomery and Alice Kessler-Harris in selecting those who delivered papers and the other participants.

Perspectives on American Labor History

· INTEGRATING ·
THEMES
AND
APPROACHES

· L E O N   F I N K ·

Looking Backward

Reflections on Workers' Culture and Certain Conceptual Dilemmas within Labor History

S trikingly similar themes dominate recent studies of working people on both sides of the Atlantic. Although framed necessarily within a specific national, regional, and local context, labor history scholarship increasingly reveals a common understanding of the logic of collective action, particularly of the cultural currents of working-class life that have operated to sustain or inhibit organized protest. For United States labor historians recognition of this trans-Atlantic congruence has had a particularly buoyant and liberating effect. The burden of American exceptionalism—the idea that U.S. history was relatively unmarked by the class conflict and class consciousness manifest in Europe, an assumption that tended to belittle the significance of American labor history—has been considerably lightened. The Social Question has been restored to center stage of nineteenth century American historical investigations, and workers' distinct responses—manifest in community, organization, ideology, or politics—treated with a new subtlety and respect. Such reevaluation of American workers' history has taken place against the backdrop of a conscious if vague awareness that the definitions of European workers' histories were also changing. The new literature, while acknowledging diversity in economic development and political situation, has, in fact, discovered remarkable parallels in labor movements, worker culture, and popular aspirations otherwise separated by geographical distance, national identity, and political autonomy.

It is this common cultural paradigm in the new labor history that I should like to explore here. The triumph of a shared perspective has offered promising opportunities to recast traditionally more insular assumptions within a comparative framework. At the same time, the discipline internationally may now confront both the strengths and weaknesses of its common models of explanation. Some of the most fertile of recent basic concepts, for example, hatched as they have been in nineteenth century studies, are particularly troublesome in dealing with the twentieth century.

One sign of the developing integration of U.S. labor history with trends in Europe is the effective breakdown of any notion of a "regular" or "normal" path of class conflict from which the Americans strayed. Indeed, one might even suggest that as the trumpets of American exceptionalism have been muted, evidences of individual British, German, and French historical exceptionalism or "peculiarities" are flourishing. To be sure, the question of why the United States did not develop a mass labor-based or socialist-oriented political party still provokes scholarly argument. However, in place of Sombart's (or Hartz's or Lipset's) assumptions about an ideologically conciliated working class with a consensus culture based on "roast beef and apple pie," speculation today is more likely to turn either on structural anomalies of American business, government, and labor markets or on the difficulties of mobilizing a disaffected but fragmented working class. To put it differently, the question for historians is less why there has been no socialism or class consciousness—questions of political culture—in America than why the considerable labor conflict that took place did not assume a lasting, institutionalized form.[1]

At the same time, the "politicization" (or perhaps more accurately, "state orientation") of the German working classes from which Sombart drew his normative base has, for some time now, drawn historical scrutiny as the product of peculiarly German (indeed, perhaps more accurately, Prussian) circumstances. Historians now, for example, attribute the early split-off of labor-based radicals from middle-class liberal connections less to natural or inevitable class formation than to the weakness of German liberals, the dependence of German industrial capitalism on state funding, the retardation of national integration, the lack of parliamentary sovereignty, and finally, as a logical response to Bismarck's antisocialist persecutions. German workers (and their unions), ghettoized by a state system but also dependent upon that system for a broad program of social insurance, in the context of the German *Sonderweg*, turned peculiarly but logically to a statist strategy, whether reformist or revolutionary, to deal with their problems.[2]

But, if the United States and Germany somehow constitute the opposite extremes of political development in the world's Gilded Age, the other two of the big four industrial powers seem hardly to constitute a golden mean. England, the classic first site of the Industrial Revolution, of course, never provided much of a textbook political model. While Chartism, as the world's first mass working-class movement once seemed roughly correlated to socioeconomic development, connections always broke down after the 1840s. One had to wait another half-century for a labor movement with a radical political form and, indeed, considerably longer before one could speak confidently of the Labour party as a major political force. Even such episodic demonstration of class conflict and consciousness, however, draws a skeptical eye from recent British commentators. Chartism, to begin with, according to Gareth Stedman Jones's reevaluation, was less a class movement than the culmination of eighteenth century radical political dissent. The very constitutionalist ideals that infused this "people's" movement, according to Jones, obstructed its capacity to confront the industrialist and to take advantage of the positive uses of state power. Patrick Joyce, who focuses explicitly on the factory districts of the later nineteenth century, moreover, finds industrial "paternalism," rather than autonomous worker culture, the norm. In a recent article he speaks of the "ambivalence of the worker-employer relationship," 1880–1920, rooted in the belief of most workers that the employment situation should be "consensual" in form. The analytic retreat from ascriptions of class solidarity perhaps reaches its apotheosis in Alastair Reid's warning against the notion of any naturally revolutionary working class: "On the contrary defeat is the normal not the abnormal condition of the working class under capitalism, for in the absence of consciously formulated politics and carefully constructed alliances, it is only able spontaneously to sustain temporary sectional revolts." It is seemingly against this sober if not downright pessimistic portrayal of the British working class that Richard Price issued his reemphasis on continuing historical struggles over the labor process and protested the "tendency nowadays to emphasize the internal weaknesses and fractures that make it [i.e., working class] ultimately impotent against a dominant capital."[3]

Might France then at least qualify as the point of departure for studies of class-based labor movements? Perhaps. France certainly provided the standard scale of European political values in the nineteenth century, offering an ideological identity to conservatives, moderates, and left radicals alike. As Eric Hobsbawm put it, "A tricolor of some kind became the emblem of virtually every emerging nation, and European (or indeed world) politics between 1789 and 1917 were largely the struggle for and against the principles of 1789 or the even more incendiary ones of 1793." The revolutionary consolidation of the French bourgeoisie, unlike the British and German, also self-consciously crystallized political oppositions along lines of social class. Following the Revolution of 1830, according to William Sewell,

> the workers created a new type of opposition to the dominant state and society, an opposition that proclaimed the workers' specific identity as laborers, opposed individualism with an ideal of fraternal solidarity, promised an end

to the tyranny of private property, and implied the legitimacy of a revolution to achieve these ends. They created, in other words, what would today be called a class-conscious workers' movement.

Focusing on the mass strikes of 1890–1914, Michael Hanagan suggests that "there were more politicized worker-militants in France than in either England or the United States."[4]

The problem with the French experience as a way of saving some notion of expected political-ideological response to the Industrial Revolution is that the latter was, in comparative terms, missing. Indeed, E. P. Thompson's categorization of certain eighteenth century English events as "class struggle without class" might also apply to nineteenth-century French radicalism. France was by far the slowest of the four great Western powers to industrialize (Hanagan called the nineteenth-century economy one of "substantial growth but little fundamental transformation") and remained, according to Bernard Moss, mostly a nation of small workshops until 1900. This paradox of the least industrially developed nation setting the terms of political discourse for "modern industrial" societies generally wreaks havoc with the entire edifice of classical expectation in the relationship of economics and politics, or society and culture. When France is the norm, then indeed, not only the Sombartian answer but the question itself is thrown into doubt.[5]

While undermining a pseudocomparative history of national "outcomes," recent labor history scholarship nevertheless points to some congruities that, more often than not, link North American and European developments. This is particularly true with regard to the sociology and ideology, broadly speaking, of worker movements. By the end of the nineteenth century, for example, Western working-class movements seemed to have passed through two phases of development. The first rested on the organization of skilled workers, artisanal values of production, and republican (or democratic-nationalist) political ideals; the second on an accommodation to industrial production, recruitment of factory workers, and a break—whether conservative or radical—with republican political tradition. In the United States, I would argue, the first phase spanned roughly the years 1830–1890, with a break appearing by the mid-1890s. The 1880s and 1890s, by this schema played out both the highest phase and the disintegration of a social and intellectual formation rooted in the pre-Civil War decades.

In the United States, the coherence of the first phase may be seen to rest on several measures, but the ideological unity of the period is perhaps the most obvious. From journeymen's protests of the 1830s through the Eight-Hour Workday campaigns of 1886, the labor movement made explicit appeal to republican values vested in the American revolutionary settlement itself. These values included an explicit small-producer work ethic, the combination of claims of citizenship and economic value, and an identity of social worth with social utility. Fending off the advocates of unrestricted industrialization in the United States, Massachusetts shoeworkers' leader, Seth Luther, in 1832, was determined "no longer to be deceived by the cry of those who produce *nothing* and who enjoy *all*, and who insultingly term us—the farmers, the mechanics and labourers, the Lower Orders—and exultingly claim our homage for themselves as the Higher Orders—while the Declaration of Independence asserts that 'All Men Are Created Equal.'" William Sylvis, architect and leader of the first national amalgamation of trade unions in the 1860s, would reassert the first principles of a common-sense labor theory of value: "[Labor is] the foundation of the entire political, social, and commercial structure. . . . It is the base upon which the proudest structure of art rests—the leverage which enables man to carry out God's wise purposes." George McNeill, who would draft the preamble to the Knights of Labor constitution, declared "an inevitable and irresistible conflict between the wage system of labor and the republican system of government." As late as 1890, Edward Bellamy spoke for the vast mainstream of labor reform thought in America when he identified himself with the

> true conservative party . . . because we are devoted to the maintenance of republican institutions against the revolution now being effected by the money power. We propose no revolution, but that the people shall resist a revolution. We oppose those who are overthrowing the republic. Let no mistake be made here. We are not revolutionists but counter-revolutionists.[6]

Such moral-philosophical claims, to be sure, carried an ambivalent political message, particularly with regard to the operation of markets and the role of government in the regulation of marketplace activity. By defining workers at their existing work as the sinews rather than the victims of society, labor republicanism implied a somewhat restricted, self-administered remedy to be all that was necessary for contemporary social ills. Give workers the minimal resources necessary to sustain their productive activities (e.g., credit, land, the ballot, and cooperatives) and control those parasitic or monopolistic elements that would destroy or hoard society's resources, then civil society could carry on with a minimal state.[7]

The twin emphases on national political traditions and economic associationalism (or workers' self-organization with a minimum of state intervention) were by no means a peculiarly American phenomenon in the nineteenth century. British Chartism's political critique of social problems combined with a minimalist view of government responsibility seems in important respects to have foreshadowed the movement around the Knights of Labor a few decades later. French labor and socialist movements, perhaps as late as 1914, likewise combined elements of republicanism with a social

critique based on artisanal craft solidarity and protectiveness. "Trade socialism" or the socialism of skilled workers, which Bernard Moss argues defined
the nineteenth century French labor movement, centered on "the belief that
workers could only end their exploitation through their acquisition of the
means of production and that the form or unit of such acquisition should
be the organized body of the trade." Their ideal, argues Moss, represented
a "transitional phase" in the history of socialism. "If they accepted some
features of industrialism—the concentration of capital, the use of power
tools, an increased division of labor—they were aiming to stop the process
midway before it destroyed the remaining privileges of the craft." Maurice
Agulhon, in his influential study of the Var, first highlighted the integration
of artisanal cooperative values and republican thought as the building
blocks of French socialism.[8]

It was perhaps not so much the organizational base nor the core ideology
of French labor radicals that distinguished them from their American contemporaries, but rather a changing *strategy* toward those ends borne of *political* events beyond their control. Thus, a cooperative strategy toward a
"social republic," uniting workers with progressive middle-class allies,
collapsed, argues Moss, in the open betrayal of labor forces by the "oppor-
tunist republicans" of the Third Republic. One result was the revolutionary
socialism of Jules Guesde's Parti Ouvrier formed in 1879, a more class-
conscious adaptation of the trade socialist idealism and skilled trade constituency of earlier years. Not until the rise of a united Socialist party (SFIO)
did political socialism win mass support from French workers, however,
and even then, according to Yves Lequin's majesterial work on Lyon, the
underlying democratic-nationalist proclivities of the French working class
prevailed: "The republican reflex remained the dominant motif of political
conduct, in 1914 as in 1848: has it ever ceased to be?"[9]

The German movement, as well, emerged from guild centers of artisans
and skilled industrial workers. Even the "German model" of an early and
clear split between middle-class and working-class organization and ideology, recent scholarship suggests, was less a function of a radically different
consciousness than of national and even regional variations in economic development and state influence. Thus, although the Rheinland, characterized
by a relatively early, intense industrialization as well as an authoritarian
Prussian state administration, seems to "fit" the national image of class polarization and political socialism (it was here that Ferdinand Lassalle's
Allgemeine Deutsche Arbeiter Verein arose in the 1860s) a state like
Wurttemburg (or German-Austria as well) with slower economic transformation and a more liberal-democratic constitutional regime tended to per-
sist in the more republican-oriented labor politics common to France, Britain, Canada, and the United States. It is noteworthy here, that in his
synthetic review of European labor protest, 1848–1939, Dick Geary settled

on structural political factors (over cultural or even economic differences) to account for the variations in labor radicalism: "Differing degrees of governmental repression do seem to correlate with levels of working-class radicalism: autocratic Russia produced an unambiguously revolutionary movement, liberal England witnessed strongly reformist labor politics, whilst semi-autocratic Germany gave birth to a working class which was neither uniformly revolutionary nor reformist."[10]

Despite variations in form and strategy, the first phase of modern labor movements was characterized by simultaneous assertion of citizenship rights and attempts to defend or reassert claims to control over the labor process. Internationally, workers laid claim to the "democratic promise" (whether or not their own governments had democracy in mind) and to a measure of both economic and social recognition accruing to their skills (whether or not the marketplace still respected or required their abilities). Such workers, one knows, were not the only ones to take part in contemporary protest, but they stamped the struggle in their image. In their world view, the self-activity of workers both as producers and citizens was not only important, it was *all* that mattered to set the world right. Eric Hobsbawm has noted that by the mid-nineteenth century, the contending ideologies of social change—liberalism, socialism, communism, anarchism —all posited a kind of "gentle anarchy" as their utopian end. If both aspects of this utopia appeared increasingly irrelevant to labor movements by the turn of the century, traces of the core beliefs remained, perhaps nowhere more steadfast than in the United States.[11]

Within the broad outline of common, Western labor developments, a few assertions about the peculiar strengths and weaknesses of the American movement, at least for discussion's sake, are worth advancing. On the plus side, one wonders whether, within the limits of the first phase of labor movements generally, working-class organization in the United States did not advance further than in any other nation. In particular, a republican aversion to all vested interests and social privilege (as well as awareness of pragmatic necessity in a nation of many peoples) seems to have engendered in the United States a comparatively early and even crusading *universalism* in labor organizing. From the Lynn shoeworkers through the Knights of Labor, *inclusiveness* characterized not only labor ideology but organizing practice during decades in which European movements, by custom if not principle, were still more restricted to craft workers. Jurgen Kocka, for example, has drawn our attention to the hold of *handwerk* (craft) and "journeymen" identity over "class" identity in mid-nineteenth century Germany. Sewell's study, likewise, suggests the persistency of the older craft estates as both the radical core and social boundary of the nineteenth-century French movement. My initial reading of the literature suggests no ready European equivalent to the ideological and organizational dynamic that would hoist blacks, women, and the unskilled into the main body of the American labor movement in the 1880s. As a direct consequence, perhaps, no contemporary European labor organization approached the size or influence of the Knights of Labor.[12]

To the extent that this argument is valid, doubt immediately envelops the claim that American society, by its very nature, was peculiarly unsusceptible to polarization by social class. Indeed, it would tend to stand the argument made most clearly by Seymour Martin Lipset and Louis Hartz on its head. Instead of "depriving" the culture of a clear-cut model of social divisions (i.e., one that could be readily updated into worker vs. bourgeois antagonisms), the very absence of feudal *staende* (estates) in the United States may have left fewer barriers to organization among the nation's working people.[13]

But the weaknesses of the American republican political culture in building a workers' movement should also be taken into account. Republican ideology offered not only a potentially radical social-political critique, but also a badge of merit to be hallowed rather than contested. The eagerness with which immigrant workers, for example, seized on the symbols of the American revolutionary past may have had not only to do with the consonance between U.S. ideals and their own, all-too-often frustrated hopes for democratic self-rule in their home countries but also with the functional uses of republicanism as a ticket of acceptance and legitimacy in their adopted land. Thus, although republicanism undoubtedly possessed a radical cutting edge, it likely acted also as a "civil religion" or form of nation-worship, cloaking established political institutions with a sacrosanct untouchability. Of the two (or more) "uses" of republican faith, labor historians in recent years (myself included) have been more successful in exploring the radical than conservative side. A most useful study, for example, would focus on the successful appeal, circa 1880–1920, of the two major political parties to urban workers; in particular, with what ideological message as well as organizational strategy did the Republican party win the masses away from radical alternatives? One would want to explore, for example, as Nick Salvatore has done so well, not only the roots of Eugene Debs's socialist republicanism but also the limits of its appeal.[14]

One might well recognize the need for a more "Gramscian" (or in American terms, perhaps, "Genovesian") approach to working-class culture; that is, one that seeks a clearer and more careful reading of the distinctions and commonalities of working-class and elite meanings. The extent, as well as the limits, of hegemony might be imaginatively probed not only in studies of politics but also in examinations of popular leisure, religious life, educational experience, and familial expectations. Certainly at the workplace, what Richard Price has called the "relationship between resistance and subordination" might also be more assiduously cultivated.[15]

Despite such deficiencies the new labor history of the nineteenth century has registered one stunning achievement—successfully projecting heretofore invisible working people as conscious historical actors. Evident in a variety of national literatures, this "culturist" thrust has newly defined the ideas, attitudes, and motivation within workers movements and laboring communities.[16] In generalizing from the literature, one finds two themes paramount in the explanation of workers' collective action: the vanguard role of the craft sector within industrial settings, and, closely related, the "autonomy" of the workers' community. So thoroughly have the twin currents of the defense-of-labor-process and defense-of-community been driven home in studies of labor protest that they may well be said to constitute the central paradigm of the discipline.

In an important sense both aspects of the prevailing wisdom rest on a single insight about the subjectivity of worker movements. Namely, both angles of explanation converge on the *residual* nature of collective action, the ability to draw on the past in confronting the present and future. Thus, skilled workers or "industrial artisans," when attacked from above, drew on "residual" strengths both in the protection of craft or industrial skill and in their inheritance (familial, communal, or intellectual) of a tradition of political activism. This same set of resources seems also to figure in (if only by transference) politicization of semiskilled workers. To take a few prominent examples, just as Dawley's early shoe artisans handed on traditions of equal rights to semiskilled, heavily Irish factory workers, and Yankee farmers passed on notions of independence to their daughters in Dublin's Lowell mills, so do Walkowitz's Troy iron molders set the pace for local shirt collar makers and Michael Hanagan's glassworkers in Rive-de-Gier provide the critical sustenance for the town's metalworkers. In each case, skill or the independence of the artisan tradition offer the sources of pride, group identity, and ultimately, politicization. Artisanal and industrial skill constitute politicization, a kind of lifeline to working-class mobilization, in the sense that those who lose contact with it are likely to perish. Thus, in their comparative community approach, the relatively isolated factory workers in Walkowitz's Cohoes and Hanagan's Saint-Chamond do not generate or sustain the effectiveness of protest evident in settings still influenced by the organizing skills of "threatened artisans."[17]

A similar picture (often linked to the skilled worker paradigm) emerges with respect to community autonomy and labor protest. Organization, the literature suggests, is likely to be strongest where the workers' community attained the most autonomy or relinquished the least control to industrialists. Herbert Gutman's early study of the Tioga and Johnstown County lockouts of 1873–1874 perhaps first set the terms for such discussion. The pivotal distinction between Johnstown workers' defeat and Tioga workers' successful resistance, according to Gutman, "was neither the stand of the miners nor that of the operators." "It was the behavior of the non-mining population of Tioga County." An already established community, in short, effectively blocked the path to hegemonic control from above. Since Gutman's seminal local studies, the community as the fulcrum of labor struggles has received heavy emphasis. Two tendencies in this evolving work are worth noting. One is the general tendency to see strength in community autonomy and tradition. Autonomy is often implicitly defined in terms of *distance* from the capitalistic-modernizing "center," whether physical distance as in Gutman's initial but later-rejected emphasis on the small town or cultural distance as in Gutman's analysis of the slave family or others' emphasis on the tenacity of ethnic communalism. The second general tendency is the obverse of the first; that is, to analyze the collapse of mass movements in terms of the destruction of earlier community environments and cultural traditions. The received community, like the traditions of the skilled worker, appears as a lifeline without which labor is unlikely to stir itself. In such terms, for example, John Cumbler contrasted labor strength in Lynn and Fall River, Massachusetts. To quote reviewer Mike Davis, Lynn's "working class was unified by a highly integrated relationship between leisure, work, and the home. Fall River, on the other hand, lacked such cohesive class-based community institutions, and its workforce was decentralized among relatively isolated work and residential areas." In similar terms, Patrick Joyce, in his study of late-Victorian British workers, explains greater radicalization of West Riding vs. Lancashire in part on the basis of less-disrupted traditions and community in West Riding, a less pervasive "culture of the factory."[18]

Closely related to the residualist explanations of the capacity of nineteenth century workers is the theme of the "breakdown" of that capacity. One finds the common threads of this analysis applied first to the turn-of-the-century period, but then, episodically, to later decades as well. The break with nineteenth century conceptualization is ordered on at least two counts. First, the variously labeled ideology of the social republic, labor republicanism, and associationalism universally lost its ability to inspire and direct mass labor movements. In Europe class-conscious socialism or a more inwardly turned laborism replaced the cross-class peoplehood of an earlier era. Equally, in the United States, the simultaneous rise of big-city political machines (ethnic politics) and business unionism on the one hand and a socialist movement on the other suggested the passing of labor's identity with radical republicanism or, as older labor historians called it, "reform-minded unionism." In part, this loss of faith in the older message was likely due to the crushing defeats dealt to the instruments that had carried the message forward. It is more than coincidence, I suspect, that the time between the collapse of Chartism and the remobilization of British workers in the New Unionism and Independent Labour politics approximately equals the time span between the disintegration of the Knights of Labor and the rise of successful industrial unionism in the 1930s. Social movements and their regeneration, one might speculate, have a life cycle of their own. As it happens, another analytic thread also seems to connect post-Chartist and post-Knights of Labor eras. The essential critique that each movement made—resting in both cases on ideals of individual rights, artisanal pride in productive work, and attacks on upper-class corruption of the social and political order—must, as Stedman-Jones has suggested, have lost a degree of forcefulness over time. If Chartism failed to address the plight of the permanent factory worker, the Knights equally ignored market tendencies toward oligopoly as well as the emergent "managerial revolution." The socialism of the European workers' parties, whatever its intellectual deficiencies, at least took as a starting point the class division (and consequent subordination of labor) that labor republicanism had struggled vainly to transcend. In the United States, disillusionment with the older nobility-of-toil ethic was equally evident in Wobbly Big Bill Haywood's admonition, "the less work the better" and in Samuel Gompers' advice that "the way out of the wage system is through higher wages."[19]

Ironically, the social changes that accounted for the declining capacities of nineteenth-century workers, resources upon which recent labor history has concentrated, also gave birth to the modern industrial working class. Increasingly, we know something of the conditions, the outer trappings, the environment in which that process occured. Richard Johnson has drawn our attention to the homogeneity and distinctiveness of international working-class culture, "more so 1880–1930 than [in] any period before or after." To the extent that there was ever a classic era of the industrial proletariat, this was it, throwing together (sometimes uniting) skilled industrial tradesmen, semiskilled operatives, and congeries of laborers as well as penny-ante, neighborhood entrepreneurs in concentrated urban-commercial settings. Indeed, the settings themselves (i.e., the spatial and functional differentiation of specific industrial cities) often take on explanatory power of their own for historians of the period. In the United States, social historians have fruitfully concentrated on this changing material environment and as well upon the aggregate profile of an urban working class shaped through a complicated combination of immigrant acculturation, mobility, and labor force segmentation. The work of Harry Braverman, David Montgomery, and David Noble, moreover, has focused attention on the radical redesign of work process undertaken by modern management and workers' efforts by the mass strike to resist or transcend corporate discipline. In the United States as in Europe the political chapters of the era—the institutionalization of workers' political parties and national trade unions and rise of government-sponsored welfare and regulatory measures followed (selectively) by insurrectionary conflagrations during the war years—are due for more serious historical attention. Forming part of the heritage out of (and to some extent against) which the new labor history took wing, the political history of the "classic" proletariat has yet to undergo systematic reinterpretation.[20]

Whereas the changing parameters of this second (in the United States, post-1890) phase of labor history have not gone unexplored, a peculiar lacuna nevertheless separates twentieth-century studies from those of the earlier period. In particular, the culturalist synthesis exploring the subjectivity of labor mobilization so fertile in nineteenth century research is largely missing in work on the twentieth century. Indeed, many of the conceptually most arresting works ignore, or at least downplay, worker culture in favor of other emphases, especially the state, legal-administrative forms, economic cycles, and managerial ideology. When invoked at all, reference to a workers' culture in the recent period, so unlike the references to the nineteenth (or even eighteenth) century past, is used less to account for *capacity* or *empowerment* than for *somnolence* or *passivity*. Perhaps precisely because of the seeming correspondence of new cultural forces with the absence of a politicized labor movement, the cultural "taming" of the working class carries a long thematic pedigree in the United States. The classic formulation was perhaps that of the Lynds' *Middletown*, which tells us that over the period 1890–1925, a vibrant associational life resting on artisan republican ideals and giving rise to strong Knights of Labor locals, succumbed to a consumerism, where "people don't have to think too much" and were satisfied to remain in "the thick blubber of custom that envelops the city's life." Whether the emphasis be on consumerism (as with the Lynds), consumption tied to labor control (as in Gramsci's notion of "Fordism"), the success of welfare capitalism (Brody), Americanization from above (Meyer), the "urban trenches" separating work and community experience (Katznelson), community fragmentation (Cumbler's Fall River; Oestreicher's Detroit), or skill, ethnic, and gender divisions (Gordon, Edwards, and Reich), the cultural situation of twentieth-century American workers seems to take a sharply downward slide. To be sure, Americans do not suffer alone from this encumbrance: Stedman-Jones, likewise, has stressed the privatizing, deradicalizing impact of commercial leisure on late-nineteenth century London workingmen, and Yves Lequin refers to the "banality of political life and union struggles" in the twentieth century industrial suburb.[21]

It is ironic, to say the least, that a historiographic tendency that began in the 1960s with great hope of exploring "alternative" and "oppositional" cultural forms should end up in something of a tunnel of twentieth century pessimism. At one level, of course, the analysis reflects the political realities of the current century against the rosier expectations once projected by some for the working classes. At the same time, the climate of the immediate present likely helps frame the interpretation of the past. Just as the hopes of the later-1960s encouraged the discovery of a "new America" buried in the old, so, too, perhaps does the reigning conservatism of the present day produce resignation before the process of cultural "incorporation of America." In Europe, one suspects, a similar gloom gathers around the eclipse of social democratic and labourist experiments.[22]

Aside from such extraacademic influences, however, I suggest that a certain analytic hurdle also bars the path to a cultural explanation of modern worker movements. In one sense the very insights of the residualist perspective as applied to the earlier period may be part of the problem. An overemphasis on roots, sources, and tradition blinds us to the dynamic and creative contributions within worker culture. Looking backward for the cultural bases of collective action, we tend to enshrine a preindustrial, artisanal, worker-controlled, or community-centered past and villify the impact of cultural as well as economic disruptions.

There is, in short, a danger of a blanket antimodernism in our approach as labor historians to cultural process. By focusing on workers' culture almost exclusively through traditions, origins, and inheritances, workers themselves become "traditionalists," threatened by what is new and changing around them. On balance, it is not surprising that two recent attempts to generalize from the new labor history build their arguments (albeit from quite different political angles) around the virtues of tradition. Craig Calhoun (who might be considered a "left" residualist) makes use of the concepts of the "radicalism of tradition" and "reactionary radicals" to account for capacities of mobilization among artisans and peasants that seem to have dried up in modern times. In a thoughtful review of the literature on collective action, he concludes that "traditional communities" "give their members the social strength with which to wage protracted battles, the 'selective inducements' with which to ensure full collective participation, and a sense of what to fight for that is at once shared and radical. This sets traditional communities apart from the modern working class." If Calhoun's conclusions point to what he considers the inevitably changed forms of working-class movements (i.e., from popular insurgency to organized, bureaucratic reformism), Aileen Kraditor (by contrast, a "right" residualist) views much of the same literature in The Radical Persuasion as proof of the irrelevance altogether for workers of radical social movements. Celebrating the traditional, familial and ethnic-centered communities she finds described in the literature, Kraditor sees little indigenous impetus (or need) for change. Socialist agitation, in particular, is presented as an alien, unwelcome, and unnecessary incursion on traditional norms. If few labor historians would adopt either generalization, they should perhaps be more aware of the logical implications of their arguments.[23]

Current working assumptions leave us with no satisfactory view of workers' consciousness and culture in an age of mass production and mass consumption, except for what we can borrow from earlier constellations. There exists, to be sure, a suggestive literature on "mass culture," but it is far stronger as social critique than as social history. Without exploration of popular responses to centrally produced products and images or of the relation of social movements to mass commercial culture, we are prone to fall back on rather schematic generalizations. Stuart Hall has offered a pointed comment on the problem in relation to modern British history:

> One of the main differences standing in the way of a proper periodisation of popular culture is the profound transformation in the culture of the popular classes which occurs between the 1880s and the 1920s. . . . Without in any way casting aspersions on the important historical work which has been done and remains to do on earlier periods, I do believe that many of the real difficulties (theoretical as well as empirical) will only be confronted when we begin to examine closely popular culture in a period which begins to resemble our own. . . . I am dubious about that kind of interest in 'popular culture' which comes to a sudden and unexpected halt at roughly the same point as the decline of Chartism. It isn't by chance that very few of us are working in popular culture in the 1930s. . . . From the viewpoint of a purely 'heroic' or 'autonomous' popular culture, the 1930s is a pretty barren period.[24]

It is no wonder that labor historians, who dispatch with early nineteenth century and even eighteenth century lower-class worlds with increasing confidence, seem positively uncomfortable in pushing cultural analysis, except most selectively, past the late-nineteenth century. The most subtle recent studies of twentieth century American workers (e.g., Montgomery, Brody, Schatz, and Lichtenstein) largely eschew the cultural interests in consciousness, community, and identity of much of "first phase" labor history. Exceptions like John Bodnar's *Immigration and Industrialization* and David Corbin's *Life, Work, and Rebellion in the Coal Fields* choose subjects where the strengths of the residual perspective continue to be applied with skill. The difficulties inherent in transporting the standing culturalist categories forward in time, however, are evident in one of the few "new histories" of the 1930s. Although providing a fascinating description of rank and file mobilization, Peter Friedlander's *Emergence of UAW Local, 1936–1939* is hobbled by its explanatory reduction of culture to ethnic origins and of actors to character types. Why, in principle, is it easier for us to assess the world of the New York journeyman mechanic in 1830 than that of the Schenectady electrical worker or the Detroit wildcat striker of the 1940s? Can it be in part that the cultural apparatus at our disposal—with its tight-knit communities, ethnic neighborhoods, moral codes, and skilled-worker republicanism—no longer fits but, except for notions of mass embourgeoisement and depoliticization, we have little to put in their place.[25]

A residualist focus on traditional culture at odds with a modernizing re-ordering of daily life will no doubt continue to offer a useful framework for the study of working-class collective action. So, too, the critique of mass culture may continue to guide us toward some of the explanations for popular apathy and inertia in our century. At the same time, a few straws in the wind (and others waiting to be rustled) point in another direction. It is the direction of culture (and consciousness) in the making rather than on the run. The objects of possible focus, either in a national or comparative context, are numerous. One obvious subject is the rise of mass leisure, the historical concomitants of which surely are not restricted to social control, general stupefaction, and the evaporation of class consciousness. Another subject surely in need of revision is an assessment of government's expanded role in industrial relations and social welfare. The reigning paradigm, concentrating on an era of comparative workers' autonomy, tends to stop at the water's edge of "state" intervention. While seizing readily on the grim consequences of state reform for plebian culture and labor's general room to maneuver, we have not gone far toward exploring the inner tensions within and between politics, government administration, the labor movement, and workers' culture. Institutions of mass socialization—including schooling, military service, and public health programs—likely also deserve fresh scrutiny. Even the skilled male worker, whose "demise" forms the backdrop to so much discussion of twentieth century labor history, might reenter the picture from new angles. As Bernard Sternsher suggests in a recent review essay, skilled workers have too often been placed in a backward-looking framework, linking them to their artisan antecedents, summoning up the "deskilling" paradigm of the skilled worker as dying breed, and reinforcing the resistance-followed-by-decline-and-fall plot structure of labor history. He suggests that by the training involved in the mastery of their craft, skilled industrial workers possessed not only economic ancestors but progeny among a latter-day educated, technical elite. One might ask, as well, whether the artisanal work ethic had any historical relationship to the "culture of professionalism" and "middle-class" occupational self-definitions of the twentieth century's rising white-collar sectors, which are normally treated as entirely distinct subjects.[26]

As a sign of the interpretive possibilities available within a more modernist framework, let us concentrate on the rise of commercial mass culture. Patrick Joyce offers some tantalizing leads in referring (at the very end of his book) to a transformation from "status" to "class" politics (including the emergence of the Labour party). The breakdown of factory, paternal culture he attributes in part to the fact that the "scope of peoples' lives grew larger." Commercialization pierced an old order of ritual life and set expectation. Not only the growth of cities but travel through and out of them affected worker consciousness. So, too, did the breakup of family firms and often-sudden imposition of more instrumental management. Finally, the rise of women's employment outside the home, argues Joyce, also helped to erode an earlier nexus of authority relations that ran from community patriarchs down through workers' families. If Joyce points to the liberating influence of late-nineteenth century commercial forms on earlier provincial and status divisions among workers, two essays by Eric Hobsbawm set further guideposts toward understanding modern working-class culture. Although continually disappointing Labour's "elite of militants," the discreet way of life that developed between the 1880s and the early 1950s was rooted in "us" vs. "them" antimonies generated both at work and away from work. One reading of Hobsbawm's material analysis of working-class life would stress the very *imperfect* absorbtion of workers into consumer capitalism as an essential starting point for understanding twentieth century class conflicts.[27]

That the radical political edge of working-class life depended as much on the forces of cultural modernism and breakdown as on instincts toward tradition and preservation is apparent in other ways in the recent literature. Bob Holton's work on British syndicalism, for example, stresses the seeds of foreign ideas planted among the miners of South Wales, as when James Connolly returned from the United States by 1910 a sworn Wobbly. Ronald Schatz's emphasis on a vanguard of families possessing "union traditions" in the organization of American electrical workers in the 1930s and 1940s is also relevant. Although mostly "highly skilled men . . . who were in their forties and fifties, had families, and were well-established in the community," this unionizing leadership, as secularists or Catholic anticlericalists who "nearly all belonged to the C.P. or the International Workers Order" were also cultural nonconformists. Moreover, as Alice Kessler-Harris suggests for an earlier period, the women among unionizing pioneers openly broke with their families, came from nontraditional families (e.g., were divorced, lived with an aunt, etc.), or grew up in the special "union tradition," minority cohort.[28]

The invocation of women's roles in the labor movement, in fact, more generally summons up an alternative approach to cultural process than the one most commonly adopted by labor historians. In women's history, it appears, the cultural focus has often been inverse to that of the new labor history. Because the traditional, autonomous ideals of male culture (including but not limited to the working class) served to mask and mystify the reality of female experience, feminist historians have long adopted a more ambivalent and skeptical attitude toward the received culture and likewise a more optimistic view of post-Victorian possibility. A classic work like Sara Evans's *Personal Politics*, for example, sets for its task the exploration of "new" consciousness and how such cultural transformation occurs in the course of a specific set of lived experiences.[29]

Recent research on working-class women likewise tends to challenge assumptions within traditional worker culture and to welcome evidence of cultural re-ordering from modernist impulses. While Mary H. Blewett's study of New England shoemakers, for instance, argues that gender-based divisions within artisan ideology effectively "cut women off" from traditions of collective action, other studies by Susan Porter Benson, Patricia A. Cooper, and Dorothy Sue Cobble point to the mutability of concepts like "skill" and "work culture." In the latter works, women workers in new or traditionally 'unskilled' jobs are seen to create parallel mechanisms of craft control and group pride to those of traditionally skilled male workers. Women's historians have also explored cultural change beyond the workplace. Despite the harshness of industrial New York in the antebellum years, Christine Stansell discovers a "dialectic of female vice and female virtue," where in the "ebb and flow of large oppressions and small freedoms, poor women traced out unforeseen possibilities for their sex." Likewise, exploring the impact of commercial culture on the once "homosocial" world of working-class leisure, Kathy Peiss leaves open the question of whether consumerism "diverted working women from their class interests or heightened expectations of the 'good life' in such a way as to encourage collective action and unionization." Perhaps Jacquelyn Hall's study of the 1929 Elizabethton strike offers the most subtle accounting to date of traditionalist and modernist influences on an episode of labor protest. On the one hand old communities of creek-bed farmers stood fast behind the strikers. On the other hand, young women were particularly prominent in the disturbances "perhaps because the peer culture and increased independence encouraged by factory labor stirred boldness and inspired experimentation." Emphasizing the "dynamic quality of working-class women's culture," Hall characterizes the Elizabethton stalwarts as "'new women,' making their way in a world their mothers could not have known but carrying with them values handed down through the female line."[30]

While not yet fully integrating workers' industrial and political history with the worlds of popular culture and leisure, recent works in twentieth century American cultural history suggest some revisionist openings. While Pittsburgh's passage from the nineteenth century Craftsmen's Empire to the early-twentieth century Steel City clearly represents for historian Francis Couvares a loss of working-class power and control, it is not an unambivalent descent into doom. Couvares describes a dignity carved out in the midst of an "unconsolidated" mass culture, a way of life created "by alternately retreating into ethnic enclaves and foraying into the still-marginal world of the free and easy." Coping as best they could amidst "the massed power of corporate capital," the pre-1919 worker generation is usefully located by Couvares between their "plebeian predecessors" who "could . . . count on the [integrating] power of a local culture" and their "successors in the thirties" who partook in a "wider culture" that could affirm "a pluralistic version of American nationality." It was during this difficult interlude, notes Couvares, that "the terse aggressiveness of a Honus Wagner [Pittsburgh Pirate baseball star of immigrant origins] and subversive autonomy of a Charlie Chaplin" came to mean "something special to their working-class audiences," and when, "cultivating a realm of spontaneity and drama within a framework of subordination and tedium, . . . commercial amusements won mass audiences before they won the compliment of elite criticism."[31]

If American workers through the 1920s would make use of mass culture largely in a defensive and nonpolitical way, their very assimilation of common forms of communication, socialization, and technological innovation may ultimately have carried considerable political meaning. Roy Rosenzweig notes that the rise of dance halls and amusement places led in the 1920s both to "embourgeoisement" and to "countervailing forces" catalyzed by the breakdown of an inwardly turned, ethnic workers' culture. "Workers who had spent their time in the movie theater in the 1920s might find their way to the union hall in the 1930s and 1940s, as they sought to achieve what the movies promised but the larger society failed to deliver and as they became increasingly able to make common cause with workers from different ethnic and religious groups." Labor activists in the Southern Piedmont similarly took hope from the cultural changes of the 1920s. Jacquelyn Hall, Robert Korstad, and James Leloudis in a sweeping restatement of southern textile workers' history acknowledge a cultural component behind the strike wave of the late 1920s and early 1930s. Higher wages, greater literacy tied to compulsory education, newspapers and magazines, and "perhaps most important," the advent of radio and its projection of their own popular music instilled pride and the expectation of "better times ahead" within a generation that came of age after World War I. The pent-up hopes and aspirations of this regional culture were ultimately manifest in mass strikes and demonstrations, campaigns in which "automobile caravans" spread walkouts from town to town.[32]

The accent laid here on the positive potential for labor of twentieth century cultural change is offered in a provisional and tentative way. I mean neither to discount the "degradation of labor" thesis, nor to deny the relevancy of other, equally sobering and "critical" interpretations of cultural transformation. I certainly do not want to initiate a new labor history whiggism based on workers' expanded access to technology, prosperity, and Mickey Mouse. I do think that investigations of the carving out of room to maneuver in "modern" times, however halting and defused such efforts may have been, requires a closer and more nuanced look than we have seen to date. Whether out of such efforts anything like a revised culturalist synthesis will emerge and whether any such approach could offer a useful comparative index for workers' history across the dislocations of depression, war, and the determinacy of political events are questions for the future.

If I have raised an implicit criticism of the so-called culturist thrust in recent labor history, it is obviously from a different basis than that of several other recent critics. The return to an institutional or economic focus counseled by some, and the search for a more thorough-going class analysis encompassing the study of domination as well as resistance advanced by others, strike me as healthy signs of pluralism within the field. I should hope, however, that in this unquiet young adulthood of the new labor history we will not fail to advance our work in areas that have already seen major breakthroughs. It is worth remembering, as Richard Johnson has noted, that the "second great era of working-class history" (an era highlighted by E. P. Thompson's work in Britain and Herbert Gutman's in America) constituted a "rediscovery of class through culture."[33] In North America, consensus history was punctured by the study of consciousness, and from consciousness and revised understandings of a diverse culture, conflict in American history was given new meaning. Far from a flight from class analysis, the so-called culturalists threw open a door nailed shut by conservatives, consensus liberals, and corporate liberal critics alike, making class conflict (as well as other social divisions) again worthy of study. Based on this foundation there are now real opportunities for comparative studies of class formation, labor movements, and popular cultures. For labor historians, the study of culture always begins with the study of possibility, with the assumption that there is "life below." Rather than bring down the final curtain on culturalism, let us instead have the second act.

NOTES

The ideas for this essay emerged from a Fulbright year of teaching at the Amerika-Institut of the University of Munich, West Germany. I should like in particular to acknowledge the influence of two seminars in which I collaborated with German colleagues: one on the rise of mass culture with Berndt Ostendorf, director of the Amerika-Institut, the other on comparative labor history with Irmgaard Steinisch of the Institut für Neurere Geschichte. An early version of the essay was presented as a comment at the International Conference on Critical Theories of Society and Culture, Center for North American Studies and Research, University of Frankfurt (Main), June 18–23, 1984. For helpful comments and suggestions along the way to the DeKalb conference I would like to thank Hartmut Keil, Daniel Rodgers, Susan Levine, James Epstein, and Donald Reid. In revising the DeKalb draft of the paper, I have profited especially from the counsel of Geoff Eley, James Epstein, James Leloudis, and Donald Reid, and also from the encouragement, just before his untimely death, of Warren Susman.

In preparing the essay for the current volume, I am aware that the literature has proceeded beyond issues I discussed at the conference. The central challenge of my remarks, however, I believe is still relevant. With one exception, therefore, I have maintained the basic integrity of the original presentation, while offering a few historiographic updates in the footnotes.

1. John H. M. Laslett and Seymour Martin Lipset, *Failure of a Dream? Essays in the History of American Socialism* (Berkeley, CA, 1984); Louis Hartz, *The Liberal Tradition in America* (New York, Harcourt, Brace, 1955); see, e.g., David Montgomery report on Why No Socialism in America conference, *ILWCH* 24 (Fall 1983): 67–70; Eric Foner, "Why Is There No Socialism in the US?" *History Workshop* 17 (Spring 1984): 57–80; and Sean Wilentz, "Against Exceptionalism: Class Consciousness and the American Labor Movement, 1790–1920," *ILWCH* 26 (Fall 1984): 1–24.

2. Jurgen Kocka, "Die Trennung von burgerlicher und proletarischer Demokratie im europaischen Vergleich. Fragestellungen und Ergebnisse," in Kocka, ed. *Europaische Arbeiterbewegungen im 19. Jahrhundert* (Gottingen, 1983), pp. 5–20. David Blackbourn and Geoff Eley's revisionist, *The Peculiarities of the German History: Bourgeois Society and Politics in Nineteenth Century Germany* (Oxford, 1984), while challenging the conventional *Sonderweg* thesis, does so, it is worth noting, not in the name of establishing a new model of social-political development but rather by exploring expectations for historical ideal types upon which exceptionalism or *Sonderweg* theories are built: "In order to have an aberration, it is clearly necessary to have a norm. . . . [Historians] should not speak of German peculiarity but of British, French, and German *particularities*" (pp. 10, 154).

3. Gareth Stedman Jones, *Languages of Class: Studies in English Working Class History, 1832–1982* (Cambridge, 1983), pp. 90–178; Patrick Joyce, *Work, Society and Politics: The Culture of the Factory in Late Victorian England* (New Brunswick, NJ, 1980); "Labour, Capital, and Compromise: A Response to Richard Price," *Social History* 9 (January 1984): 70–71; Alastair Reid, "Politics and Economics in the Formation of the British Working Class: A Response to H. F. Moorhouse," *Social History* 3 (October 1978): 361; Richard Price, "The Labour Process and Labour History," *Social History* 8 (January 1983): 72; See also Sidney Pollard, "England: Der unrevolutionare Pionier," in Kocka, *Europaische Arbeiterbewegungen*, pp. 21—38; and Ross McKibbin, "Why Was There No Marxism in Great Britain?" *English Historical Review* 99 (1984): 297–331: Re Jones's thesis, see also the provocative critique by James Epstein, "Rethinking the Categories of Working-Class History," *Labour/Le Travail* 18 (Fall 1986): 195–208.

4. Eric Hobsbawm, *Age of Revolution* (London, 1975), p. 53; William Sewell, *Work and Revolution in France: The Language of Labor From the Old Regime to 1848* (New York, 1980), p. 282. Michael P. Hanagan, *The Logic of Solidarity: Artisans and Industrial Workers in Three French Towns, 1871–1914* (Urbana, IL, 1983), pp. 24–25.

5. Edward P. Thompson, "Eighteenth-Century English Society: Class Struggle without Class?" *Social History* 3 (May 1978): 133–65, esp. 148–49; Hanagan, *Logic of Solidarity*, p. 6; Bernard Moss, *The Origins of the French Labor Movement 1830–1914: The Socialism of Skilled Workers* (Berkeley, CA, 1976), pp. 156–58; see also Ronald Aminzade, "Reinterpreting Capitalist Industrialization: A Study of

Nineteenth-Century France," *Social History* 9 (October 1984): 329–50. For an exemplary, and reinforcing, treatment of this general theme, see Aristide R. Zolberg, "How Many Exceptionalisms?" in Ira Katznelson and Zolberg, eds., *Working-Class Formation* (Princeton, 1986), pp. 397–456.

6. "An Address to the Working-Men of New England . . ." Boston, 1832 (unpublished document, courtesy Herbert Gutman); Daniel T. Rodgers, *The Work Ethic in Industrial America* (Chicago, 1978), p. 175; George McNeill, *The Labor Movement: The Problem of Today* (Boston, 1887), p. 459; John L. Thomas, *Alternative America: Henry George, Edward Bellamy, Henry Demarest Lloyd and the Adversary Tradition* (Cambridge, MA, 1983), pp. 274–75.

7. See, generally, the author's argument in Chapter 2, *Workingmen's Democracy* (Urbana, IL, 1983), pp. 18–37.

8. Moss, *Origins of the French Labor Movement*, pp. 156, 160; Maurice Agulhon, *Une Ville ouvriere au temps du socialisme Utopicque. Toulon de 1815 a 1851* (Paris, 1970); for his overview of French historiography, I am indebted here to Donald Reid's paper, "Local History and Labor History in France," Southern Historical Association meeting in Houston, November 1985.

9. Moss, *Origins of the French Labor Movement*, p. 73; Dick Geary, *European Labour Protest 1848–1939* (London, 1981), p. 48; Yves Lequin, *les Ouvriers de la région lyonnaise (1848–1914)* (Lyon, 1977).

10. See Dieter Dowe, "Deutschland: Das Rheinland und Wurttemberg im Vergleich," in Kocka, *Europaische Arbeitbewegungen*, pp. 77–105, and Helmut Konrad, "Deutsch-Osterreich: Gebremste Klassenbildung und importierte Arbeiterbewegung im Vielvolkerstaat," in ibid., pp. 106–28; Geary, *European Labor Protest*, p. 63.

11. Lawrence Goodwyn, *Democratic Promise: The Populist Moment in America* (New York, 1976); Geary, *European Labor Protest*, pp. 70–80; Hobsbawm, *Age of Revolution*, p. 243.

12. See Alan Dawley, *Class and Community* (Cambridge, 1976) and Paul Faler, *Mechanics and Manufacturers in the Early Industrial Revolution* (Albany, NY, 1981); Geary, *European Labor Protest*; Kocka, *Lohnarbeit und Klassenbildung. Arbeiter und Arbeiterbewegung in Deutschland, 1800–1875* (Berlin and Bonn, 1983), pp. 134–37; see also, Barrington Moore, Jr., *Injustice, the Social Bases of Obedience and Revolt* (New York, 1978), esp. pp. 185–90; Sewell, pp. 154–61, 211–18; Cf., e.g., the author's *Workingmen's Democracy* (Urbana, IL, 1983), pp. 220–25, Richmond, Virginia Knights' call for a movement "irrespective of party, color or social standing," p. 157; Paul Krause, "Labor Republicanism and 'Za Chlebom': Anglo-American and Slavic Solidarity in Homestead," in Dirk Hoerder, ed., *"Struggle a Hard Battle": Essays on Working-Class Immigrants* (DeKalb, 1986), pp. 143–69, esp., the call for an "amalgamation" of laborers regardless of "creed, color or race"; and Susan B. Levine, *Labor's True Woman: Carpet Weavers, Industrialization, and Labor Reform in the Gilded Age* (Philadelphia, 1984).

13. See, e.g., Seymour Martin Lipset, "Radicalism or Reformism: The Sources of Working Class Politics," *American Political Science Review* 77 (1983): 1–18; Louis Hartz, *Liberal Tradition*.

14. Cf., e.g., Bruce Carlan Levine, "Free Soil, Free Labor, and Freimanner:

German Chicago in the Civil War Era," in Hartmut Keil and John Jentz, eds. *German Workers in Industrial Chicago, 1850–1910* (DeKalb, IL, 1983), pp. 163–82; Elise Marienstras, "State-Building and Civil Religion in the Revolutionary Era," (unpublished ms., 1984); Nick Salvatore, *Eugene V. Debs: Citizens and Socialist* (Urbana, IL, 1982).

15. See esp. Eugene D. Genovese, *Roll, Jordan, Roll: The World the Slaves Made* (New York, 1976); Cf. Geoff Eley and Keith Nield, "Why Does Social History Ignore Politics?" *Social History* 5 (May 1980): 249–71; Bryan Palmer's review of *Eight Hours for What We Will* and *The Remaking of Pittsburgh* in *Social History* 10 (October 1985): 400–404; Price, "Labour Process," p. 62. For illustrative recent histories of education, see David John Hogan, *Class and Reform: School and Society in Chicago 1880–1930* (Philadelphia, 1985) and Julia Wrigley, *Class Politics and Public Schools: Chicago 1900–1950* (New Brunswick, NJ, 1982).

16. I am adopting Richard Johnson's term here but "Americanizing" it, giving it a looser, more pluralistic set of references. See "Edward Thompson, Eugene Genovese, and Socialist-Humanist History," *History Workshop* 6 (Autumn 1978): 79–100.

17. Dawley, *Class and Community*, pp. 148, 177, 248–49; Thomas Dublin, *Women at Work: The Transformation of Work and Community in Lowell, Massachusetts, 1826–1860* (New York, 1979), pp. 86–107; Daniel Walkowitz, *Worker City, Company Town: Iron and Cotton-Worker Protest in Troy and Cohoes, New York, 1855–84* (Urbana, IL, 1978), pp. 249–250, 252; Hanagan, *Logic of Solidarity*, pp. 209–17.

18. *Work, Culture and Society in Industrializing America* (New York, 1976), pp. 321–43, quotation p. 340; "The Worker's Search for Power: Labor in the Gilded Age," in H. Wayne Morgan, ed., *The Gilded Age: A Reappraisal* (Syracuse, NY, 1963), pp. 38–68; *The Black Family in Slavery and Freedom, 1750–1925* (New York, 1976); cf. the author's comments in "A Symposium on Gutman's *The Black Family*," in *Radical History Review* 4 (Spring–Summer 1977): 77; reference to Cumbler's *Working Class Community in Industrial America* in "Why the US Working Class Is Different?" *New Left Review* 123 (September–October 1980): pp. 3–44; Joyce, *Work, Society, and Politics*, esp. pp. 201–39, 331.

19. See Gerald N. Grob, *Workers and Utopia* (Chicago, 1969), pp. 3–10; Stedman Jones, *Languages of Class*; Joyce, *Work, Society, and Politics*, pp. 313–14; Rodgers, *Work Ethic*, p. 156; Alan Trachtenberg, *The Incorporation of America: Culture and Society in the Gilded Age* (New York, 1982), p. 95.

20. John Clarke, Charles Critcher, and Richard Johnson, eds., *Working-Class Culture: Studies in History and Theory* (London, 1979), p. 235. On U.S. workers in the industrial city, see, e.g., Keil and Jentz, *German Workers*, pp. 163–82, and Oliver Zunz, *The Changing Face of Inequality: Urbanization, Industrial Development, and Immigrants in Detroit, 1890–1920* (Chicago, 1982). For a comparative perspective on urban community and worker protest, see James E. Cronin, "Labor Insurgency and Class Formation," in Cronin and Carmen Sirianni, eds. *Work, Community, and Power* (Philadelphia, 1983); Harry Braverman, *Labor and Monopoly Capital* (New York, 1974); David Montgomery, *Workers' Control in America: Studies in the History of Work, Technology and Labor Struggles* (New York, 1979);

David Noble, *America by Design* (New York, 1977); cf. Geoff Eley, "Combining Two Histories: The SPD and the German Working Class Before 1914," *Radical History Review* 28–30 (1984): 13–44.

Fortunately, several recent contributions have substantially enhanced our understanding of workers' social and political history for this period. For the United States the most important is David Montgomery, *The Fall of the House of Labor: The Workplace, the State, and American Labor Activism, 1865–1925* (New York, 1987). For Britain, see David Howell, *British Workers and the Independent Labour Party, 1888–1906* (Dover, NH, 1984); Richard Price, *Labour in British Society: An Interpretive History* (Dover, NH, 1986); and James E. Cronin, *Labour and Society in Britain, 1918–1979* (London, 1984). For rare comparative insight, see Jeffrey Haydu, *Between Craft and Class: Skilled Workers and Factory Politics in the United States and Britain, 1890–1922* (Berkeley, 1988). For France, a major work establishing the twentieth-century terrain is Lenard R. Berlanstein, *The Working People of Paris, 1871–1914* (Baltimore, 1985). On the "re-making" of the French working class, see Gerard Noiriel, *Longwy: Immigrés et Prolétaires, 1880–1980* (Paris, 1984). Among recent German labor-political studies, Mary Nolan, *Social Democracy and Society: Working Class Radicalism in Dusseldorf, 1890–1920* (New York, 1981), is exemplary.

21. *Middletown* quotation in Richard Wightman Fox, "Epitaph For Middletown," in Fox and T. Jackson Lears, eds., *The Culture of Consumption* (New York, 1983), pp. 103–41, esp. 135; Antonio Gramsci, *Selections from the Prison Notebooks* (New York, 1972); David Brody, *Workers in Industrial America: Essays on the Twentieth Century Struggle* (New York, 1980); Steven Meyer, *The Five Dollar Day: Labor, Management and Social Control in the Ford Motor Company, 1908–1921* (Albany, NY, 1981); Ira Katznelson, *City Trenches: Urban Politics and the Patterning of Class in the United States* (New York, 1981); Richard Oestreicher, "Industrialization, Class, and Competing Cultural Systems: Detroit Workers, 1875–1900," in Keil and Jentz, *German Workers*, pp. 52–69; John Cumbler, *Working Class Community in Industrial America*, (Westport, CT, 1979); David Gordon, Richard Edwards, and Michael Reich, *Segmented Work, Divided Workers* (New York, 1982). See Geary, *European Labor Protest*, pp. 111–15; Gareth Stedman Jones, "Working-Class Culture and Working-Class Politics in London, 1870–1900; Notes on the Remaking of a Working Class," *Journal of Social History* 7 (Summer 1974): 460–508. Yves Lequin, "Social Structures and Shared Beliefs . . ." *ILWCH* 22 (Fall 1982): 8–12. Among the most stimulating (but non-culture-centered) recent works are: David Gordon, Richard Edwards, and Michael Reich, *Segmented Work, Divided Workers* (New York, 1982); Christopher L. Tomlins, *The State and the Unions: Labor Relations, Law, and the Organized Labor Movement in America, 1880–1960* (New York, 1985); Victoria C. Hattam, "Unions and Politics: The Courts and American Labor, 1806–1896," (PhD diss., MIT, 1987); Sanford M. Jacoby, *Employing Bureaucracy: Managers, Unions, and the Transformation of Work in American Industry, 1900–1945* (New York, 1985). Similarly, for France, see Donald Reid, *The Miners of Decazeville: A Genealogy of Deindustrialization* (Cambridge, MA, 1985) and Luc Bultanski, *Les Cadres: la formation d'un groupe sociale* (Paris, 1982). In contrast to the prevailing trends, one recent work is

noteworthy for addressing the culture question in a "positive" way: see Vernon L. Lidtke, *The Alternative Culture: Socialist Labor in Imperial Germany* (New York, 1985).

22. James Weinstein and David W. Eakins, eds., *For a New America* (New York, 1970); Trachtenberg, *Incorporation of America*. See also the Perry Anderson-Marshall Berman encounter, "Modernity and Revolution" and "The Signs in the Streets," *New Left Review* 144 (March-April 1984), pp. 96–123.

23. Craig Calhoun, "The Radicalism of Tradition," *American Journal of Sociology* 88 (March 1983): 886–914, quotation p. 900; see also *The Question of Class Struggle* (Chicago, 1981); Aileen Kraditor (Baton Rouge, LA, 1981), esp. pp. 55–85; see also the author's review, "My Dinner with Aileen," *The Nation* 236 (June 18, 1983), pp. 770–73; for distinct and original variations on the theme of tradition within workers' culture and (at least implicitly) its juxtaposition to socialist-rationalist radicalism, see John E. Bodnar's *Immigration and Industrialization: Community and Protest in an Industrial Society, 1900–1940* (Baltimore, 1982) and William M. Reddy, *The Rise of Market Culture* (New York, 1984).

24. The canonical and formulaic wisdom is evident in the following passage on working-class life in the post-World War II period: "First, there had been a pronounced tendency under the impact of social and technological change for the traditional institutions of private life, especially the traditional working class family, to disintegrate. ... This, in turn, is related to a second tendency, toward the replacement of all the traditional forms of proletarian culture and everyday life—which gave working class communities their coherence and provided the underpinnings for the traditional forms of proletarian class-consciousness—with a new, manipulated consumer culture which for convenience's sake we will call mass culture." Stanley Aronowitz, *False Promises, the Shaping of American Working Class Consciousness* (New York, 1973), p. 95; Stuart Hall, "Notes on Deconstructing the 'Popular'," in Raphael Samuel, ed., *People's History and Socialist Theory* (London, 1981), pp. 229, 231.

25. Montgomery, *Workers' Control in America*. Montgomery's studies, which run from skilled nineteenth century workers through an analysis of New Deal unionism, in and of themselves suggest the changing first stage–second stage change of emphasis. The "cultural" characterization of workers'–work ethic, sense of respectability, male identity, and "ethical code" that appears in the seminal first chapter on the industrial craftsman is never reexamined in the light of twentieth century experiences; Brody, *Workers in Industrial America*; Ronald Schatz, *The Electrical Workers, A History of Labor at General Electric and Westinghouse, 1923–60* (Urbana, IL, 1983); Nelson Lichtenstein, *Labor's War at Home: The CIO in World War II* (New York, 1982); Peter Friedlander, *Emergence of a UAW Local, 1936–1939* (Pittsburgh, 1975).

26. For a recently renewed focus on the state, see Geary, *European Labor Protest*; James E. Cronin and Carmen Sirianni, *Work, Community, and Power*; Bernard Sternsher, "Great Depression Labor Historiography in the 1970s: Middle Range Questions, Ethnocultures and Levels of Generalization," *Reviews in American History* (June 1983): 300–19, esp. 304.

27. Joyce, *Work, Society, and Politics*, pp. 337–40; Eric Hobsbawm, *Workers: Worlds of Labor* (New York, 1984), pp. 176–214, esp. 190–92.

28. Bob Holton, *British Syndicalism 1900–1914 Myths and Realities* (London, 1976), p. 50; Schatz, *Electrical Workers*, pp. 36–37, 80–101; Alice Kessler-Harris, "Organizing the Unorganizable: Three Jewish Women and Their Union," *Labor History* 17 (Winter 1976): 5–23.

29. Sara Evans, *Personal Politics: The Roots of Women's Liberation in the Civil Rights Movement and the New Left* (New York, 1979).

30. Mary H. Blewett, "Work, Gender, and the Artisan Tradition in New England Shoemaking, 1780–1860," *Journal of Social History*, 17 (Winter 1983): 221–48. See also the excellent discussion of the development of the male as breadwinner in Sonya O. Rose, "Gender Antagonism and Class Conflict: Exclusionary Strategies of Male Trade Unionists in Nineteenth-Century Britain," *Social History* 13 (May 1988): 191–208; Susan Porter Benson, *Counter Cultures: Saleswomen, Managers, and Customers in American Department Stores, 1890–1940* (Urbana, IL, 1986); Patricia A. Cooper, *Once a Cigar Maker: Men, Women, and Work Culture in American Cigar Factories, 1900–1919* (Urbana, IL, 1987); Dorothy Sue Cobble, "Craft Unionism Revisited: The Case of the Waitress Locals," Paper delivered to the American Historical Association, Cincinnati, Ohio, Dec. 27–30, 1988; Christine Stansell, *City of Women: Sex and Class in New York, 1789–1860* (Urbana, IL, 1987), quotation p. 221; Kathy Peiss, *Cheap Amusements: Working Women and Leisure in Turn-of-the-Century New York* (Philadelphia, 1986), quotation p. 188; Jacquelyn Dowd Hall, "Disorderly Women: Gender and Labor Militancy in the Appalachian South," *Journal of American History* 73 (September 1986): 354–82, quotations pp. 372, 379.

31. Francis G. Couvares, *The Remaking of Pittsburgh* (Albany, NY, 1984), p. 126; "The Triumph of Commerce: Class Culture and Mass Culture in Pittsburgh," in Michael Frisch and Daniel Walkowitz, eds., *Working Class America* (Urbana, IL, 1983), p. 142.

32. Roy Rosenzweig, *Eight Hours for What We Will, Workers and Leisure in an Industrial City 1870–1920* (New York, 1983), pp. 227–28; Jacquelyn Hall, Robert Korstad, and James Leloudis, "Cotton Mill People: Work, Community, and Protest in the Textile South, 1880–1940," *American Historical Review* 91 (April 1986): 245–86. For an example of one attempt at a positive reevaluation of working-class creativity within a modern setting, see George Lipsitz, *Class and Culture in Cold War America: A Rainbow at Midnight* (New York, 1981).

33. Richard Johnson, "Culture and the Historians," in Clarke, Critcher, and Johnson, *Working-Class Culture*, p. 65. See, e.g., David Brody, "The Old Labor History and the New: In Search of an American Working Class," *Labor History* 20 (Winter 1979): 111–26; Elizabeth Fox-Genovese and Eugene D. Genovese, "The Political Crisis of Social History," *Journal of Social History* 10 (Winter 1976): 205–20; and Lawrence T. McDonnell, "'You Are Too Sentimental': Problems and Suggestions For a New Labor History," *Journal of Social History* 17 (Summer 1984): 629–54.

· M I C H A E L R E I C H ·

Capitalist Development, Class Relations, and Labor History

*I*n this essay I discuss an approach to class and labor history that integrates both old and new labor history themes with a new interpretation of the dynamics of capitalist development and class conflict in U.S. history. To situate this approach in relation to recent scholarship, I first contrast the principal explanatory orientations of the old and the new labor histories and suggest how a synthesis might be developed. I then introduce a stage theory of capitalist development and class conflict; this theory provides a framework for the analysis of labor history. In the third section of the essay, I summarize the application of this theory to U.S. labor history from the early nineteenth century to the 1980s, presenting three stages in the history of the U.S. working class. Finally, I discuss the implications of this theory for alternative periodizations of U.S. labor history.

MODES OF EXPLANATION IN U.S. LABOR HISTORY

The outpouring of scholarship in labor history and in social history in recent decades has literally turned two old fields upside down, in each case changing the focus of the subject matter and the principal explanatory orientation used to analyze it. The change in the subject matter is so well-known that it needs little recapitulation here.[1] The old labor history focused primarily upon the evolution of U.S. labor unions and the experiences of organized workers in relation to their union leaders. Labor history was identified primarily with the history of official labor organizations.

By contrast, the subject matter of the new labor history has drawn attention to the diversity of U.S. workers' experiences, whether unionized or not, and the new social history has drawn attention to the everyday lives of all kinds of ordinary Americans, whether articulate or not. The new scholarship has provided a more rounded view of all Americans' historical experiences. It has given voice to hitherto neglected groups and shown how the working class and other groups have affected the historical process.

In particular, the new scholarship has uncovered many positive features in working-class culture. Culture not only provided ordinary Americans with the tools to construct their own sense of meaning in their lives. It also provided the means to comprehend, confront, and sometimes transform the social order in which they lived. By expanding the subject matter in these directions, the new scholarship has made important intellectual advances.

The shift in the principal explanatory approach of the new scholarship is equally important but less frequently discussed. As I see it, the principal explanatory orientation of the old labor history involved an articulated theoretical framework of industrial and labor development. Rapid and prosperous industrialization, together with the early achievement of liberal democratic political institutions, inevitably produced a working class, industrial relations system, and labor leadership with a specified functional character. Initial conditions in the United States differed from those in Europe and explain the differing characteristics of labor movements in each area.[2]

In contrast, the new labor and the new social history utilize a theoretical framework that emphasizes historical contingency, with culture and consciousness rather than iron laws of macroeconomic or political development as the primary generating factors. Historical change is seen as contingent upon human action, which itself is informed by consciousness. Working-class culture, consciousness, and organization are seen as developing in a conflictual context, created by the unequal class relations and institutionalized power of industrializing capitalism. But the outcome of this process is not preordained, one way or another, and need not conform to any functional fit.

The theoretical reorientation represented by the new labor history is just as significant but much less noticed than the spectacular achievements of the shift in the subject matter. In his MARHO interview, Herbert Gutman provided a clear, forceful, and I believe, representative theoretical perspective on the new labor history. In this interview Gutman affirms the role of culture, the aridity of deterministic models of capitalist development, and the falseness of deterministic theories of working-class consciousness, structure, or development.[3] The contrast with the explanatory orientation of the old labor history is evident and provocative.

The attention to contingency and culture certainly constitutes an important and welcome corrective to the theoretical approach of the old labor history. Yet, what has become of the economic forces and systematic determinants that loomed so large in the old scholarship? To some extent, they seem to be returning in the latest wave of the new labor history.[4] In a recent review essay, Gutman characterizes the newest labor history as showing how culture and politics arise not in a vacuum but in relation to changes in class structure and economic development. This intellectual trend indicates that attempts to integrate the old and the new labor history are already underway.[5]

Economics and technology also appear increasingly in the new labor history, with the greater recent emphasis on the organization of work as an important topic of study in itself. One strand of this literature presents a new twist on an old labor history theme: changes in the organization of work during the process of industrialization displaced skilled artisans and small workshops and replaced them with less-skilled mass production workers employed in massive factories. But the changeover took much longer and was less linear in progression than was once thought, and skilled workers played a more active and class-conscious role than was previously thought. The historical diversity of the working class is thus now understood as partly rooted in the diversity of the labor process. Another strand reproduces some central themes of the new labor history: workers' culture at the workplace; the culture they bring to the workplace as well as the culture they create there, and not just economics and technology, play a constitutive role in the organization of work and the conflictual politics of industrial relations.[6] The new historical scholarship is also returning to the political history of labor unions themselves, also a focus of the old labor scholarship.[7]

Whereas the link to economic factors and the old labor history seems to be in the process of reconstruction, it does not yet seem to have been made in a systematic or synthesizing manner. That a gap remains is apparent from complaints that the new labor and social history now suffer from excessive internal fragmentation.[8] The new scholarship, goes the complaint, has been primarily addressed to microscopic case studies to the neglect of the recasting of grand and overarching themes. A new periodization and synthesis are needed.[9]

The development of an integrative theoretical framework within which we could reinterpret the new scholarship certainly sounds desirable. But, how can it be constructed? My account of the importance of contingent rather than systematic factors in the new labor history suggests obstacles from within that might block such a synthesis. It is tempting to then suggest that a synthesis could be developed through a merger of the old labor history with the new.

Such a merger would have to proceed at two levels. First, it would require an integration of the somewhat separate subject matter of the old and new scholarship. I see no basic obstacles here, and as I indicated earlier, such a process already seems underway. Second, a merger would require an integration of the widely different explanatory approaches of the old and the new scholarship. Can an integration of economics and systematic forces with culture and contingency be developed in a satisfactory manner? I am rather doubtful. I propose that an entirely different, alternative synthesis is needed, possible, and fruitful.

This essay suggests that a new labor history synthesis must not only integrate culture and economics. It must also rest upon a more articulated overall conception of U.S. capitalist development than the new labor history has utilized thus far. To do so we need not return to the overly linear, deterministic, and functional theory of capitalist development of the old labor history. Proponents of a new radical political economics, including myself, have been working to improve and broaden our theories of capitalist development. Our approach emphasizes the constitutive importance of culture and politics in the evolution of economic structures. It is, I believe, complementary with the central contributions of the new labor history.

In a recent book, David M. Gordon, Richard Edwards, and I have tried to construct the outline of such an analysis.[10] We developed a political-economic theory of macroeconomic development and drew from both the old and the new labor scholarship to offer an integrated interpretation of the history of the U.S. working class. Labor history, we proposed, should be embedded in a larger account of the dynamics of capitalist development and class conflict. The history of labor and labor struggles can be understood only if linked to macrodynamic developments, not just at the level of individual communities or workplaces but in the social and political order as a whole.

Our theory proposes that the interaction between historically specific social structures of accumulation and the activity and organization of various classes best accounts for the history of U.S. capitalist development and the history of the U.S. working class. Such an approach helps to reperiodize class and labor history and highlights the changing character of the central actors, institutions, and conflicts that have dominated U.S. labor history. I present a summary of our account in the next section.

A STAGE THEORY OF CAPITALIST DEVELOPMENT AND CLASS CONFLICT

It is common to view capitalism as a distinct stage of human history. Yet, capitalism itself has undergone several decisive qualitative transformations, suggesting that capitalism has passed through successive stages of development. Since the 1820s, U.S. capitalism has undergone three major historical changes, each involving a new stage of development. The first stage, competitive capitalism, lasted until the 1890s. In this period slavery was abolished and the capitalist form of organizing production emerged dominant over production by independent artisans or family labor. This period was a stage of competitive capitalism because competition among capitalists became increasingly prevalent in most industries.

Competitive capitalism gave way to the second stage, monopoly capitalism, around the turn of the century, when immense concentrations of capital emerged. The large capitalists now became dominant not only over artisans and family labor but also over small capitalists and industrial workers. The Great Depression of the 1930s challenged this dominance, and a new stage of capitalism, contemporary capitalism, then followed.

In order to understand these decisive changes in U.S. capitalism, we need a theory of the stages of capitalist development that emphasizes the broader environment within which accumulation and change take place. The theory presented here begins with the observation that the institutions surrounding the process of capitalist accumulation must make a coherent structure, called the *social structure of accumulation*, or SSA, for successful capitalist accumulation to proceed.

The social structure of accumulation consists of the specific political, economic, social, and cultural environment within which the capitalist accumulation process is organized. These institutions include "economic" structures, such as the organization of producing firms and markets; the sources of raw materials, labor, and capital; the monetary and credit system; the pattern of state involvement in the economy; and the organization of work and the structure of labor markets. They encompass such international institutions as the organization of international trade, finance, and investment. Equally important, the institutions of the SSA crucially include "cultural" and "political" institutions such as the character of class consciousness, organization and conflict, and the nature of political coalitions and parties.

Once constructed, a social structure of accumulation passes through a life cycle that is connected to its ability to facilitate the capitalist accumulation process. A period of rapid economic growth depends upon the creation of a favorable SSA. But successful capital accumulation ultimately runs into its own limits, the limits imposed by the existing institutional structures or the limits created when it begins to destabilize those structures. With the onset of economic stagnation, the institutions of the structure of accumulation become further undermined. Class conflict is likely to intensify, as each group attempts to defend its existing position and offer and struggle for a vision of an alternative institutional arrangement.

A difficult and lengthy period of institutional reconstruction ensues, requiring experimentation with alternatives, collective action, and the forging of a new political consensus. This new consensus emerges when one class or coalition either overwhelms or reaches a compromise with competing classes or coalitions. Once put into place by the new consensus, the new institutions become consolidated and promote the next long boom. The key institutions continue to evolve during the boom, but in an already set framework.

The rise and decline of successive SSAs give rise to successive stages of capitalist development. Each SSA follows a life cycle characterized initially by exploration, next by consolidation, and finally by decay; the decay of one SSA overlaps with exploratory efforts to construct a new one. The new SSA is unlikely to resemble that of an earlier era because of changes in economic institutions, class structure, and political organization. Each period is likely to exhibit different structural dynamics.

The SSA approach, then, attempts to strike a balance between deterministic and contingent explanations. The boom comes to an end because of internal limits, specific to the period. But the resolution of the crisis, both the timing and terms on which it is resolved, are historically contingent. Consequently, the duration of both the boom and crisis periods are likely to be of uneven length.

The SSA approach offers several additional advantages. For economists, it raises historically contingent social and political factors to a greater level of importance than in conventional macroeconomic models. For historians, it allows us to examine what distinguishes different stages of capitalist development while also permitting variation across countries in the character of that development. The multidimensional approach contrasts with previous stage theories, which focused on technological spurts, movements in the relative prices of primary products, demographic shifts, or other single-factor explanations.

The life cycle of each distinct SSA produces, as a consequence, a specific long swing of the capitalist accumulation cycle. Long swings in capitalist development consist in alternating periods (of about twenty-five years each) of sustained relative prosperity and sustained relative stagnation. These have characterized the world capitalist economy since at least the early nineteenth century. I stress here relative prosperity and relative stagnation because the periods of stagnation that we identify exhibit relatively slow growth rather than no growth at all. Similarly, the periods of prosperity contain some years of recession and no growth, but these are not as frequent, severe, or sustained as in a period of relative stagnation.

The dates for these long swings, which in our theory are of uneven length, are provided in the first two columns of Table 1. For each long swing, the phase of rapid growth is denoted by the letter A and the phase of slow growth by the letter B. Table 2 summarizes some of the quantitative

TABLE 1

Forces Shaping Labor in the United States

Long Swings and Phases	Approximate Timing	Initial Proletarianization	Homogenization	Segmentation
I A	1790s–circa 1820			
B	1820–mid-1840s	Exploration		
II A	Mid-1840s–circa 1873	Consolidation	Exploration	
B	Circa 1873–late 1890s	Decay		
III A	Late 1890s–World War I		Consolidation	Exploration
B	World War I–World War II		Decay	
IV A	World War II–early 1970s			Consolidation
B	Early 1970s–present			Decay

TABLE 2
Evidence for Long Swings

Long swing	Years	Average Annual Percentage Growth in Real Output				
		United States	United Kingdom	Germany	France	Weighted Average
II A	1846–1878	4.2	2.2	2.5	1.3	2.8
B	1878–1894	3.7	1.7	2.3	0.9	2.6
III A	1894–1914	3.8	2.1	2.5	1.5	3.0
B	1914–1938	2.1	1.1	2.9	1.0	2.0
IV A	1938–1970	4.0	2.4	3.8	3.7	3.8

Note: For further details and sources, see Gordon, Edwards, and Reich, *Segmented Work, Divided Workers*, Table 2.1.

indicators of their existence. The dates in this table refer to the world capitalist economy; they also fit the U.S. experience reasonably well.[11]

THREE STAGES IN U.S. LABOR HISTORY

Three qualitatively different social structures of accumulation have characterized the labor process and labor markets of the United States in the period from 1820 to the present. These three different (but overlapping) stages, in turn, have each proceeded through exploratory, consolidated, and decay phases. The interaction of macroeconomic dynamics and labor organization provide in each stage the mechanisms that lead to exploration, consolidation, and decay.

The first stage of the history of the U.S. working class consists of a period of initial proletarianization; its exploratory phase begins in about the 1820s, its consolidation in about the mid-1840s, and its decay phase lasts from the early 1870s to the mid-1890s. This process of initial proletarianization accompanied the development of competitive capitalism, the first stage of capitalist development in the United States.

In this period two great changes affected the development of the U.S. labor force: the abolition of slavery and its replacement by sharecropping in the cotton South, and the emergence of wage labor as the dominant form of employment in the rest of the nation. Our focus here is on the development of wage labor.

The initial scarcity of dependent wage labor forced employers to explore and ultimately rely upon diverse sources of labor supply: native white male farmers, young native women, children, immigrants, and artisans. These labor sources and the wage-labor market developed slowly and at uneven rates throughout the initial proletarianization period. The labor process in the capitalist factories remained equally diverse and in many instances untransformed from the precapitalist period; artisans in particular frequently retained considerable control over the organization of work.

In the period of relatively rapid growth, from the mid-1840s to the early 1870s, diverse internal systems of employer control over labor coexisted, corresponding largely to the respective characteristics of the labor supply. Small workshops typically were supervised by individual entrepreneur-owners, whereas larger factories often employed subcontracting schemes to organize the labor process. Labor markets also remained fragmented and highly imperfect in their competitive structure, divided into relatively distinct pockets. Competition among capitalists, however, began to grow over this period and became increasingly intense from the 1870s on.

The growth of intercapitalist competition, while providing an initial source of great dynamism, led first to increasing economic instability and then to stagnation. Especially after 1873, laissez-faire competition generated increasingly frequent and serious economic fluctuations. Since the national economy was becoming increasingly interdependent, farmers, workers, and businesses faced greater insecurities. Intense competition contributed to falling profit margins during the phase of relative stagnaion, but widespread labor resistance, the growth of unionism, and traditional craft control over the labor process inhibited employer attempts to increase productivity or to cut real wages. The institutions of the competitive capitalist period did not permit employers to restore profit margins easily.

The social structure of the cotton South, it should be noted, also became less suited to facilitating national capitalist accumulation. The profits from slavery were both substantial and tended to mingle in a circulatory process with the profits from trade and wage labor. But the economic surplus generated in the postbellum era was scantier, reflecting both the growth of competition from foreign cotton suppliers and internal impediments inherent in the sharecropping system. Moreover, what little surplus was produced was less likely to enter the national banking system and become available for capitalist accumulation.

Seeking to construct a new SSA, employers began to search for means to restrain competition through mergers and tariff policy and to reduce the power of craft workers. Capital's search for a new social structure of accumulation was at first stimulated by declining profit rates and increased economic instability. It was given a further push by the spread of labor unrest from the 1870s on and by the rise of farmer movements in the 1880s and early 1890s.

But, in the crisis of the 1890s, the old institutions and coalitions broke up and new ones began to be formed, leading to a new SSA. Decisive labor defeats at Homestead and elsewhere in 1892, the electoral defeats of Populism and of an emergent farmer-worker coalition in 1896, the subsequent merger wave, and the drive for higher tariffs and overseas expansion each represent important events in the creation of this new social structure of accumulation, which we call the stage of monopoly capitalism.

Corresponding to this new stage of capitalist development, the second stage in the history of the U.S. working class consists in a period of homogenization. Its exploratory phase begins in the 1870s, a consolidation phase begins in the mid-1890s, and decay takes place in the period between the two world wars. Employers responded to their labor productivity problems in the late nineteenth century by reorganizing the workplace—mechanizing, increasing direct supervision of workers, and decreasing their reliance on skilled labor.

This reorganization, which later came to be called the *drive system*, increased capital-labor ratios, plant size, and the proportion of operatives in industry. Skill differentials fell slightly, a nationally competitive labor market was established, and employers now drew upon a vastly greater supply of labor. Although the ethnic and racial composition of the working class became much more diverse, the working conditions faced by the vast majority of workers became much more similar. For this reason, we describe the drive system as a homogenizing force.

The drive system alone did not constitute a sufficient innovation to usher in a new period of rapid capital accumulation. The new policies that consolidated the homogenization era centered on mechanisms to undercut worker opposition to the drive system: centralized personnel departments, cooperation with and cooptation of existing craft unions, and manipulation of ethnic and racial differences among workers. Such policies required enormous corporate size and were applied only after the great merger movement at the turn of the century. Once it was victorious over labor, big business still had to contend with opposition from other quarters: small business, middle-class Progressive reformers, and urban Socialists. These challenges were resolved during World War I.

The U.S. economic boom of the 1920s was largely made possible by the wartime consolidation of the victory of capital over labor. The boom nonetheless contained its own limits. Given the weak state of labor organization, the rapid growth of labor productivity generated by the drive system far outpaced the growth of wage rates. At the same time, the oligopolistic structure of industry prevented prices from falling; profits soared as a result, and income became distributed much more unequally. By the end of the decade, the consumer boom became based increasingly on debt and decreasingly on real consumer income. As a consequence, the level of economic activity became increasingly subject to the volatility of investment demand.

Economic contradictions, developing in the sociopolitical context of the second social structure of accumulation, made the economy vulnerable to a major crash. With the international economic rivalries of the period, the international institutions of the SSA were as seriously decayed as the domestic ones. The Great Depression then provided the context for the ensuing conflict over the content of the next social structure of accumulation.

In the 1930s class conflict intensified in both the industrial and political arenas. The primary industrial conflict involved, of course, the successful organization of unions among mass production industrial workers. The political conflict produced a realignment of political parties by 1936, analogous to but different in outcome from the realignment of 1896. Neither set of conflicts was resolved decisively until the war.

The third social structure of accumulation, which we call the stage of contemporary capitalism, was formed during and immediately after World War II. It was built upon three principal institutions that each differed substantially from their interwar counterparts. These consisted of a government commitment to avoid depressions and manage aggregate demand by active use of the tools of fiscal and monetary policy; U.S. military and economic leadership to stabilize and dominate the world market in a liberal world order; and the establishment of a limited capital-labor accord, a new system of labor relations that integrated the new industrial unions into a corporatist system of collective bargaining but excluded those groups that the industrial and craft unions had still failed to organize. The compromises inherent in the limited capital-labor accord meant that the postwar SSA was constructed on more favorable terms for a section of labor than was the prewar system.

Corresponding to this third stage of capitalism, the third stage in the history of the U.S. working class consists in a period of segmentation, with exploration beginning after World War I, consolidation beginning around World War II, and decay developing from the early 1970s to the present. The segmentation of labor both accompanied and helped facilitate the period of rapid growth in the United States after World War II. Large corporations had already explored segmentation mechanisms in the 1920s and early 1930s, but these were necessarily put aside for most of the Depression, as the conflict over the contours of industrial unionism became paramount. This conflict over the character of emergent industrial unionism gave way by the early 1950s to conflict within a contained and institutionalized system of collective bargaining that reflected major concessions to the unions.

In the postwar period of segmentation, greater distinctions emerged among unionized industrial workers, professional and technical workers, and workers in the secondary labor market. The expansion of the secondary labor market was facilitated by the break-up of sharecropping systems in the South, the extraordinary productivity growth of agriculture in all regions, and the rapid entry of women into wage labor. The development of divergent labor processes, pay rates, and skill levels and barriers among the three labor submarkets proceeded along both industrial and occupational lines.[12]

By the early 1970s, this system of segmentation and the postwar institutional structure of accumulation more generally were showing signs of serious strain. The system of aggregate demand management, the structure of the international political economy, and the domestic limited capital-labor accord each were no longer functioning to promote prosperity, and a variety of alternative institutions were being explored.

In each period, then, the decline of a social structure of accumulation involved a shift from contained to disruptive class conflict. To be sure, the shift to a new social structure of accumulation did not occur as a mechanical process. Opposing groups presented and struggled for alternative visions of a new set of institutions that would resolve the current crisis. The institutions constructed were not the only ones that would have worked; they were put into place because they did work and because they expressed the political power and success of a new governing coalition. In these ways, the changing character of labor-capital conflict was partly shaped by the macroeconomic context and partly helped to shape that context.

PERIODIZATION IN LABOR HISTORY

This quick summary necessarily represents a highly abbreviated, oversimplified presentation of a complex, extensively documented historical account. The summary also gives more attention to economics and less to culture and consciousness than would be dictated by a proper balance. Nonetheless, I believe that this account provides a framework within which the new labor history's findings on culture and consciousness can be periodized and reinterpreted. Equally important, by theorizing anew the role of historical contingency in capitalist development, I maintain an active and constitutive role for culture and consciousness.

Rather than develop these or other broader theoretical issues in this essay, I prefer here to discuss several specific issues that touch more directly upon the periodization of labor history.[13] In particular, the periodization just presented departs the most from other widely held periodizations for the years 1865 to 1920. The Progressive Beard-Hacker approach saw the Civil War and the CIO–New Deal era as key turning points in U.S. history, while the corporate liberal Weinstein approach saw the development of oligopolistic industry and the interventionist state at the turn of the century as a key turning point. The periodization in this chapter builds upon but differs from both of these.

In order to provide some focus, my discussion shall pertain only to events within the period 1865 to 1920. I consider in turn the impact of the Civil War on industrialization, the growth slowdown and the character of technological change at the end of the nineteenth century, and the meaning of the upsurge in labor revolt in the first two decades of the twentieth century.

The Civil War and Industrialization

In the periodization just presented, I avoided any sustained discussion of the impact of the end of slavery and the Civil War because I focused my attention upon on the wage-labor sector of the economy. For similar reasons, I paid little attention to agricultural labor in general and agrarian conditions and the growth of agrarian protest in the last decades of the nineteenth century in particular. Yet these important events can easily be incorporated into the SSA framework.

A standard historical approach views the Civil War as the great divide in the nation's history. This certainly is undeniable; no other crisis within the country required an internal war for its resolution. I wish to discuss here a more specific proposition: the Beard-Hacker thesis that the North's triumph in the Civil War constituted a capitalist revolution and that industrialization was given a big spurt by the Civil War.

In this view, the era from the Civil War to the Great Depression represents a single period; each decade of the period is characterized by rapid technological change, high rates of growth, and the rapid development of an industrial labor force and economy. The old days of an artisan-based, small-scale manufacturing age gave rise to the big trusts, mass production workers, and the growth of highly capitalized industry. According to this conception, labor struggles surged upward from the onset of the postbellum era, repeatedly but always temporarily defeated by a hostile business class until the great watershed of the 1930s.

My view of this era is more differentiated and leads to an alternative periodization of labor history. The U.S. economy did grow rapidly after the Civil War, assisted by the institutional transformations that had been blocked by the antebellum slavery-capitalism conflict. But the North's victory in the Civil War did not, contrary to the Beards and Hacker, usher in industrial capitalism, which was already well in place. It did, however, permit the final step in the consolidation of the existing social structure of accumulation.

The new elements and their impact are well-known. Most important, of course, the North gained control over national government. During and after the war, northern industrialists were able to implement a long-stalled agenda that consolidated the national economy and promoted rapid industrial growth. Higher tariffs on industrial goods, encouragement of land development for western agriculture, subsidies for railroad expansion, the development of a national banking system, the encouragement of immigration, and support for education all had the effect of integrating national markets, expanding the labor supply, and promoting rapid capital accumulation.[14]

These consolidations of the capitalist order permitted dramatic growth for a time, consistent with the Beard-Hacker thesis. Table 3 indeed shows that GNP, productivity, and industrial production grew quite rapidly in the early 1870s, evidence of the vitality of the consolidated social structure of accumulation in this period. This growth was nonetheless unstable and unsustainable: the first social structure of accumulation was in deep crisis by the time of the Great Depression in 1893–1896. As I will document further, it is misleading to see a single period of U.S. capitalism or of labor history stretching from the Civil War until the Great Depression of 1929.

The Late-Nineteenth Century Crisis

The period from 1873 to 1896 is marked by increasing cyclical economic instability and progressively slower trend growth rates. Economic growth did not stop altogether, as the term stagnation might imply, for growth occurred in every decade, and particularly in the 1880s. But a slowdown in growth did occur from 1873 to 1896, marked by a profit squeeze, productivity bottlenecks, and the increasing frequency of stock market panics and serious business cycle downturns. Instability in the 1870s and 1880s gave way to crisis in the 1890s; the resolution of the crisis involved the defeat of insurgent farmers and workers and the construction of a new set of institutions for accumulation. Only then could rapid capital accumulation resume.

The evidence for the slowdown in growth is reviewed in our book in some detail. However, labor historians David Brody and Frank Wilkinson have each cited extensive data to deny the existence of such a slowdown.[15] Both seem to prefer the alternate Beard-Hacker periodization. I present additional evidence for the slowdown here because the Brody-Wilkinson challenge is crucial for our account, and the issues are consequential for a correct periodization of labor history. In order to avoid repetition, the quantitative evidence I present here is restricted to sources that we have not used previously.

In determining whether a slowdown in the trend rate of growth occurred in a certain period, it is crucial to separate cyclical and trend movements. This separation is usually accomplished by dating the starting and ending points of the period in years that fall in similar phases of the short-run business cycle or by smoothing cyclical variations through the use of moving averages of annual data. Although both Brody and Wilkinson use the same output series that we draw upon in the book, they fail to carefully separate trend from cycle. We do so in our book, and additional evidence supports our conclusions.

Critical of previous estimates, W. Arthur Lewis has developed his own industrial production indices for this period.[16] Using Lewis's series, my own calculations of the trend growth rate show a consistent slowdown in industrial growth from the 1870s to the 1890s (see Table 3). Throughout the period, and even in the boom 1880s, Lewis finds (p. 102) a falling profit rate.

From the early 1870s on, the U.S. economy grew at a slower rate than in the preceding long upswing. Jeffrey G. Williamson shows that the trend rates of growth of both output and productivity slowed further with each successive short-term cycle.[17] As Table 2. 3 indicates, real GNP was growing

TABLE 3

Output and Productivity Growth Rates, 1869–1908

Years	GNP (1860 prices)	GNP per Worker	Industrial Production*
1869/78–1874/83	5.58%	2.66%	2.47%
1874/83–1879/88	4.76	2.11	3.30
1879/88–1884/93	3.68	0.40	2.52
1884/93–1889/98	2.55	0.19	1.11
1889/98–1894/1903	3.39	1.61	2.37
1894/1903–1899/1908	4.31	1.94	3.00

Note: Figures represent per year compound growth rates and are based on the Gallman-Kuznets GNP series, the Lebergott labor force series, and the Lewis industrial production series.
* Manufacturing, mining, and construction.

Sources: GNP and GNP per worker from Jeffrey G. Williamson, *Late Nineteenth Century American Development: A General Equilibrium History*, (New York, 1974), Table 4.2B, p. 70. Industrial production calculated by the author from W. Arthur Lewis, *Growth and Fluctuations 1870–1913* (London, 1978) Table A7, p. 273.

at 5.58 percent per year in the 1870s, 4.76 percent in the early 1880s, 3.68 percent in the late 1880s, and 2.55 percent in the early 1890s. Productivity growth in the same period slowed down from 2.66 percent per year in the 1870s to 0.19 percent per year in the early 1890s. These downward trends were reversed after the recovery from the Great Depression of 1893–1896, when the next long upswing began.[18]

I conclude that the growth retardation thesis rests on a persuasive evidential basis. A relative stagnation did occur, culminating in the economic crisis of the late-nineteenth century. The years from 1865 to 1920 should be divided into two periods, with a major turning point near the end of the century.

Of course, demonstrating the existence of relative stagnation does not amount to explaining the cause of the economic crisis of the late-nineteenth century. Our analysis suggested specific factors: a profit squeeze caused by increasing intercapitalist competition in a labor-management regime that sustained considerable worker power. In this period, I suggest, prices were falling and workers were able to increase their real wages while employers were inhibited from further advancing labor productivity. In order to support this argument beyond the tentative suggestions offered in our book, I have drawn together several pieces of the relevant quantitative material. I present and discuss this evidence in an appendix to this essay.

The Character of Technological Change

An issue related to growth retardation concerns the pace of technological change affecting the labor process in this period. According to our schema, mechanization remained surprisingly limited until the decay of homogenization in the 1880s. At that point, employers became increasingly concerned with cutting labor costs and consequently began to experiment with new means of wresting control over the labor process from skilled workers. Mechanization increased labor productivity in the first instance, but the associated homogenization of the labor force created unintended and unforeseen problems: increased solidarity and resistance from industrial workers. Mechanization really accelerated only after employers learned how to resolve such labor problems.

In his review of our work Brody remarks that technological change was developing rapidly in the postbellum era in such industries as meat processing and iron and steel, contradicting our analytical framework and rendering it suspect. The alternative hypothesis seems to be that technological change was dynamic through the 1920s, in keeping once again with the Beard-Hacker periodization. The alternative hypothesis also sees the character of technological change as cause, and the organization of work as effect, whereas we were stressing the causal role of the labor process and technological change as the response.

In assessing this issue, it is first of all useful to distinguish between individual cases and the central tendencies of a distribution of individual cases. Although simultaneously addressing developments in a wide range of industries, our argument of necessity must be intended to apply to central tendencies and not to every single case. We would expect some variation around the mean, because technological change never occurs at the same rate in all industries. Our account need not apply precisely to every single industry in order to be correct overall.

In any case, I remain convinced of the usefulness of our periodization of the process of mechanization. As I suggested, our account stresses the unintended and unforeseen labor problems created by the increases in mechanization that began in the 1880s. The rate of mechanization grew dramatically faster once capital began to resolve these problems after the turn of the century.[19] Thus, unlike Brody, we see a discontinuity in the 1890s that fits our general account.

1900–1920: Labor Upsurge or Labor Defeat?

Our account of the stages of capitalist development and class conflict in the United States claims that an economic boom began in the late 1890s because a new social structure of accumulation was put into place at that time. But labor unrest and labor revolts, by many accounts, including ours, continued their upward rise through the record-breaking strike wave of 1919. For example, both Brody[20] and *Segmented Work, Divided Workers* (p. 122) cite the rapid growth in union membership, from 447,000 in 1897 to over 2 million in 1904. And David Montgomery has drawn attention to the militancy of the "new unionism" of 1909–1922.[21] It thus seems that one of the central institutions in the social structure of accumulation was not in place until 1920. How does this apparent anomaly affect our theory?

In answer, I would supplement the extensive discussion of exactly this issue in our book by again suggesting the importance of the discontinuity of the 1890s. A brief review of the political crisis of the 1890s and the manner in which it was resolved will help in periodizing the labor struggles of the subsequent two decades. I suggest that capital's resolution of the political crisis of the 1890s did in fact constitute a decisive victory over labor, and that the many labor struggles of the subsequent years were fought in a less favorable structural context.

The political crisis of the 1890s represented a major challenge for capital. The dimensions of the crisis were apparent in the growth of agrarian protest, labor unrest, and business bankruptcies in what was then the worst time of economic troubles the country had ever experienced. Already, in 1892, the Populist party had mounted a serious political challenge and was reaching out to urban workers to construct a potentially formidable farmer-labor alliance. Workers themselves were engaged in new forms of struggle after the disastrous defeats of the 1892 strike wave. Industrial unionism grew rapidly among railway workers and miners and political action also exploded; one indicator is provided by Coxey's Army, another by the support the AFL gave to a socialist platform in 1894 and its efforts that same year on behalf of Populist candidates. Capitalists were painfully aware that something had to be done, and quickly; and they focused their efforts on dividing industrial workers from agrarian Populists.

Promising workers a tariff and stable currencies, capital mobilized on a tremendous scale to defeat the widespread popular revolt. In the 1896 election business contributions to the Republicans doubled over the 1892 level and the Republicans spent five times what the Democrats could muster. The political challenge was defeated, and the potential farmer-labor coalition divided. A critical realignment of the political party system toward the Republicans was thus effected; the "System of '96," as it was called, registered the political dominance of big business.[22]

The swing to the Republicans was further solidified by the removal of blacks and poor whites from southern electoral politics. During this period such Supreme Court decisions as Plessy vs. Ferguson (1896) and Williams vs. Mississippi (1898), as well as a series of state disfranchising conventions, made interracial class alliances opposed to business close to impossible in the South.

Having achieved political dominance, business turned to the difficult task of building a new social structure of accumulation. It first of all went through a frenzied merger wave designed to reduce the level of inter-capitalist competition. At the same time, it promoted overseas expansion to restimulate economic growth, and then, beginning especially with the employer offensive of 1903, it turned its attention to the continuing labor unrest that had been the unintended consequence of homogenizing tendencies.

As we discuss in our book, the consolidation of the period of homogenization involved a lengthy and arduous process. During the Progressive period, big business faced opposition from small business, urban reformers, and other quarters. This was also a period of growing AFL strength, syndicalist upsurges, and socialist insurgencies. Much has been made of the fact that many of these conflicts were not resolved until World War I. However, the length and number of struggles should not obscure the central tendency of this period: because of the groundwork laid down in 1896, the terrain of these contests was basically much more favorable to big business.

The heightened labor struggles of this period illustrate this point. After 1903 business was able to defeat the labor challenges in a decisive manner. This defeat of labor in this period is registered in a variety of indicators, including the quantitative strike data. Although the frequency of strikes stayed at high levels between 1900 and 1920, the percentage of strikes won by workers declined sharply after 1900. By 1921, it stood at half the rate of the early 1880s.[23] Brody rightly characterizes the Progressive era as a period of retreat for the labor movement.[24]

The explanation of these defeats and the associated economic boom, it seems to me, is provided by our SSA account. But, a key turning point, the election of 1896, needs to be further identified and discussed. Although the institutions surrounding labor continued to evolve and undergo consolidation during this period, their basic framework had been constructed earlier. The key turning point had been reached with the defeat of the potential farmer-worker alliance in 1896. After that point, a broad oppositional coalition with an alternative vision was not on the immediate agenda.

As we lay out in detail, except in the cases of coal mining and apparel, business policies to reinforce the drive system overwhelmed labor. The labor movement and its allies, whether socialist, syndicalist, or whatever, were forced into more particularistic and defensive positions, and could not regain the offensive until after the collapse of the second social structure of accumulation in 1929. The further defeat of the labor Left during and after World War I represented a continuation of the trends of this period, rather than an accident of the war.

These brief remarks on the impact of the Civil War, the late-nineteenth century crisis and the labor struggles of 1900 to 1920 suggest how the account in *Segmented Work, Divided Workers* might be expanded to present a fuller view of the historical transformation of labor between 1865 and 1920. The structure of our argument concerning the relation between social structures of accumulation and labor history emerges elaborated in important specifics and intact in broad outline. The periodization suggested here seems useful.

More generally, in this essay I have tried to indicate how labor history can be enriched by a greater integration with an institutional analysis of the macrodynamics of capitalist development. The integration I propose here involves both structural determination and historical contingency. Thus, although the social structure of accumulation that developed after the 1870s involved a growing and more homogeneous working class, its structure did not favor a growth in working class power. At the same time, the discontinuity of the 1890s and the creation of the second social structure of accumulation was a historically contingent rather than predetermined event.

In lieu of a fuller conclusion at this point, I might simply suggest that this illustrates a main theme of this essay. The economic forces and institutions that connect with labor history and give rise to distinct historical periods are not themselves determined by some objective laws of motion, as was once thought. They result from the historically contingent efforts of a variety of actors, not the least of which is labor.

APPENDIX: CAUSES OF THE LATE-NINETEENTH CENTURY SLOWDOWN

The literature on the Great Depression of the 1890s is notably more descriptive and less analytical than the literature on the 1930s. Historical economists have not engaged in the same kind of econometric hypothesis-testing and debate exemplified by Peter Temin's *Did Monetary Forces Cause the Great Depression?*[25] Still, a number of explanations have been offered, corresponding to the usual list of suspects: monetarist, neoclassical, Keynesian, and traditional Marxist (by which I mean the rising organic composition of capital theory). I compare in this appendix the neoclassical explanation (exemplified in Williamson's causal emphasis on investment and the closing of the frontier), the traditional Marxist explanation (exemplified in the causal emphasis on the rising capital-output ratio), and an alternative profit-squeeze mechanism (exemplified in increasing price competition and capital-labor conflict).

Jeffrey Williamson has argued that the crisis of the 1890s was due to a decline in the rate of capital accumulation, itself caused by the exhaustion of profitable investment opportunities.[26] Williamson suggests that a temporarily large set of profitable opportunities arose immediately after the Civil War, but this argument can also be cast in terms of later diminishing opportunities, such as the closing of the frontier and the completion of the national railway net. The decline in investment is then said to cause the decline in productivity and output growth noted in Table 2.3. Using the Kuznets capital stock series, Williamson presents decadal data (based on five-year moving averages) on the rate of growth of the capital stock that seems to bear out this decline. He also points out that the decline in the rate of investment occurred despite a substantial increase in the rate of savings.[27]

Williamson is correct to identify a fall in the rate of profit and in the rate of growth in the late-nineteenth century. But he is wrong to attribute the economic retardation primarily to a decline in the rate of capital accumulation. My own examination of the Kuznets investment series, but drawing upon quinquennial rather than decadal differences and gross rather than net investment, provides a very different picture. Real investment, as Table 4 shows, was increasing in each five-year period from 1869 to 1896, not decreasing. Moreover, investment was increasing at an accelerating rate. This finding of a speed-up of investment is consistent with Williamson's calculations showing that the capital-labor ratio was increasing during this period.[28] It seems unlikely that a *decline* in investment could have been the primary culprit in the growth slowdown.

Traditional Marxian economics suggests that the increase in investment might have been the cause of the growth slowdown. Williamson reports that the capital-output ratio fell between the 1870s and 1880s and then rose until the mid-1890s, as the traditional Marxian account predicts. This declining effectiveness of increased investment might explain the growth slowdown, for the growth rate can be expressed as the ratio of the propensity to save (and invest), which was rising slowly, to the capital-output ratio, which was rising much faster. These considerations support the traditional Marxian explanation.

But a rising capital-output ratio is also consistent with a profit-squeeze theory of the crisis. The rising capital-output ratio need not have resulted from diminishing returns, in the technological sense of the term. A productivity slowdown associated with increased capital-labor conflict could also

TABLE 4
Investment Growth Rates, 1869–1906

1869/73–1872/76	3.4%
1872/76–1877/81	3.9
1877/81–1882/86	4.7
1882/86–1887/91	6.2
1887/91–1892/96	7.0
1892/96–1897/1901	1.0
1897/1901–1902/06	7.3

Note: Figures refer to per year compound growth rates of real gross domestic private fixed nonresidential investment and were calculated by the author from *Historical Statistics of the United States* (1976), Series F98–124. To smooth out short-term business cycle effects, beginning and ending points of each period are four-year averages. The underlying source for these data is Simon Kuznets, *Capital in the American Economy: Its Formation and Financing* (Princeton, NJ, 1961), Appendix C.

diminish the output-enhancing effects of investment and raise the capital-output ratio. Then the profit rate would be squeezed by a different mechanism.

The traditional Marxian and profit squeeze theories seem difficult to distinguish empirically. A look at the movement of real wages in relation to productivity may provide some clues. Lebergott's series on real wages indicates that annual earnings of nonfarm employees fell from 1872 to 1876, were stagnant from 1876 to 1880, rose substantially from 1880 to 1892, fell from 1892 to 1894, and rose steadily in the subsequent decade.[29] Note that the growth in real wages during 1880 to 1892 occurred at a time of slowed productivity growth.

Two additional calculations further support the profit-squeeze hypothesis. First, drawing from the periodic manufacturing censuses, I have calculated trends in the wage share of net output (value-added) for a sample of industries over this period. I find declining profit margins (rising labor shares) from the 1880s until the 1890s and increasing profit margins subsequently. Second, using Frickey's index of annual production and annual data on industry employment generated by Williamson, I have calculated an *annual* output per worker series for 1870 to 1907. These calculations show that productivity growth in industry was rapid between 1876 and 1882, considerably slower between 1882 and 1896, and then most rapid from 1896 to 1907. Moreover, productivity grew faster than real wages from 1876 to 1882, whereas wages grew faster than productivity from 1882 to 1896; after 1896 productivity growth again outpaced real wage growth.

In sum, the evidence presented here is consistent with two hypotheses. First, profits were squeezed in the period up to 1896, and then grew thereafter. Second, growing capital-labor conflict in the workplace or increasing national and international competition, or a combination of these two factors, provided the initial source of the profit squeeze and crisis. If this hypothesis is correct, the investment decline that took place in the 1890s resulted from these sources of a squeeze on profits rather than causing it in the first place. However, these bits of evidence are only suggestive and must be supplemented by further research.

NOTES

Acknowledgments: I am grateful to S. William Segal for excellent research assistance; to the Institute of Industrial Relations, University of California, Berkeley, for research support; and to Samuel Bowles, David Brody, Nancy Chodorow, David M. Gordon, Joan Underhill Hannon, David M. Kotz, Carl Mosk, and Thomas E. Weisskopf for stimulating discussions.

1. Recent reviews of this shift are provided by David Brody, "The Old Labor History and the New: In Search of an American Working Class," *Labor History* 20 (Winter 1979): 111–26; David Montgomery, "To Study the People: The American Working Class," *Labor History* 21 (Fall 1980): 485–512; and Michael H. Frisch and Daniel J. Walkowitz, ed., *Working-Class America: Essays on Labor, Community and American Society* (Urbana, IL, 1983).

2. Selig Perlman, *A Theory of the Labor Movement* (New York, 1928); and Lloyd Ulman, *The Rise of the National Trade Union* (Cambridge, MA, 1955).

3. Interview with Herbert G. Gutman in MARHO, *Visions of History* (New York, 1983), pp. 187–216. Gutman's innovation is not just to emphasize the positive and significant role of cultural factors. He also wants the explanation of the experiences of U. S. workers to be constructed on its own terms, without holding up English, French, or Russian workers as a comparative standard. Gutman is certainly correct that our historical explanations must permit the evolution of working-class structure, organization, and consciousness to vary across the core capitalist countries.

4. See, for example, Frisch and Walkowitz, *Working Class America*.

5. See for example, Gutman's "Working Class Heroes," a review of Sean Wilentz, *Chants Democratic*, in *The New Republic* (July 7, 1984), pp. 33–36; also see his comments in the MARHO interview.

6. For example, see David Montgomery, *Workers' Control in America: Studies in the History of Work, Technology, and Labor* (New York, 1979). A similar emphasis appears in the work of radical political economists.

7. Frisch and Walkowitz, *Working Class America*.

8. See the essays by Brody, Montgomery, and Gutman cited in note 1.

9. Frisch and Walkowitz suggest that the new scholarship is trying to be more integrative (*Working Class America*, p. xi), but I think this is true only in a limited sense.

10. David M. Gordon, Richard Edwards, and Michael Reich, *Segmented Work, Divided Workers: The Historical Transformation of Labor in the United States* (New York, 1982).

11. I include these tables here because two prominent labor historians, David Brody and Frank Wilkinson, have questioned the relevance of long swings to the U.S. case. I present a more detailed discussion of this controversy later in this chapter.

12. For further analysis of this period, extending the discussion and documentation in our book, see Samuel Bowles, David M. Gordon, and Thomas E. Weisskopf, *Beyond the Waste Land: A Democratic Alternative to Economic Decline* (Garden City, NY, 1983); Nelson Lichtenstein, "UAW Bargaining Strategy and Shop-Floor Conflict, 1946–70," *Industrial Relations* 24 (Fall 1985): 360–81; and Michael Reich, "Segmented Labor: Time Series Hypotheses and Evidence," *Cambridge Journal of Economics* 8 (March 1984): 63–82.

13. Several broader issues bear elaboration in another essay. We present a lengthy list of the institutions that constitute the social structure of accumulation, but we do not theorize which are the most important, how many must be in place before a boom period can begin, nor what changes in these institutions are possible or expected during the boom. Moreover, because the book was primarily a history of the transformations of labor, we did not present as rounded an account of each social structure of accumulation as might have been possible in a broader account. In particular, we could have elaborated more fully the political party realignments and changes in the financial system that accompanied each new social structure of accumulation. We could also have said more about the role of U.S. imperialism in constructing the second social structure of accumulation at the turn of the century and then emphasized the decline of U.S. internationalism in subsequent decades as a factor that undermined accumulation in the period.

14. The outcome for the South was different, of course. I generally follow Barrington Moore's suggestion, in his *Social Origins of Dictatorship and Democracy* (Boston, 1967, Chapter 4), that the Civil War constituted an incomplete capitalist revolution. I would add to this story the important work of David Montgomery, *Beyond Equality: Labor and the Radical Republicans, 1862–1872* (New York, 1967), and Jonathan Wiener, *Social Origins of the New South: Alabama, 1860–1885* (Baton Rouge, LA, 1978).

15. David Brody in *Journal of Interdisciplinary History* 14 (Winter 1984): 701–05; and S. F. Wilkinson in *Contributions to Political Economy* 2 (March 1983): 92–98.

16. W. Arthur Lewis, *Growth and Fluctuations, 1870–1913* (London, 1978).

17. Jeffrey G. Williamson, *Late Nineteenth Century American Development: A General Equilibrium History* (New York, 1974).

18. The idea that instability in the 1880s was giving way to crisis by the 1890s also receives confirmation from the work of David M. Gordon, Thomas E.

Weisskopf, and Samuel Bowles, "Long Swings and the Nonreproductive Cycle," *American Economic Review* 73 (May 1983): 152–53. These authors suggest that "normal," short-term business cycles in U.S. economic history are reproductive of the profit rate. In a reproductive business cycle, the downturn acts to re-create the conditions of profitable accumulation that had been eroded during the short-term upturn; the profit rate is higher at the end of the downturn than at its beginning. But in a nonreproductive cycle, the conditions of profitable accumulation are not re-created; the profit rate does not consistently recover in the downturn. Gordon, Weisskopf, and Bowles show that the major depressions of the 1890s, the 1930s, and the 1970s were each preceded by nonreproductive downturns, signaling that the current social structure of accumulation was no longer working, and that major institutional restructuring was needed to re-create profitable conditions for rapid capital accumulation.

19. For further corroborating evidence (not previously cited by us) that supports the periodization of the labor process and technological change presented in *Segmented Work, Divided Workers*, see the following fine studies: Robert C. Allen, "The Peculiar Productivity of American Blast Furnaces, 1840–1913," *Journal of Economic History* 37 (September 1977): 605–33; Steve Fraser, "Dress Rehearsal for the New Deal: Shop-Floor Insurgents, Political Elites, and Industrial Democracy in the Amalgamated Clothing Workers," in Frisch and Walkowitz, *Working Class America*, pp. 212–55; John James, "Structural Change in American Manufacturing, 1850–1890," *Journal of Economic History* 43 (June 1983): 433–59; Christine Stansell, "The Origins of the Sweatshop: Women and Early Industrialization in New York City," in Frisch and Walkowitz, ibid., 78–103; and Sean Wilentz, "Artisan Republican Festivals and the Rise of Class Conflict in New York City, 1788—1837," in ibid., pp. 37–77. On the other side, Peter Nolan and P. K. Edwards ["Homogenize, Divide and Rule: An Essay on Segmented Work, Divided Workers," *Cambridge Journal of Economics* 8 (June 1984): 197–215] mysteriously criticize our periodization of the labor process, and of homogenization in particular, as lacking in documentation. But they fail to notice most of the documentation we cite. They mention only one case study that allegedly contradicts our account—Keith Dix's analysis of the coal industry. However, even a cursory look at this essay reveals that Dix's argument is precisely the opposite of what Nolan and Edwards attribute to him. Nolan and Edwards repeatedly misrepresent what we have to say as well.

20. David Brody, *Workers in Industrial America* (New York, 1980), Chapter 1.

21. David Montgomery, *Workers' Control in America*, Chapter 4; and "New Tendencies in Union Struggles and Strategies in Europe and the United States, 1916–1922," in James E. Cronin and Carmen Sirianni, eds., *Work, Community, and Power: The Experience of Labor in Europe and America, 1900–1925* (Philadelphia, 1983), pp. 88–116. Melvyn Dubofsky in "Abortive Reform: The Wilson Administration and Organized Labor, 1913–1920," in ibid., pp. 197–220, sees a growth in the power of organized labor during the Wilson years.

22. See Bowles, Gordon, and Weisskopf, *Beyond the Waste Land*, pp. 242–49; and Walter Dean Burnham, *Critical Elections and the Mainsprings of American Politics* (New York, 1970).

23. Nolan and Edwards, "Homogenize, Divide and Rule," Table 2. See also pp. 155–57 of *Segmented Work, Divided Workers* for a more detailed discussion of strike trends.

24. Brody, *Workers in Industrial America,* Chapter 1.

25. New York, 1976.

26. Williamson, *Late Nineteenth Century American Development,* p. 111.

27. Ibid., p. 72.

28. Ibid., p. 73.

29. The Lebergott series is reproduced in ibid., p. 79.

· MARI JO BUHLE ·

Gender and Labor History

The new labor history and women's history have developed along parallel lines and at times enjoyed a healthy symbiotic relationship. Both fields, as we now construe them, appeared as by-products of major changes in the profession since World War II, as leading historians departed from the established forms of political or institutional narrative and searched for updated definitions of their interpretive tasks. Both fields gained perhaps even greater inspiration and sustenance from the well-known events of the 1960s; in their wake the most innovative scholars resolved to broaden the subject of history by placing at the forefront the experiences of "ordinary" people. I plan to discuss in this essay some of these common points of reference, to assess the current state of cross-fertilization, and to pinpoint a few potentially fruitful as well as problematical areas of scholarship.

Like new labor historians, recent scholars of American women's history set in by defining their goals against those of their predecessors. Although their counterparts grappled with the collective bargaining and trade union heritage of the Commons-Perlman-Taft school, women's historians examined the relevant scholarship produced before World War II. Their forerunners had not achieved the academic respectability of the pioneering labor economists, but the early historians had produced, as mainly lay practitioners, a sizable body of literature similarly bound by the prevailing institutional framework and whiggish assumptions. Where the old labor history recorded the (purported) maturation of the labor movement and its accession of a significant place in the corporate state, the "old" women's history detailed the contributions of the women's movement to the expansion of women's role in civil society, especially in securing political representation through suffrage. In both cases the legacy proved insufficient. In the first place, the premise informing these early studies, that institutional achievement equaled progress, lacked credibility to a generation coming to intellectual maturity during the 1960s. Second, their institutional frameworks seemed too confining. The radical democratic impulses of the 1960s had revitalized the imperative of retrieving the history of those who stood outside the relatively privileged ranks of the labor aristocracy or organized feminism, and scholar-activists complained readily that "ordinary" people, be they workers or women, appeared too rarely in the early histories. Neither unions nor women's organizations, the major subjects of scholarship, reflected adequately the experiences of the majority, they charged. In reviewing their respective canons, then, both new labor historians and women's historians demanded "a new approach."[1]

American labor historians took their cue, in part, from the British and European social historians Thompson, Hobsbawm, Rude, and others. Thompson in particular helped to transform the field into working-class history at the same time he altered the very meaning of class. Since the landmark publication of The Making of the English Working Class in 1963, American scholars have emulated the Europeans' empirical style and, most important, made workers and work, rather than primarily institutions and events, the subject of their studies.

Labor historians have routinely charted this well-known intellectual odyssey, most by quoting salient passages from Thompson's now-classic preface to The Making of the English Working Class. They hold out the conventional wisdom that "class experience is largely determined by the productive relations into which men are born—or enter involuntarily." They affirm even more readily Thompson's important statement that class consciousness is "the way in which these experiences are handled in cultural terms: embodied in traditions, value-systems, ideas, and institutional forms."[2] During the past two decades, American scholars have been wrestling with the provocative notion that class implies not a categorical grouping but a relationship among people, that its quality cannot be determined simply by inference from economic arrangements, and that its conscious or collective expressions take many forms beyond trade unions and political parties.

Women's historians found a lesson analogous to Thompson's in Mary Ritter Beard's Woman as Force in History. Published originally in 1946 in the shadow of the military defeat of fascism, Beard's book appeared more distant from the sensibilities of the 1960s scholars than did the new European social histories of peasants and workers. Woman as Force in History in its 1962 edition nevertheless sparked interest because Beard, like Thompson, challenged conventional modes of inquiry, in her case by questioning the standards historians employed in measuring contributions to the commonweal. Too often, Beard complained, historians had deemed significant only those arenas where men governed. As a result the majority of writers recorded history within a narrow political space and inadvertently excluded women; or, with the best intentions, others documented the injustice of women's exclusion from this space and portrayed their valiant efforts to gain entry. Beard advised scholars to reject this male paradigm, to enlarge the boundaries of historical significance, and to identify and document women's essential and unique contributions.

Like Thompson, Beard suggested the possibility of a new approach. Although many of her own specific examples of women's role in civilization revealed her unintentional bias for, as Berenice Carroll pointed out, "taking men as the measure," Beard inspired a generation of women's historians in the 1960s to identify new research goals, to look beyond the conventional emphasis on political history, and to search carefully the interstices of everyday life.[3] As Thompson helped to weaken the nexus between trade-union and working-class history, so, too, did Beard set scholars to reconsider history outside the institutional domain defined by men's achievements. Both historians helped, in different ways and for different purposes, to tip the balance from society to culture.

Although most women's historians aspired to follow Beard's lead in redefining historical significance, few adopted her conceptual framework. Beard's thesis was that woman's capacity for maternity fostered a desire for peace and harmony and consequently rendered woman the prime agency of cultural preservation; and upon this thesis she rebuilt a grand historical narrative with women placed at the center. Admiring her intention, scholars of the 1960s nevertheless rejected the earlier historian's tendency toward gender essentialism—a notion undoubtedly more appealing to some scholars today than twenty years ago—and sought to define *sex* with fewer allusions to nature. As a category of social thought, they averred, "sex" might serve properly only if it did not represent a natural condition immune to the ravages of history. Thus, as new labor historians strove to envision "class" as a culturally as well as materially constructed phenomenon, women's historians likewise sought to rid *sex*, or more appropriately *gender*, of static, sterile meanings. Like their peers, women's historians sought nonreductionist concepts to inform their analysis and for theoretical guidance turned away from Beard.

The new labor history suggested possible models. As Joan Kelly pointed out, the most heuristic scholars were in practice adapting the new techniques of class analysis to their special study of women. Not that women's historians merely substituted "sex" for "class" or claimed that women constituted a class. Rather, their determination was to place *social relations* at the center of their historical narrative, which suggested a complementary mode of analysis. New labor historians studied not merely workers' oppression and heroic struggles for liberation; women's historians similarly rejected a paradigm focused on women's subordination and efforts at liberation. Scholars in both camps took up the study of the *process* by which social relations, class or sex, changed; *how* this process conditioned an awareness of social relations; and equally important, *how* actual people in particular situations, workers or women, acted upon this understanding.[4]

For this reason, the framework of the new scholarship in women's history bears an apparent resemblance to that of the new labor history. During the developing stages of the 1960s and early 1970s, scholars in both fields studied most enthusiastically the era of the Industrial Revolution and plotted the course of changes in social relations accompanying the major economic reorganization, particularly the decline in household production and the rise of the factory system. Where labor historians studied the disjunction between master and journeyman, women's historians documented the distancing of men from women and the emergence of "separate spheres." Historians in both fields considered the impact of this epochal event on the status of their respective subjects, but rather than positing a simple decline and tracing a collective response in the form of parties or movements, as their predecessors had done, the younger generation paused to examine the specific forms of cultural mediation that fed this collective consciousness and identified new forms of expression. Labor historians produced richly detailed descriptions of artisanal culture, ranging from, for example, firehouse gangs, sports, tavern life, parade iconography, and religious revivals to the work ethic itself. In examining the cultural by-products of the removal of production from the household, women's historians focused on the emergence of domesticity and its corollary definitions of gender. The major areas of investigation included female friendship and the rituals of sisterhood, relations between mothers and daughters and various aspects of female bonding, "Victorian" sexual mores and behavior, and the "feminization" of religion—in short, the various cultural forms that would provide the mediations between economics and politics.[5]

Although most commentators applauded the overall accomplishments of scholars in these two fields, some noted a few knotty points that fell eventually under the general charge of "culturalism." Labor historians, it was said, sometimes tended to romanticize the preindustrial past and celebrate without sufficient reservation the survival of its customs into the nineteenth century. Women's historians fell into a similar trap by indulging in unwarranted reveries about the transcending nature of nineteenth century sisterhood, underestimating the more important differences between women based on race, class, ethnicity, or region. Other critics evinced impatience about the scale of research and interpretation. Labor historians, some concluded, had become too intensive in their localized pursuits of workers' culture and in producing dozens of "community studies" had short-circuited the goal of fashioning a narrative history of *the* American working class. Women's historians, on the other hand, veered toward grand generalizations based on materials culled mainly from the New England archives of the white middle class.

Perhaps it was inevitable that some historians would claim that their colleagues had gone too far in their neglect of institutions and politics. In a major address in 1978, David Brody urged labor historians to reconsider "the powerful logic behind an economic approach to the history of American workers" and to admit that "the job concerns of American workers were largely bound up with, and sometimes observable to us only through collective activity and labor organizations."[6] Just two years later, women's historians read a similar complaint. Ellen C. DuBois warned that an increasingly narrow focus on women's culture ran the risk of robbing scholars of their original feminist agenda. DuBois, like Brody, reaffirmed the importance of studying organized political movements and gave witness in her own masterful analysis of the nineteenth century woman suffrage movement.[7]

In actuality, sizable numbers in both fields had maintained a perspective on politics. The most inventive scholars identified new institutional forms, but the majority nevertheless acceded the importance of conventional measures. The landmark community studies of nineteenth century working-class life featured strikes, unions, and local parties, whereas the equally pathbreaking workplace studies of the twentieth century emphasized the connections between informal and formal work rules and collective resistance to management strategy. Recently, historians have restored trade unions and political parties to a place of prominence, albeit on different ground; new publications on the Knights of Labor, the Socialist and Communist movements, and specific national or international unions suggest a discernible trend. Women's historians, for their part, have not lagged behind. In numerous essays and monographs published since the mid-1970s, a link between culture and politics serves to hold together the various narratives. Recent studies of religious revivalism, abolitionism, urban philanthropy, temperance and prison reform, health care, and radical movements indicate a continuing interest in politics, broadly defined.[8]

In addition, leading scholars in both labor history and women's history continue to concede the centrality of economics in any analytical schema. As Brody has pointed out, new labor historians might reject the specific teleological slant of Commons et al., but they have not abandoned the materialist underpinnings of the original scholarship.[9] Indeed, empirical data accumulated as well as shaped by the pioneers continue to inform recently published monographs. New labor historians undoubtedly write more eloquently and profusely about the mediations between culture and society in shaping identity, ideology, and behavior; they nevertheless root their descriptions in a close reading of productive and property relations. Such is also the case among the many women's historians who have benefited directly from the early researches of Commons's contemporaries Alice Clark, Edith Abbott, and Helen Sumner. In even the most cultural studies, women's relationship with production serves as baseline in analysis. One might go so far as to assume that it is as much this attention to economics as shared interest in culture that links these fields of scholarship.

The methodological congruence of women's history and the new labor history represents only one aspect of their parallel development. Another reflects the generational experiences of the historians themselves. As is well-known and sometimes decried, initially these two fields attracted an inordinate number of students who sought in history a political purpose and who shocked their more reserved colleagues by stating explicitly their desire for relevance. The problematic nature of this quest aside, a large component of the dynamism that marked these two fields during their formative years flowed directly from an almost utopian faith in the power of historical understanding to change the very social relations under examination.[10]

This process took place as much outside the classroom as within. In the 1960s, when the works of Thompson and Beard found receptive audiences, readers considered their contributions mainly in informal study groups. These groups comprised mostly graduate students, a few young faculty members, and a handful of undergraduates who commonly sought to fill out a new agenda. Self-directed classes on corporate liberalism, imperialism, social movements, and popular protest constituted an alternative curriculum and, in some cases, the pivotal experience of graduate training. Rejecting the consensus interpretations of their regular professors, these students pursued instead the more credible theme of conflict in American history and shaped their studies under the rubric of radical history.

Newly published works on the corporate state and European social history or the out-of-fashion Progressive classics represented only one element in this education. Works on theory played a no less important role. Fledgling radical historians tackled Marxist philosophy and cultural anthropology and helped to create new journals specializing in synthesis across several disciplines. Informal study groups thus augmented reading lists in history with selections from anthropologists Mintz, Geertz, and Levi-Strauss; the leading contributors to the Frankfurt school; the "early" Marx and the modernists who refashioned his ideas in the pages of *Telos* and *Radical America*; the structuralists and neomaterialists who hammered out their differences in *New Left Review*; and the political economists writing in *Socialist Revolution* and *Monthly Review*.

The events of the times—the Vietnam War, revelations about social injustice at home, large-scale protest and liberationist movements—served to heighten the consciousness of such historians. Most came to recognize the dual implications of "radical history": that radicalism played a major part in shaping American history; and that radicalism had a powerful appeal to historians. This realization fed expectations. Perhaps each generation believes itself invested with the responsibility to remap the contours of the existing canon. But not since the era of the Progressives did a generation sense not only a necessity but a possibility of breaking through the confines of the academy. Radical historians aspired to be truly sophisticated and skillful at their craft, to be pathbreaking. They also felt an imperative to apply their talents outside the immediate setting of the classroom and to take advantage of opportunities to make public statements. The then-popular slogan "Power to the People" legitimated this desire. Historians, despite their training and dedication, did not aspire to draw the lessons for the masses; rather, in the spirit of Carl Becker, they sought to engage people directly in the study of history, of a truly relevant history, of their own history.

There was, in sum, a pervasive belief that the discipline of history was tremendously important. Among radicals, history was *the* conception of the age, as much as literary criticism or psychology had been to radicals of the 1910s and 1930s, and at the cutting edge of scholarship were students of social relations. Labor historians and women's historians, as specialists in class and sex relations, respectively, thereby assumed major roles in defining the terms of discussion within the growing, self-confident circles of radical historians.

Although both groups felt the immediacy of the moment and anticipated great conceptual advances, women's historians in particular set very high standards. They aspired to reconceptualize the very foundations of historical inquiry and, in so doing, revitalize the role of theory. By placing gender at the center of analysis, they believed, scholars would necessarily discover the means to recast the entire narrative structure of American history. But to some, even this goal was in itself insufficient. The most far-reaching intended to give coequal attention to the process of class formation in American history.

Among radical historians, specialists in women's history demanded the ultimate synthesis. Joan Kelly wrote:

We have made of sex a category as fundamental to our analysis of the social order as other classifications, such as class and race. And we consider the relation of the sexes, as those of class and race, to be socially rather than naturally constituted, to have its own development varying with changes in social organization. Embedded in and shaped by the social order, the relation of the sexes must be integral to any study of it. Our new sense of periodization reflects an assessment of historical change from the vantage point of women as well as men. Our use of sex as a social category means that our conception of historical change itself, as change in the social order, is broadened to include the relation of the sexes.

After defining this basic tenet, Kelly specified the larger goal. "If the relationship of the sexes is as necessary to an understanding of human history as the social relation of classes," Kelly explained, "what now needs to be worked out are the connections between changes in class and sex relations."[11]

It would be naive, of course, to claim that all scholars toed this line. A tendency toward radical feminism had already developed, and heated discussions about the "unhappy marriage" of Marxism and feminism, while sharpening the terms of dialogue for some, moved others to contemplate divorce.[12] Certainly not all women's historians, perhaps not even the majority, reached toward a synthesis of class and gender analysis. Nevertheless, the number who aspired to reach this goal was large and influential within the field of women's history during its formative period.

By the early 1970s, then, many women's historians shared with labor historians not only techniques of analysis or methodology, intense interest in theory and desire for relevance, but also *substance*—the history of class relations. For these reasons perspicacious scholars tried to keep up with the outpourings in labor history. Many believed labor historians were their closest allies in the theoretical tasks at hand, and they hoped to carry their insights and empirical contributions into their own special researches on women.[13]

This affinity in methodology and subject matter between the two fields abetted the development of one of the most innovative and rich subfields: women's labor history, or the history of women and work. Specialists in this area have produced a sizable body of literature that spans American history from the preindustrial arrangements of colonial New England to detailed studies of recent events, such as the Great Depression and world wars. Historians have considered the major areas of women's employment, from domestic service, the textile and apparel industries, to clerical, retail sales, and health service work. Women's professional occupations stand prominently in recent studies of librarians, physicians, and scientists. And the long-standing issues of women's participation in trade unions and labor organizations have inspired a wealth of studies.[14] In no other area of women's history—sexuality, family, politics, or popular culture, for example—is the picture drawn as completely or finely. One might even claim that contributions in this area, as methodologically rigorous as numerous, constitute the backbone of the new scholarship in women's history.

A central theme in these publications is the gendered division of labor and its implications for women's status in the labor market. In pursuing this matter, historians have built upon the important contributions of their forerunners Sumner, Abbott, and Clark, but have also delved into more recent research into women's labor-market activity. Drawing on the work of their peers in related disciplines, such as sociology and economics, they have considered the persistent wage differential between men and women, the clustering of women into few occupations, and women's underrepresentation in labor unions—in short, the discriminatory aspects of women's experience in wage labor. The interdisciplinary orientation has served scholars well in this investigation: theories of status attainment and of dual labor markets have proven useful to varying degrees in framing in new ways old questions about women's subordinate status. As a result, formulations concerning women's wage labor during recessions, depressions, and wars is much more complex and interpretations more sophisticated than, for example, the formerly popular "reserve army" paradigm.[15]

The chief innovations stem, however, from recent research into the link between women's place in the labor market and their equally unique role at home. Building on, and contributing to, the rich studies of nineteenth century domestic life—the structural as well as cultural redefinitions of womanhood associated with the rise of industrial capitalism—women's historians have enlarged their conception of labor history to incorporate the "nonproductive" labor of women in their homes. And this aspect of their research separates them from their forerunners as well as the vast majority of their contemporaries in labor history.

Whereas labor historians, including Commons's colleagues who researched women's history, focused on workers in relation to production (meaning those men and women engaged in social production or the production of exchange value), most contemporary women's historians acknowledge the importance of women's work in the home and shape their analyses around this important insight. In 1969 Margaret Benston set scholars moving in this direction. In a provocative essay, she argued that women's domestic work—household maintenance, the care of boarders, consumer functions, emotional and sexual service to husbands, care and socialization of children, and so on—shaped female identity as well as influenced market relations; and, second, that women's domestic work was not marginal but necessary in the overall schema of capitalist production.[16] In the decade following the publication of Benston's essay, scholars in several disciplines refined and elaborated upon the significance of the dual nature of capitalist production, such that it is now commonplace to assert the simple but previously obscured premise that women, even if not wage earners for most of their history, have always worked and that this work is central to the development of both class and gender relations.[17]

Historians of women's work insist, then, that a full study comprises an equally close examination of those areas of labor classified as "social reproduction" or "the reproduction of labor power." This aspect of research and analysis concerns not merely the central place of housework, however broadly defined, but sexual relations, particularly as ordered within the family.

Most women's historians define two sets of social relations, separate but interrelated, each historically specific and dynamic—capitalism and patriarchy. Building upon the recent contributions of mainly feminist anthropologists, many historians now readily accede the importance of patriarchy, or what is more broadly termed the sex-gender system. According to Gayle Rubin, the sex-gender system comprises "the set of arrangements by which a society transforms biological sexuality into products of human activity, and in which these transformed sexual needs are satisfied." Kinship systems, Rubin explains, are the "observable and empirical forms" of this aspect of social organization, including various relational categories and status hierarchies. The particular, historically determined form of a sex-gender system marked by domination by men and oppression of women is termed *patriarchy*. Extending this line of analysis, most women's historians agree with Heidi Hartmann's provocative thesis that a patriarchal sex-gender system, wherein men dominated in an unequal division of labor within the family, not only predated capitalism but contributed to its development. The status of women and the sexual division of labor in American society is the result, in Hartmann's opinion, "of a long process of interaction between patriarchy and capitalism."[18] Historian Linda Gordon draws out the implications of this insight:

> the situation of women cannot be fully explained in terms of the capitalist mode of production—the subject central to Marxist thought. Our sex/gender system has roots in the organization of reproduction, which appears to have predated all forms of class society. Capitalism has not itself completely individualized people, and production relations are often mediated by other social relations created by reproductive forms of organization—by friendship, kinship, informal work groups.[19]

This assumption has moved scholars of women's work along lines of investigation less readily associated with labor history, into matters related to sexual rather than to specifically economic arrangements.

The examination of the relationship of production and social reproduction surfaces in a variety of ways in recent publications. Women's historians no longer ask only the familiar questions about the impact of wage-earning on women's status. Following the lead of European historians Joan Wallach

Scott and Louise Tilly, they now routinely consider the particular character of the family economy and examine their subjects' understanding of domestic work; their identity as wives, mothers, or sisters; and the impact of both on their marketplace behavior and status. Despite important differences in interpretation, historians agree about the reciprocity inherent in these two roles. Where one assumes that young working women's realistic expectations about a future defined by marriage and motherhood—as well as the accompanying segregation into low-paying, low-status occupations—inhibit their consciousness as wage earners, others contend that the experience of wage earning itself alters fundamentally a woman's options as well as aspirations about her domestic future.[20] Scholars specializing in "workers' culture" and resistance to management strategy have been especially attuned to the ways in which women's sexual identity impinges on their behavior in the workplace; they have contributed greatly to our understanding of the unique ways in which women have organized, informally as well as formally, to control the conditions of their labor. More than other historians of the twentieth century shop floor, they have managed to reunite the public and private aspects of daily life, to sketch a fuller consciousness of their subjects than those aspects determined apparently by productive relations.[21] In fact, these studies together underscore and enlarge the thesis that working-class consciousness cannot be extracted from workers' relation to production alone.

Those historians who have pursued more conventional matters—collective actions, strikes, unions, and so on—have also utilized this growing body of research on women's familial and reproductive roles, including their extension into friendships, networks, and popular ideologies. We have, as a result, more multidimensional answers to such nagging questions as "where are the organized women workers?" We know, as Alice Kessler-Harris and Ruth Milkman have documented, that both the structure of the capitalist labor market and the patriarchal attitudes of male workers and unionists have mitigated against women's participation in the organized labor movement. Kessler-Harris has explained additionally that women's primary attachments to home and family often countered their impulse to join and sustain unions, and that the popular ideology associated with women's reproductive roles served as the rationale for the protective legislation that further ensured women's secondary status in the labor market. But Kessler-Harris has also suggested that these same sensibilities—women's recognition of their differences from men and their potential for motherhood—could at other times, such as during the decade of peak labor activity before World War I, foster rather than inhibit trade union solidarity.[22] Research into such historical phenomena as female bonding, friendships, and networks as well as the ideology of sisterhood has given us new perspectives on those organizations that stand out in women's labor history, such as the Knights of Labor, the Women's Trade Union League, and the International Ladies' Garment Workers' Union.[23] We are also beginning to understand the moments when middle- or upper-class women supported wage-earning women in their organizational struggles. Some historians even postulate that, at times, the class struggle bore a distinctive gender character in the form of a "cross-class sisterhood" uniting activists from church, temperance, or philanthropic societies and trade unionists.[24]

The value of research along this line is readily apparent in recent work on collective actions or strikes involving women. Although labor historians have long recognized the importance of neighborhood or community mobilization in behalf of union-sponsored or spontaneous turnouts, research centered on women's role has provided new perspectives on familiar events. Take, for example, the Lawrence textile strike of 1912, a landmark in twentieth century labor history. The conflicts between opposing philosophies of unionism, the issues associated with an unskilled, new-immigrant work force, and the complex political implications have featured prominently in the scholarship for decades. Recently, however, Ardis Cameron has provided a strikingly fresh analysis. Through painstaking reconstruction of working-class communities, Cameron uncovered a network of women that spanned neighborhood and factory and played the pivotal role in organizing and sustaining the strike. Some of the most militant "strikers," Cameron found, were women who were not working at the time in Lawrence's factories. Many, of course, had known life on the shop floor in years or months past, or expected to return to the mills in the near future; others vicariously shared the experiences of wage-earning friends and relatives. By showing how these bonds among women functioned to solidify class consciousness and encourage labor militance, Cameron exposed the crucial link between women's traditional sphere, the home, and working-class activism.[25]

In light of these recent contributions, one might conclude that this special subfield, the history of women's work, has flourished perhaps above all others. Drawing on the conceptual advances associated with the new labor history, employing some of the most innovative paradigms of the new scholarship in women's studies, historians in this area have explored with determination and with impressive results the possibilities of scholarly cross-fertilization. They have directed their research toward achieving a full history of social relations embracing both class and sex, and have gained apparent methodological sophistication in the complementary modes of analysis. One might conclude further that the notorious "unhappy marriage" provided just the right amount of tension—for historians, at least—for nearing the fulfillment of its promise.

To the major question, How have these contributions influenced American labor history in general? Without doubt, labor historians have profited from these advances. Few now follow directly in the footsteps of mentor E. P. Thompson who, in Ann Lane's words, "pulled the English working class from a world of silence [but] left women out."[26] Rather, they note the presence of women in the industrial work force and record assiduously the exclusivist rhetoric of old-time craft unionists. The community-based studies of the nineteenth century have included references to women's domestic role or to the "cult of true womanhood," if only to distinguish between the experiences of middle- and working-class women or to discuss the decline in household production. Indeed, the noninstitutional tendencies of the new labor history is conducive to explorations in this direction and has allowed historians to define more broadly working-class culture and consciousness. Whereas in the many monographs inspired by the Commons school, women were negligible, save perhaps in the textile or garment industries, and their roles in trade unions, although occasionally heroic, were in actuality minimal for well-known reasons, recent publications provide considerably more space for women as actors. Gender has emerged, in other words, as a significant factor.

Although most labor historians now recognize gender as a means of differentiating among distinct groups of workers and of assigning specific characteristics to each, the majority has not gone very far in incorporating the deeper meanings of the new scholarship in women's history. Few show any predilection to alter basic categories of analysis, and the principal subjects—workers and work—continue to gain definition only in relation to capitalist production. The ways in which culture mediates this relationship are more far-reaching, of course, for most historians reject simplistic connections between material conditions and behavior or ideology, be it collective or individual. And, for this reason, situations outside the workplace, in the community, neighborhood, or family, play a role in explaining working-class activity and in drawing even nonwage earning women into the narrative. But this tendency is slight. Despite the important conceptual advances in both labor and women's history, the narrative baseline remains productive relations, traditionally defined. The family economy, the nonwage labor performed in the household, may appear but only peripherally to the main analysis, and the organization of reproduction, if mentioned, derives almost entirely from its allegedly subordinate relation to the system of production. For this reason, recent scholarship in American labor history varies *in essence* only slightly from the earlier model. Despite the novel emphasis on cultural mediation in the new scholarship, the moorings in the materialist paradigms developed in the late-nineteenth century and focused on production alone remain firm; and these moorings continue to secure the major inquiry in the old, conceptually limited categories. Good intentions notwith-

standing, too many historians still incline to view women as secondary actors in the class struggle, as auxiliaries to the main event, or as "factors"
to be integrated into predesignated categories.[27]

If, then, American labor history stands at a crossroad, the problem ahead
is not merely one of synthesizing the major contributions in the field.
Through the power of collective imagination, scholars might unite the methodologically discrete community and workplace studies, break through the
boundaries of localized research, figure out more precisely the connections
between culture and politics, and finally, create a narrative structure on a
grand scale. The foundation in the form of brilliant essays and monographs
certainly exists and grows sturdier at an increasing rate. This is not to say
that the task is a simple or easy one. But if scholars can resist the temptation
to lighten their labors by returning to the safer economism of earlier times,
the promise inherent in the works accumulating since the 1960s might still
be realized. But even this particular task of synthesis, as monumental as it
may at times seem, falls short of the goal set by women's historians: to
reconceptualize basic categories of analysis to include the processes of class
formation *outside* capitalist production, as traditionally defined.

Is the moment propitious for just such a conceptual leap? Scholarship
in both women's history and labor history is rich, and these two fields now
stand as respected establishments within the larger historical profession.
New contributions appear almost daily, and despite the comparatively low
prestige of the humanities today, interest among students has not waned
to a life-threatening degree. Especially at the graduate level, scholars in
training represent a reassuring constituency. But many things have changed
since the heady days of the 1960s and early 1970s, when these two fields
presented their initial challenges before the profession. On the one hand,
the magnitude of achievement has legitimated the inquiry into the history
of these formerly marginalized subjects, such that a trend toward professionalism, so-called, carries with it some well-known and perhaps inevitable
consequences. A tendency toward a narrow empiricism, of knowledge seemingly for its own sake, shows itself in some recent publications just at a time
when the necessity for further theoretical speculation looms paramount.
Certainly, the earlier visionary expectations about history in relation to
praxis have quelled to some extent, even among some now-aging enthusi-
asts. Faith in the relevance of historical research seems less functional as
a motivating factor, and in its place stands, to some degree, an appreciation
of the philosophical elegance of the new scholarship. In terms of continuing
institutional support, little needs to be added about the potential ramifications of the political climate of the 1980s.

In addition to these weighty matters are other developments of perhaps
overwhelming significance, shifts in orientation within the field of women's
history. As mentioned earlier, only a minority of women's historians ever

perceived an affinity with the methodological and theoretical agendas of the new labor history. This group, despite its size, nevertheless proved highly influential within its field, such that it might not be too much to contend that publications in women's history informed by class served in the early 1970s as the centerpiece of the developing scholarship. It would be more difficult to make this claim today, when scholars in women's studies, including younger historians, seem less committed to the philosophical imperative of class analysis and present other priorities, ranging from a poststructuralist emphasis on psychosexual formations to an insistence on a more-informed consideration of the category of race.

Students of Afro-American history, through a growing list of publications, are questioning the validity of existing scholarship on women. Although scholars have regularly issued statements on the theoretical importance of social categories outside gender, they note, few actually designed their research strategies to include the readily recognized but insufficiently explored differences in the historical experiences of black and white women. As a result, the bulk of monographs produced in the past fifteen years concerns the history of mainly white, middle- and working-class women.

Even more problematical than a dearth of information on the specific history of Afro-American women is the often-unacknowledged weakness in the conceptual frameworks built on this narrow evidential base. To a large extent, women's historians have linked shifts in sex relations and roles to developments in industrial capitalism and sex-gender systems common to Europe and North America. This practice necessarily excludes a study of American black women, whose specific experiences are tied more to agriculture than industry, and equally important, to a sex-gender system that originated in Africa rather than Europe. At a theoretical level, this practice additionally conflates the history of industrialization and capitalism and thereby blunts our tools of analysis. And it inadvertently presumes a universal form of patriarchy.[28]

Historians of Afro-American women are currently exploring more fully the sexual division of labor within the black family and its significance within the larger system of capitalist production. Here Angela Y. Davis's early contribution on women's role in the community of slaves gains new meaning, as historians reexamine Afro-American kinship structure in relation to the political economy of slavery. Jacqueline Jones's *Labor of Love, Labor of Sorrow* takes a first, monumental step in this direction, documenting the "peculiar configuration" of economic and sexual relations governing the lives of Afro-American women. By situating slavery squarely at the center of American capitalist development, Jones underscores the unique and essential part played by black women's labor. Jones does not deny the importance of industrialization or place black women outside its framework. But, by focusing on agricultural labor, both slave and free, she brings the majority of black women into the larger narrative of capitalist development.[29]

The implications of new research along this line are manifold. By enlarging the existing set of social categories to include not only class and gender but race, we may sharpen our analytical tools. The Industrial Revolution, and New England, may play a less prominent role as researchers uncover a larger material base. Historians may finally uncover the unique contours of the history of Afro-American women and at the same time create new conceptual frameworks for the history of American women in general.

Labor historians need only to consider recent works on systems of labor to appreciate the importance of such shifts in analysis. Despite the efforts of W. E. B. DuBois and C. L. R. James, to name only the most prominent Pan-Africanist scholars, American slavery continues to appear in most historical works as a national or even regional event, tragic for its human toll but hardly instrumental in determining the course of American history. Immanuel Wallerstein among others has suggested a different perspective: slave-labor as engine for saving Europe from economic stagnation, one element in a tripartite division of the world's labor force, fuel for industrial capitalism.[30] Such a view assumes a systemic relationship between slavery and capitalism and counters the prevailing emphasis on the specific history of (mainly white) industrial workers.

It remains to be seen, of course, if established historians of women or labor are ready to meet the tough challenges posed by these developments. Empirical research is still at a very elementary stage, certainly insufficient for constructing grand narratives or sophisticated analyses. But if the new social history is to survive, a massive dose of theoretical revitalization is needed. Historians must satisfy a deep-seated yearning for broader analyses, or they will cease to play a role.

Historians are already losing ground within the field of women's studies. Previously, historians, especially those material feminists with eyes fixed on the dual nature of capitalist production, stood at the forefront; now they occupy a position mainly in the wings as scholars with other perspectives capture audiences with theoretical forays into gender essentialism, or what is sometimes called a *woman-centered analysis* or *perspective*. In this view, the female experience rather than social relations stands as the principal locus of inquiry, and historical analysis seems less vital than alternative disciplinary modes that seem more amenable to an examination of the sexual-psychological makeup of women. Upcoming scholars, more attuned to radical rather than socialist-feminist thought, focus on the universal elements of the female experience as located in individual psychology or motherhood and deemphasize the larger social and economic context of this experience. Some in fact, serve as archcritics of historians, dismissing their work by naming it a system of inquiry shaped by patriarchy and marked by phallogocentrism.[31]

One may sense the implications of this shift by considering the current status of history within women's studies. Once the building block of the field, history now seems to pale before the other allegedly more theoretical disciplines, such as literary criticism. In fact, charges of "vulgar empiricism" are not uncommon. To established scholars, who for years have prided themselves precisely on the uniquely theoretical and interdisciplinary quality of scholarship in women's history, such accusations seem both shocking and nonsensical. Eventually, however, they decode the message: women's history is too materialist and not sufficiently psychoanalytic; it centers on systems of oppression rather than repression; and its conceptual framework concerns productive relations rather than sexual systems, or capitalism rather than the phallus. To those with lingering respect for history's pioneering role, it is not so much the case that women's history is nontheoretical, merely old-fashioned in its theory.

The larger implications of this reordering of disciplines are manifold. On the one hand, historians have benefited conceptually from research and paradigms developed by scholars outside the area of history. The contributions of anthropologists to our understanding of the relationship between public and private spheres and women's status have been enormous. The research by psychologists into mother-daughter bonds and the process by which sexual identity forms cannot be underestimated. By the mid-1970s, the interdisciplinary quality showed itself most beneficially in the pivotal work by Carroll Smith-Rosenberg, for example, which treated historically the female experience associated primarily with reproduction in its biological and social forms.[32] The research and theoretical formulations concerning reproduction have been central to the development of scholarship, so much so that most women's historians now consider matter-of-factly the interaction of, in Linda Gordon's words, "a patriarchal economy of reproduction with a capitalist economy of production."[33] Perhaps, no one illustrates the elegance of this insight with as much ease as Temma Kaplan who, in examining female consciousness emerging from the division of labor by sex, gives special attention to its content. Building on scholarship in disciplines outside history, Kaplan asserted: "all classes of women understand what their society's division of labor by sex requires of them: the bedrock of women's consciousness is the need to preserve life."[34] Perhaps, the way is now paved for a new appreciation of Mary Beard, who located in "feminine qualities" the main agency against the forces of "barbarism and pessimism wrestling for the possession of the human spirit."[35] More likely, the road leads away from historical inquiry altogether.

"Everything is word, everything is only word," writes French feminist

Hélène Cixous.[36] Paraphrasing Jacques Lacan, and appropriating his psychoanalytic method, Cixous elaborates a premise underlying much scholarship in women's studies; namely, that language constructs humanity rather than vice versa. Feminist inquiry thus focuses on the binary opposition of symbolic systems, the hierarchical oppositions of "male" and "female" as the source of women's repression. The symbolic order, its logic and linguistics as constructed by men, produces meaning. Only by decoding it, only by laying bare the phallogocentrism, can women gain subjectivity. In this "exorbitation of language," to use Perry Anderson's neologism, the strategy becomes reading the text, criticizing the text, and writing the new text.[37] Historical modes seem very much beside the point.

What does this shift mean for labor historians? One can only speculate, of course. Perhaps the scholarship on women's status in relation to the dual mode of capitalist production will finally strike a responsive chord and inspire a new era of experimentation. Certainly, the questions raised by interpreters of Afro-American history underscore the importance of kinship structure and affirm, if only implicitly, the wisdom of such a course. Perhaps a new, enlarged partnership is the best possibility. By working together, women's, labor, and Afro-American historians might provide the desirable renewal. A team effort is undoubtedly now required to construct a conceptual framework capable of spanning all fields, making actual the abstract claims of class, gender, and race as essential categories of historical analysis.

A gloomier possibility is a further fragmentation of scholarship in these three benchmark fields of social history and a foreclosure on the once-symbiotic relationship of women's and labor history. Ominous signs cloud the horizon. There is, for example, a tendency among some women's historians to regard *class* in ways that parallel most labor historians' use of *gender* (and both's of *race*); that is, as a means to differentiate among the experiences of discrete groups but not to structure a conceptual framework. *Class* becomes, in other words, a factor but *not* a category. The difference in meaning here is more than semantic, and the potential consequences greater than trifling.

It is likely that the recent (belated, by European standards) acquisition of poststructural methods ensures this latter possibility. If the recent and prestigious work in women's studies involves primarily a study of "discourse," especially of the written text, then the earlier commitment to the history of "ordinary" people, the "inarticulate," nearly vanishes. Women's and labor historians would surely benefit from more sophisticated research into popular ideologies and would gain new insights into the cultural construction of class or gender. But if the method is determined by theoretical premises ahistorical or antihistorical, the results will be incompatible with the substance of social history. Under the sign of gender essentialism, binary opposition between the sexes rules all other historic relations marginal or entirely inconsequential. Labor historians, among others, will be left out in the cold, faces pressed against the window, staring at the luxuriant feminist intellectual feastings inside.

The prospects of this spectacle should cause labor historians to reconsider their own origins. For the generation of the 1960s and 1970s, even the most complex scholarly dialogue assumed that its most erudite notions could be translated into popular forms, if not at the time, then under better conditions. Slowly, painfully, belief in (and commitment to) relevance for the sake of social change has ebbed across American university life. Semiotic scholars, in the purely intellectual sense, might be seen as mirror opposites of ourselves at an earlier age.

"History is not the soil of happiness," Hegel warned long ago, and we might add today, happy for neither participants nor historians. "In contemplating history," he went on, "as the slaughter bench at which the happiness of peoples, the wisdom of states and the virtues of individuals have been sacrificed, a question necessarily arises: To what principles, to what purpose, have these monstrous sacrifices been made?" This is a good question, better perhaps for the twentieth century than for the nineteenth. Many today would respond no purpose at all. Hegel shaped an answer that infallibly recalls the visionary zeal that inspired the social historians two decades ago: "World history is the progress of the consciousness of freedom," however *freedom* may be defined.[38]

Such faith is difficult to maintain at this time. Labor historians nevertheless await, as they must await, some sign that the present mood will pass sooner or later.

NOTES

1. This phrase appeared first in Gerda Lerner's influential essay, "New Approaches to the Study of Women in American History," *Journal of Social History* 3 (1969): 53–62; reprinted in Lerner, *Majority Finds Its Past* (New York, 1979). For a similar statement, see Ann D. Gordon, Mari Jo Buhle, and Nancy Schrom (Dye), "Women in American Society: An Historical Contribution," *Radical America* 5 (1971): 3–66.

2. E. P. Thompson, *The Making of the English Working Class* (New York, 1963), pp. 9–10.

3. Berenice Carroll, "On Mary Beard's *Woman as Force in History*," in B. A. Carroll, ed., *Liberating Women's History: Theoretical and Critical Essays* (Urbana, IL, 1976), p. 38. At the Fourth Berkshire Conference on the History of Women, in August 1978, historians discussed the influence of Beard's work at a

session entitled "Roundtable: The Legacy of Mary Ritter Beard." For selections from Beard's writings and for an assessment of their significance, see Ann J. Lane, ed., *Mary Ritter Beard: A Sourcebook* (New York, 1977).

4. Joan Kelly-Gadol, "The Social Relations of the Sexes: Methodological Implications of Women's History," *Signs* 1 (1976): 813. In an informal paper presented at the Radical Historians' session at the annual meeting of the Organization of American Historians, April 1975, I acknowledged Thompson's influence on the developing field of women's history. This essay was published as "Recent Contributions to Women's History," *Radical History Review* 2 (1975): 4–11.

5. For a fuller characterization and for specific citations, see Barbara Sicherman, "Review Essay: American History," *Signs* 1 (1975): 461–85; Mary Beth Norton, "Review Essay: American History," *Signs* 5 (1979): 324–37; and Barbara Sicherman, E. William Monter, Joan Wallach Scott, and Kathryn Kish Sklar, *Recent United States Scholarship on the History of Women* (Washington, DC, 1980).

6. David Brody, "The Old Labor History and the New," paper delivered at the annual meeting of the Organization of American Historians, April 1978, p. 10; published as "The Old Labor History and the New: In Search of an American Working Class," *Labor History* 20 (1979): 111–26. A harsh criticism of the allegedly apolitical thrust of the new social history, including labor history, appeared two years earlier: Eugene D. Genovese and Elizabeth Fox Genovese, "The Political Crisis of Social History," *Journal of Social History* 10 (1976): 205–20.

7. Ellen Carol DuBois, "Politics and Culture in Women's History: A Symposium," *Feminist Studies* 6 (1980): 28–36; and *Feminism and Suffrage: The Emergence of an Independent Women's Movement in America, 1848–1869* (Ithaca, NY, 1978). An earlier affirmation of political history came from Linda Gordon, "What Should Women's Historians Do? Politics, Social History, and Women's History," *Marxist Perspectives* 1 (1979): 133. See, also, Elizabeth Fox Genovese, "The Personal Is Not Political Enough," *Marxist Perspectives* 2 (1979–80): 94–113.

8. For examples of recently published monographs, see: Nancy F. Cott, *Bonds of Womanhood: "Woman's Sphere" in New England, 1780–1835* (New Haven, CT, 1977); Blanche Glassman Hersh, *The Slavery of Sex: Feminist Abolitionists in America* (Urbana, IL, 1978); Barbara Berg, *The Remembered Gate: Origins of American Feminism—The Woman and the City, 1800–1860* (New York, 1978); Karen J. Blair, *The Clubwoman as Feminist: True Womanhood Redefined, 1868–1914* (New York, 1980); Ruth Bordin, *Women and Temperance: The Quest for Power and Liberty, 1873–1900* (Philadelphia, 1981); Barbara Leslie Epstein, *The Politics of Domesticity: Women, Evangelism, and Temperance in Nineteenth-Century America* (Middleton, CT, 1981); Estelle B. Freedman, *Their Sisters' Keepers: Women Prison Reform in America, 1830–1930* (Ann Arbor, MI, 1981); Virginia Drachman, *Hospital with a Heart: Women Doctors and the Paradox of Separatism at the New England Hospital, 1862–1969* (Ithaca, NY, 1984); Jacquelyn Dowd Hall, *Revolt against Chivalry: Jessie Daniel Ames and the Women's Campaign against Lynching* (New York, 1974); Sara Evans, *Personal Politics: The Roots of Women's Liberation in the Civil Rights Movement and the New Left* (New York, 1978); Linda Gordon, *Woman's Body/Woman's Right: A Social History of Birth*

Control in America (New York, 1976); and Mari Jo Buhle, *Women and American Socialism, 1870–1920* (Urbana, IL, 1981). For an important essay outlining the relationship of culture and politics in women's history, see Estelle B. Freedman, "Separatism as Strategy: Female Institution Building and American Feminism, 1870–1930," *Feminist Studies* 5 (1979): 512–29.

9. Brody, "The Old Labor History and the New."

10. The historical relationship of feminism and women's history has been explored by Kathryn Kish Sklar, "American Female Historians in Context, 1770–1930," *Feminist Studies* 2 (1975): 171–84. For a statement of the contemporary relationship, see Gordon, "What Should Women's Historians Do?" pp. 128–29.

11. Kelly-Gadol, "Social Relations of the Sexes," pp. 816–17.

12. For a succinct statement, see Heidi Hartmann, "The Unhappy Marriage of Marxism and Feminism: Toward a More Progressive Union," *Capital and Class* 8 (1979): 1–33; reprinted with a series of related essays in Lydia Sargent, ed., *Women and Revolution* (Boston, 1981).

13. For examples of this scholarship, see a collection of essays published originally in Judith Newton, Mary P. Ryan, and Judith R. Walkowitz, eds., *Feminist Studies: Sex and Class in Women's History* (Boston, 1983).

14. Several full-length overviews are Alice Kessler-Harris, *Out To Work: A History of Wage-Earning Women in the United States* (New York, 1982); Julie A. Matthaei, *An Economic History of Women in America: Women's Work, the Sexual Division of Labor, and the Development of Capitalism* (New York, 1982); and Susan E. Kennedy, *If All We Did Was to Weep at Home: A History of White Working Class Women in America* (Bloomington, IN, 1979). For examples of monographs on various topics, see Laurel Thatcher Ulrich, *Goodwives: Image and Reality in the Lives of Women in Northern New England, 1650–1750* (New York, 1982); Lois Scharf, *To Work and to Wed: Female Employment, Feminism, and the Great Depression* (Westport, CT, 1980); Winifred Wandersee, *Women's Work and Family Values, 1920–1940* (Cambridge, MA, 1980); William H. Chafe, *The American Woman: Her Changing Social, Economic and Political Roles, 1920–1970* (New York, 1977); Maurine Weiner Greenwald, *Women, War, and Work: The Impact of World War I on Women Workers in the United States* (Westport, CT, 1980); Karen Anderson, *Wartime Women: Sex Roles, Family Relations and the Status of Women during World War II* (Westport, CT, 1981); Susan M. Hartmann, *The Home Front and Beyond: American Women in the 1940s* (Boston, 1982); Thomas Dublin, *Women at Work: The Transformation of Work and Community in Lowell, Massachusetts, 1826–1860* (New York, 1979); Marjorie Davies, *Woman's Place Is at the Typewriter: Office Work and Office Workers, 1870–1930* (Philadelphia, 1982); Elyce Rotella, *From Home to Office: U.S. Women at Work, 1870–1930* (Ann Arbor, MI, 1981); Mary H. Blewett, *Men, Women, and Work: Class, Gender, and Protest in the New England Shoe Industry, 1780–1910* (Urbana, IL, 1988); Susan Porter Benson, *Counter Cultures: Saleswomen, Manager, and Customers in American Department Stores, 1890–1940* (Urbana, IL, 1986); David M. Katzman, *Seven Days a Week: Women and Domestic Service in Industrializing America* (New York, 1978); Faye E.

Dudden, *Serving Women: Household Service in Nineteenth-Century America* (Middleton, CT, 1983); Barbara Melosh, *"The Physician's Hand": Work Culture and Conflict in American Nursing* (Philadelphia, 1982); Dee Garrison, *Apostle of Culture: Public Librarian and American History* (New York, 1979); Mary Roth Walsh, *"Doctors Wanted: No Women Need Apply"—Sexual Barriers in the Medical Profession, 1835–1875* (New Haven, CT, 1976); Barbara Harris, *Beyond Her Sphere: Women and the Professions in American History* (Westport, CT, 1978); Patricia Hammer, *Decade of Elusive Promise: Professional Women in the United States, 1920–1930* (Ann Arbor, MI, 1978); Barbara Wertheimer, *We Were There: The Story of Working Women in America* (New York, 1975); Nancy Schrom Dye, *As Equals and as Sisters: Feminism, the Labor Movement, and the Women's Trade Union League of New York* (Columbia, MO, 1980); and Meredith Tax, *Rising of the Women: Feminist Solidarity and Class Conflict, 1880–1917* (New York, 1980).

15. Ruth Milkman, "Women's Work and the Economic Crisis: Some Lessons from the Great Depression" *Review of Radical Political Economics* 8 (1976): 73–97; reprinted in Nancy F. Cott and Elizabeth Pleck, eds., *A Heritage of Her Own: Toward a New Social History* (New York, 1979), pp. 343–66. Alice Kessler-Harris, "Stratifying by Sex: Understanding the History of Working Women," in Richard C. Edwards, Michael Reich, and David Gordon, eds., *Labor Market Segmentation*, (Lexington, MA, 1975). See, also, M. Blaxall and B. Regan, eds., *Women and the Workplace: The Implications of Occupational Segregation* (Chicago, 1976).

16. Margaret Benston, "The Political Economy of Women's Liberation," *Monthly Review* 21 (1969): 13–27.

17. Alice Kessler-Harris, *Women Have Always Worked: A Historical Overview* (Old Westbury, NY, 1981).

18. Gayle Rubin, "The Traffic in Women: Notes on the 'Political Economy' of Sex," in Rayna R. Reiter (Rapp), ed., *Toward an Anthropology of Women* (New York, 1975), pp. 159, 169; Heidi Hartmann, "Capitalism, Patriarchy, and Job Segregation by Sex," *Signs* 1 (1976): 167.

19. Gordon, "What Should Women's Historians Do?" p. 134. Literature on this historical as well as theoretical matter is plentiful. Renate Bridenthal's "The Dialectics of Production and Reproduction in History," *Radical America* 10 (1976): 3–11, provides a succinct statement of the historical relevance. See also Joan Kelly, "The Double Vision of Feminist Theory: A Postscript to the 'Women and Power' Conference," *Feminist Studies* 5 (1979): 216–27; reprinted with other valuable essays in *Women, History, and Theory: The Essays of Joan Kelly* (Chicago, 1984). Several volumes address this issue: Annette Kuhn and Ann Marie Wolpe, eds., *Feminism and Marxism: Women and Modes of Production* (London, 1978); Zillah R. Eisenstein, ed., *Capitalist Patriarchy and the Case for Socialist Feminism* (New York, 1978); Natalie J. Sokoloff, *Between Money and Love: The Dialectics of Women's Home and Market Work* (New York, 1981); and Lise Vogel, *Marxism and the Oppression of Women: Toward a Unitary Theory* (New Brunswick, 1983). Mattaei's *An Economic History of Women in America* considers both market and nonwaged labor in the home. Literature on the history of housework is abundant. For an assessment, see Nona Glazer, "Housework: Review Essay," *Signs* 1 (1976): 905–22.

For a collection of essays, see Sara Fenstermaker Berk, ed., *Women and Household Labor* (Beverly Hills, CA, 1980). Two full-length histories are Susan Strasser, *Never Done: A History of American Housework* (New York, 1982); and Ruth Schwartz Cowan, *More Work for Mother: The Ironies of Household Technology from the Open Hearth to Microwave* (New York, 1983).

20. Louise Tilly and Joan Wallach Scott, *Women, Work, and Family* (New York, 1978), demonstrated the importance of the family economy in women's history. For examples of different emphases regarding the meaning of wage labor, see Dublin, *Women At Work*, and Leslie Woodcock Tentler, *Wage-Earning Women: Industrial Work and Family Life in the United States, 1900–1930* (New York, 1979).

21. See Susan Porter Benson, "'The Customers Ain't God': The Work Culture of Department Store Saleswomen, 1890–1940," in Michael H. Frisch and Daniel J. Walkowitz, eds., *Working-Class America: Essays on Labor, Community, and American Society* (Urbana, IL, 1983), pp. 185–211; and Mary H. Blewett, "Work, Gender and the Artisan Tradition in New England Shoemaking, 1780–1860," *Journal of Social History* 17 (1983): 221–48. See also Davies, *Woman's Place Is at the Typewriter*; and Melosh, *"The Physician's Hand."* The literature on the interrelation of women's domestic-sexual identity and class identity is growing. Virginia Yans-McLaughlin, *Family and Community: Italian Immigrants in Buffalo, 1880–1930* (Ithaca, NY, 1977) focused on the role of ethnicity, as did Miram Cohen, "Italian-American Women in New York City, 1900–1950," in Milton Cantor and Bruce Laurie, eds., *Class, Sex, and the Woman Worker* (Westport, CT, 1977), pp. 120–43; and Elizabeth H. Pleck, "A Mother's Wages: Income Earning among Married Italian and Black Women, 1896–1911," in Michael Gordon, ed., *The American Family in Social-Historical Perspective*, 2d ed. (New York, 1978), pp. 490–510, and reprinted in *A Heritage of Her Own*, pp. 367–92. See also Tamara Hareven, "Family Time and Industrial Time: Family and Work in a Planned Corporation Town, 1900–1974," *Journal of Urban History* 1 (1975): 365–89; and Barbara Klaczynska, "Why Women Work: A Comparison of Various Groups, Philadelphia, 1910–1930," *Labor History* 17 (1976): 73–87. To sense the significant change in tenor of argument since these early publications, see Christine Stansell's "The Origins of the Sweatshop: Women and Early Industrialization in New York City," in *Working-Class America*, pp. 78–103.

22. Alice Kessler-Harris, "'Where Are the Organized Women Workers?'" *Feminist Studies* 3 (1975): 92–111, and reprinted in *A Heritage of Her Own*, pp. 343–66; Ruth Milkman, "Organizing the Sexual Division of Labor: Historical Perspectives on 'Women's Work' and the American Labor Movement," *Socialist Review* 10 (1980), pp. 95–150; Kessler-Harris, "Problems of Coalition-Building: Women and Trade Unions in the 1920s," in Ruth Milkman, ed., *Women, Work, and Protest: A Century of U.S. Women's Labor History* (Boston, 1985), pp. 110–38; and Sharon Hartman Strom, "Challenging 'Woman's Place': Feminism, the Left, and Industrial Unionism in the 1930s," *Feminist Studies* 9 (1983): 359–86.

23. Susan Levine, *Labor's True Woman: Carpetweavers, Industrialization, and Labor Reform in the Gilded Age* (Philadelphia, 1985); Dye, *As Equals and as Sisters*; Robin Miller Jacoby, "The Women's Trade Union League and American Fem-

inism," *Feminist Studies* 3 (1975): 126–41; Nancy MacLean, "The Culture of Resistance: Female Institution Building in the International Ladies' Garment Workers Union, 1905–1920," *Michigan Occasional Papers in Women's Studies* 21 (Winter 1982); Joan M. Jensen and Sue Davison, eds., *A Needle, a Bobbin, a Strike: Women Needleworkers in America* (Philadelphia, 1984).

24. Cross-class alliances are examined by Tax, *Rising of the Women*; Dye, *As Equals and as Sisters*; and Buhle, *Women and American Socialism, 1870–1920*. For institutions involving women of differing classes, see essays in Joyce L. Kornbluh and Mary Frederickson, eds., *Sisterhood and Solidarity: Workers' Education for Women, 1914–1984* (Philadelphia, 1984). The importance of women's networks in the community is underscored in Judith E. Smith's "Our Own Kind: Family and Community Networks in Providence," *Radical History Review* 17 (1978): 99–120, and reprinted in *A Heritage of Her Own*, pp. 393–411; and in Smith's *Family Connections: A History of Italian and Jewish Immigrant Lives in Providence, Rhode Island 1900–1940* (Albany, NY, 1985).

25. Ardis Cameron, "Bread and Roses Revisited: Women's Culture and Working-Class Activism in the Lawrence Strike of 1912," in *Women, Work, and Protest*, pp. 42–61. For a slightly different model, see Temma Kaplan's "Female Consciousness and Collective Action: The Case of Barcelona, 1910–1918," *Signs* 7 (1982): 545–66.

26. Ann J. Lane, "Women in Society: A Critique of Frederick Engels," in *Liberating Women's History*, p. 21.

27. A recent discussion highlights the centrality of this matter in labor history as well as differences of opinion: Harold Benenson, "Victorian Sexual Ideology and Marx's Theory of the Working Class," and responses by David Montgomery and Ellen Ross, *International Labor and Working Class History* 25 (1984): 1–36.

28. Bonnie Thorton Dill, "Race, Class and Gender: Prospects for an All-Inclusive Sisterhood," *Feminist Studies* 9 (1983): 131–50; Claudia Goldin, "Historians' Consenses on the Economic Role of Women in American History: A Review Essay," *Historical Methods* 16 (1983): 74–81; Phyllis Marynick Palmer, "White Women/Black Women: The Dualism of Female Identity and Experiences in the United States," *Feminist Studies* 9 (1983): 151–70; and Bettina Aptheker, *Woman's Legacy: Essays on Race, Sex, and Class in American History* (Amherst, MA, 1982). A valuable collection of essays is Sharon Harley and Rosalyn Terborg-Penn, eds., *The Afro-American Woman: Struggles and Images* (New York, 1978).

29. Jacqueline Jones, *Labor of Love/Labor of Sorrow: Black Women, Work, and the Family from Slavery to the Present* (New York, 1985); Angela Y. Davis, "Reflections on the Black Woman's Role in the Community of Slaves," *The Black Scholar* 3 (1971): 2–15; and Davis, *Women, Race and Class* (New York, 1981). See also Herbert G. Gutman, *The Black Family in Slavery and Freedom, 1750–1925* (New York, 1976); and Suzanne Lebsock, *The Free Women of Petersberg: Status and Culture in a Southern Town, 1784–1860* (New York, 1984). For three important sources on women's wage labor, see Dolores Janiewski, *Sisterhood Denied: Race, Gender and Class in a New South Community* (Philadelphia, 1985); Beverly W. Jones, "Race, Sex, and Class: Black Female Tobacco Workers in Durham, North Carolina, 1920–1940, and the Development of Female Consciousness," *Feminist*

Studies 10 (1984): 441–52; and Rosalyn Terborg-Penn, "Survival Strategies among African-American Women Workers: A Continuing Process," in *Women, Work, and Protest,* pp. 139–55.

30. Immanuel Wallerstein, *The Modern World System,* vols. 1 and 2 (New York, 1974, 1980). See also Cedric J. Robinson, *Black Marxism: The Making of the Black Radical Tradition* (London, 1983).

31. A useful overview is Hester Eisenstein, *Contemporary Feminist Thought* (Boston, 1983).

32. Carroll Smith-Rosenberg, "The Female World of Love and Ritual: Relations Between Women in Nineteenth-Century America," *Signs* 1 (1975), 1–30; reprinted in *A Heritage of Her Own,* 311–42.

33. Gordon, "What Should Women's Historians Do?" p. 134.

34. Kaplan, "Female Consciousness and Collective Action," p. 546. Kaplan draws from the work of Nancy Chodorow, *The Reproduction of Mothering: Psychoanalysis and the Sociology of Gender* (Berkeley and Los Angeles, 1978). Also applicable in varying degrees are Dorothy Dinnerstein, *The Mermaid and the Minotaur: Sexual Arrangements and the Human Malaise* (New York, 1977); and Adrienne Rich, *Of Woman Born: Motherhood as Experience and Institution* (New York, 1976).

35. Beard, *Woman as Force in History,* p. 339.

36. Hélène Cixous, in "Le Sexe ou la tête?" as quoted by Domna C. Stanton, "Language and Revolution: The Franco-American Dis-connection," in Hester Eisenstein and Alice Jardine, eds., *The Future of Difference* (New York, 1980), p. 73. See also Elaine Marks and Isabelle de Courtivron, eds., *New French Feminisms: An Anthology* (Amherst, MA, 1980); and Ann Rosalind Jones, "Writing the Body: Toward an Understanding of L'Écriture Feminine," *Feminist Studies* 7 (1981): 247–63.

37. Perry Anderson, *In the Tracks of Historical Materialism* (London, 1983), p. 40.

38. G. W. F. Hegel, *Reason and History: A General Introduction to the Philosophy of History,* trans. Robert S. Hartman (Indianapolis, 1953), pp. 33, 26, 24.

· EXPLORATIONS ·
IN
SYNTHESIS

· SEAN WILENTZ ·

The Rise of the American Working Class, 1776–1877

A Survey

> "What was America in 1492 but a Loose-Fish, in which Columbus struck the Spanish standard by way of waifing it for his royal master and mistress? What was Poland to the Czar? What Greece to the Turk? What India to England? What at last will Mexico be to the United States? All Loose-Fish.
>
> What are the Rights of Man and the Liberties of the World but Loose-Fish?"
>
> —Herman Melville, *Moby-Dick, or The Whale* (1851)

*I*n the mid-1770s, the American colonies were a string of agrarian communities and provincial seaports of increasingly uncertain political allegiance. Their work force consisted mainly of petty producers, servants, slaveholders, slaves; only a small proportion of the population worked primarily for wages. In 1880, the United States was still largely rural but on its way to becoming the leading industrial producer on earth—a reunited nation-state of capitalists, petty producers, shopkeepers, and employees, where most gainfully employed persons were wage earners.[1] Such, at their sketchiest, are the outlines of the rise of the American working class.

The many complexities of this chapter of American labor history are all too familiar. The spread of northern capitalist wage labor alongside the rise and fall of the cotton kingdom, the expansion of democracy and party loyalties among propertyless white men, the emergence of a largely immigrant and ethnic working class—these developments and many others obstruct any tidy narrative of American class formation and development. They also preclude attempts to judge American workers on the basis of economic and political models drawn from the history of other countries. But these complexities are just that. They do not indicate, as historians once assumed, the irrelevance of class and class conflict in the United States.[2] Quite the contrary, they help us comprehend the peculiar timbre and ferocity of working-class history in the first successful modern republic, a history that led, in the 1880s and 1890s, to one of the bloodiest crescendos of industrial warfare anywhere in the world.

To understand these events, we must discard the old assumption that labor history is simply about wage earners or about life on the shop floor. Even today, that assumption remains strong. The very term, *labor history*, still conjures up a familiar set of images—brawny men and feisty women (usually white) tending huge machines or walking on picket lines. Such scenes are certainly important, but so are many others: slaves picking cotton and harvesting cane; sharecroppers tending their plots; politicians (few of them working-class) debating legislation; working people in their homes and at play as well as at work. Class formation and development were political and cultural as well as economic processes that touched every American and every aspect of American life. They were also uneven processes that affected different groups of workers in very different ways; at no point was the American working class a monolith. Reinterpreting the history of American workers means reaching for a fresh synthesis of all of American history, one that tries to connect working people's diverse experiences and activities to larger patterns of politics, ideas, and social relations.

A few recent scholars, faced with this formidable task, have tried to identify some key markers in the past in order to distinguish one era of American labor history from another. Despite their disagreements over theory and method, they have come up with roughly similar chronologies and mapped out four phases of American capitalist development prior to 1920. Phase one, spanning the years between 1500 and the coming of the American Revolution, has been described as an era of "primitive accumulation," in which British and European settlers seized land from native Americans and began exploiting the bounty of the New World, making abundant use of bound labor. Phase two, the period of ascendant merchant capitalism from the Revolution to the crisis years of the 1840s and 1850s, brought the victory, consolidation, and democratization of the republican revolution, the geographic expansion of cotton slavery, the transformation of northern wage labor into a market commodity, and the creation of the first locally based working-class movements. Phase three, from the midcentury crisis to the worldwide depression of the 1870s, saw the vindication of the free-labor republic, national political reconstruction, a virtually unrestrained burst of industrial capitalist growth, the development of a largely immigrant and ethnic industrial working class, and the first clear signs of a national working-class presence. Phase four, from the upheavals of the 1880s to the era of World War I, brought the advent of national and international monopoly capital, a remaking of the American working class, bitter conflicts between employers and workers, and a fragmentation of the American labor movement.[3]

The focus here will be on the second and third periods—on the formation and early development of the American working class. A multitude of events and social changes is contained in that phrase, some of which can only be touched on in this survey. At every point, though, the rise of the working class was intimately connected to an overriding theme of late-eighteenth and nineteenth century American history: the struggle to match contradictory republican ideals to the realities of conflict that accompanied capitalist development.

WORKING-CLASS FORMATION
IN THE AGE OF REVOLUTION, 1776–1848

1776–1815

Beginning with the arrival of the first ships of white settlers, British North America was tied to an expanding capitalist world system. Yet, even as late as the 1770s, it would have been difficult to describe America as a capitalist *society*. In contrast to the mother country, colonial American development generated not a "free" propertyless proletariat but various forms of unfree labor—slavery for Africans and some American Indians, indentured servitude for propertyless white immigrants. More fortunate "middling" settlers—northern and southern yeomen, urban craftsmen—followed forms of barter exchange and petty commerce, based in individual households, that were out of step with capitalist relations. The imperial mercantile network certainly connected the colonies to regional and international markets, primarily through London; by the outbreak of the Revolution, these connections had begun to undermine established labor regimes. But the triumph of capitalist labor and market relations—and the emergence of a working class on these shores—awaited the further decline of bound labor and the disruption of petty household production in town and countryside.[4]

The prevalence of household production did not mean that colonial society was egalitarian, even for free persons. In the countryside, marked stratification of wealth and power was evident in the staple-growing regions of the South as early as the seventeenth century. By the middle of the eighteenth, the older "egalitarian" settlements of New England and the middle colonies were increasingly dominated by local elites of exceptional wealth and power. In the infant cities, commercial growth brought even greater concentrations of wealth: in Philadelphia, for example, the wealthiest 10 percent of the population came, by the 1760s, to control two-thirds of the city's taxable resources. Nor did household production utterly preclude wage labor. Free domestic servants could be found in wealthier urban homes. The maritime, transportation, and building trades in the port cities created markets for seasonal and casual labor. Skilled journeymen, in town and country, worked for wages. Tenant farmers hired themselves out, on a temporary basis, to help with harvesting, clearing the land, and other farm chores.[5]

The main arena for labor relations, however, was the household; farmers and craftsmen exploited themselves, their families, their apprentices, and their slaves within a web of paternalist obligation quite distinct from that of an impersonal capitalist labor market. Wage earners and their families accounted for only about one-fifth of the white population at the time of the Revolution. Even in the cities, the growing inequality among free persons did not remove the abundant need for unfree labor. In 1750, black slaves represented about 10 percent of Boston's population and about 20 percent of New York's, while in Philadelphia, slaves and indentured servants made up 20 percent of the population and held almost half of all laboring jobs.[6]

The shift toward the greater use of free wage labor seems to have begun as early as the 1750s, and it quickly accelerated over the next half century. The seaboard cities, particularly in the urban crafts, were the crucibles of change. Artisan production had grown rapidly during the early and mid-eighteenth century, in step with the growth of colonial agriculture and commerce. Shipbuilders, joiners, and other maritime craftsmen supplied the merchants with necessary materièl; the expansion of urban consumer markets widened the need for building tradesmen, cordwainers, tailors, blacksmiths, and many others. Based in small workshops (often attached to the master craftsman's residence), the artisans benefited from a general scarcity of skilled labor in the colonies. Journeymen craftsmen were generally able to reach favorable wage agreements with their employers and fairly quickly set up shops of their own. Bound apprentices appear to have had a reasonable expectation of one day becoming independent artisans. Conditions were such that, as late as 1750, many independent master craftsmen, North and South, had to rely on bound white workers and slaves: "Barring any unforeseen problems," one historian has written of Philadelphia, "servants and slaves were far cheaper than wage laborers."[7]

By the 1770s, however, several factors had converged to change this situation in the chief northern cities. Continued immigration from Britain and Europe added thousands of potential wage workers to the northeastern population. Deepening fluctuations in trade and a tightening of credit resources in the calamitous aftermath of the Seven Years' War made it more difficult for journeymen to earn their competences and for master craftsmen to sustain their independence. In the last third of the eighteenth century, roughly one-quarter to one-third of the seaport free population found itself in the ranks of the laboring poor, including mariners, day laborers, hucksters, and a rising number of wage earners in such "lesser" crafts as shoemaking and tailoring.[8]

This swelling free labor supply—of women, children, and immigrants as well as of native journeymen and laborers—provided merchants and master craftsmen with enough cheap hands to abandon unfree labor and existing "just-price" wage agreements. Not all trades were affected: shoemaking, tailoring, and other consumer finishing crafts, along with printing and the building trades, bore the brunt of reorganization, as they would continue to do through the 1830s. As a rule, mechanization and concentration of the work force into centralized manufactories were of secondary importance, as the surplus labor of the seaports and the mounting costs of urban real estate offset any advantages of such innovations. Nevertheless, the changes in labor relations, although uneven and gradual, were profound. By turning apprenticeship into a glorified form of child wage labor, and by dividing and putting out as much work as possible to outworkers and other inexpensive hands, merchant capitalists and master craftsmen increased production for new regional and national markets while cutting their wage costs. Within the shell of the artisan system, masters and contractors bastardized the supposedly filial and cooperative relations of workshop production and transformed craft wage labor into a commodity, subject to the abstract justice of the labor market.[9]

Some craftsmen immediately recognized the implications of these structural changes, and fought back. As early as 1768, a "late Reduction of the Wages of journeymen Taylors" in New York led some twenty tailors to go on strike.[10] Such concerted labor action, however, remained sporadic until the very end of the eighteenth century. Of far greater importance in the 1760s and 1770s were the political repercussions of the growing imperial crisis. The urban artisans had long found their political interests subordinated to those of the mercantile and gentry elite. Although many artisans qualified to vote in colonial elections, they were expected to defer to their social betters, who actually held elective and appointive office. Growing American restiveness at British mercantile policy, culminating in the anti-British agitation of 1774–1776 and the Declaration of Independence, opened some cracks in this political establishment; masters and journeymen tended to join together, across emerging class lines within the crafts, to form the hard center of the urban plebeian democracy in opposition to British rule. Out of this experience, the artisans forged a distinctive ideology that colored their political allegiances after independence and became a focal point of early working-class understanding and action.[11]

Artisan republicanism had its distant origins in the democratic "small producer" ethic of various seventeenth-century plebeian English sects and movements. It came to the fore on these shores in the outbursts of mob action and the more formal democratic anti-British agitation led by local mechanics' committees on the eve of 1776. It matured during the war, in the democratically organized urban militia companies of Philadelphia and Baltimore and in the minds of mechanics in other cities who supported the patriot cause. And it flourished just after the war with the emergence of a distinct "mechanics' interest" in seaboard urban politics, aligned momentarily with the Federalists and then more generally with the Jeffersonians.

Couched in the rhetoric of radical Whiggery and Painite democracy, beholden to ideas enunciated by the russet-coated radicals of the English Commonwealth, the artisans' republicanism was a specific variant of broader republican views. Like other Americans, the artisans shared a basic respect for private property; many also expressed a profound distrust for the "unproductive" propertyless poor. At the same time, they proclaimed fiercely egalitarian notions of independence, citizenship, and political rights for white men, tied to an intense pride in craft cooperation and productive labor, and an abiding suspicion of the dominant mercantile elite and its professional allies. In the reflection of the Revolution, the artisans fought hard and successfully—mainly over local matters—to win a permanent place in political affairs. Portraying themselves as the very "axis of society," they articulated a political vision of the American republic akin to the Jeffersonian ideal of the noble husbandman—a vision that valued innovation, nationalism, and commercial expansion, but imagined such expansion could proceed without undermining the individual independence, social cooperation, and virtuous citizenship of the petty producer.[12]

Ironically, the very ideals that helped cement craft solidarity in politics also became a source of bitter contention in the trades, with the continuing disruption of the workshops after the Revolution. Journeymen artisans' mounting fury at the bastardized regime, and their relegation to the ranks of the permanently propertyless, led to the organization of the first recorded American trade unions in the 1780s and 1790s. As the breakdown of the seaboard crafts continued between 1800 and 1815, conflicts between masters and journeymen intensified, particularly in the needle, printing, and building trades. To a degree unacknowledged by most labor historians, the seaboard journeymen's unions exerted an effective control over local wage rates and shop conditions, despite repeated harassment by their masters and at least six major conspiracy trials. Two dozen strikes broke out in New York City alone between 1800 and 1815 to combat the subdivision and put-

ting out of work as well as to raise wages and resist reductions. The unionists of the other major seaports were no less militant.[13]

Throughout, the journeymen and their lawyers turned to artisan republican ideals and a class-aware version of John Locke and Adam Smith to pro-
claim their cause. Much as British tyrants and placemen had oppressed the
colonies, the union men argued, selfish accumulating American employers
now oppressed their men; masters, they charged, had violated the good of
all for the sake of their private profit alone and denied the journeymen's
natural rights as free Americans to secure their independent competencies.
The masters, in turn, asserted *their* prerogatives as independent Americans.
They charged the unions with tyrannical violations of private rights and of
that "tacit compact" of obligation and reciprocity that supposedly governed
the republican workshop. Class identities, although framed by a common
rhetoric, had begun to sunder the major seaboard trades.[14]

The direction of the new nation's political economy augured continued
dislocations. The Revolution had secured American independence, but there
was no clear consensus about the new republic's polity and economy. After
1783, the patriot coalition began to fragment, primarily over economic and
financial issues, paving the way for the framing and ratification of the Constitution, a nationalist compromise between urban capitalists and Southern
planters that won the wholehearted support of the urban craftsmen. Soon
thereafter, the political crises of the 1790s—sparked by Hamilton's plans
for a centralized form of capitalist development and the Federalists' increasingly Anglophilic, antidemocratic posture—threatened that compromise se-
verely and led to a new national political cleavage. Craftsmen in the larger
cities for the most part drifted into the Jeffersonian opposition, largely out
of their fears that continued Federalist supremacy would restore and then
enlarge the powers of the mercantile elite.[15]

Jefferson's election, although it doomed the Hamiltonians' finance system, did nothing to halt the early industrialization of the crafts and the
spread of capitalist wage labor. However genuine Jefferson's more radical
speculations on property and democracy may have been, neither his nor his
successors' policies attacked locally based efforts to improve manufacturing,
finance, and transportation. The first decade and a half of the nineteenth
century actually saw something of a revolution in the organization of banking and credit facilities and early manufacturing promotion. Many manufacturing entrepreneurs found the Jeffersonians' laissez-faire instincts more
congenial than Hamiltonian centralism. Jeffersonian leaders, meanwhile,
displayed little enthusiasm (and sometimes outright hostility) toward the infant craft unions.[16]

Of course, the Jeffersonians, like the rest of the country, only dimly understood the portents of working-class formation in the New World. As of

1815, the emerging American working class represented a miniscule proportion of the new republic's population. But dramatic processes, already underway in 1815, would soon begin to alter the picture even further. Rural unrest, which exploded in Shays' Rebellion, the Whiskey Rebellion, and lesser revolts in the 1780s and 1790s, bespoke the decay of rural petty production as well as agrarian fears of taxation and dependence.[17] In New England and the middle states, entrepreneurs and ambitious mechanics began to move ahead with plans to build sophisticated American factories. In the South, technical advances and expanding markets overseas inaugurated the cotton revolution and revitalized the slave economy. In Britain and Ireland, and on the Continent, the breakdown of urban crafts and recurrent agrarian hardships ensured an unending stream of immigration to America. After 1815, these developments, along with the continued reorganization of craft labor, would greatly expand the terrain of working-class formation. And as an American working class took shape, growing numbers of people—natives and newcomers, men and women, black and white—would reassess the Revolution's legacy in order to make sense of their changing circumstances.

1815–1848

The War of 1812, seemingly a tangential event in American working-class history, was actually something of a turning point. The diplomatic intrigues leading to the war—and then the war itself—forced Jefferson and his successors to back away from their more idealistic notions of a simple domestic government and a harmonious international order based on free trade. The sheer expense of the conflict, while hardly giving rise to anything like a powerfully centralized state, stimulated the revival of various Hamiltonian projects, above all the national bank. Wartime encouragement to domestic manufacturing opened opportunities for industrial investment that Founding Fathers like John Adams had once dismissed. The outbreak of peace in Europe in 1815 changed world trading patterns and intensified international competition, forcing American merchants to consider moving out of commerce altogether and into manufacturing and internal improvements. The nation's self-proclaimed military victory quickened the drive for national economic development; Andrew Jackson's very real victory at New Orleans secured the conquest of the Southwest Indians and opened up for commercial cultivation immense tracts of rich lands obtained in the Louisiana Purchase of 1803.

Over the next three decades, the nation's economy developed rapidly—not, perhaps, as Hamilton might once have envisioned, but on a dazzling scale nevertheless. George Rogers Taylor aptly dubbed these changes "the transportation revolution." After 1815, internal improvements became the main focus for new private investment and government action, state and local. The direct results of these projects were impressive. Overall, nation-wide freight rates were virtually halved between 1820 and 1860, while the speed of travel for persons and freight nearly doubled. Yet, as Taylor realized, the impact of these changes extended far beyond improved transportation. The new transport routes encouraged capital formation and helped foster a national network of merchants and financiers, headquartered in the regional commercial cities and capable of coordinating the nation's mixed economy of plantations, small holdings, and infant manufactories. The penetration of the market into the hinterland broke down some of the barriers between petty household producers and the mercantile centers and disrupted the old rural order. In the West, the construction of transport links with the major northeastern centers accelerated the pace of commercialization and strengthened interregional economic, cultural, and political bonds north of the Mason-Dixon line. These developments in turn helped spur the rise of the early factories.[18]

It is no longer as common as it used to be to concentrate the history of American industrialization on the factory system. Greater stress has fallen on the importance of other entrepreneurial strategies—above all the labor intensive division of craft work and "sweating"—through the Gilded Age. Even in the age of steam, hand technology remained essential to industrial expansion; mechanized factories generally were the exception in the nation's leading manufacturing sites, the seaboard cities, long after 1840.[19] Yet, if we remember not to equate industrialization with the mechanized factory alone, it remains clear that the cotton revolution and the very early stages of industrialization in shoemaking helped accelerate the formation of a northeastern industrial proletariat before the Civil War. More to the point, the factory was critical to working-class formation in New England, the leading manufacturing section in the antebellum United States.[20]

The coming of the factory was closely related to a deepening crisis in northeastern rural relations. Mounting demographic pressures, apparent since the early eighteenth century, placed enormous strains on customary practices of household-centered simple commodity production (above all on inheritance) between 1800 and 1840. Simultaneously, the expansion of regional and transatlantic markets for food stuffs, coupled with the transportation revolution, reoriented a growing portion of northeastern production toward commercialized farming. A consequent rise in geographic mobility and the erosion of established patriarchal household authority hastened the collapse of the social system of rural household production.[21] Migrants did reconstitute, for a time, a version of what some have called the "household mode of production" on the frontiers of early settlement in western New York, Ohio, and Illinois; in New England, some independent producers resisted entry into commercial agriculture. Nevertheless, by the 1840s, a large and growing proportion of the rural northeast found itself either liberated or cut off from earlier generations' expectations of family production and exchange. Some of these people successfully negotiated the switch to commercial farming and stayed on the land; thousands of others, like the hapless Mayo Greenleaf Patch, wound up displaced in industrial cities like Samuel Slater's Pawtucket or in the burgeoning seaports.[22] More important, the gradual commercialization of agriculture left wives and daughters open in new ways for wage labor, either to produce outwork for eastern and local manufacturers or to work in factories.

Historians of American women have explored the relationships between early industrialization and gender systems largely in terms of the extent to which female roles shifted away from production.[23] The recruitment and consolidation of the New England work force revealed even more intricate connections between class formation and the changing structure of family and gender authority in the North. Contrary to the rosier prediction of contemporary promoters, early manufacturers initially had difficulties convincing even displaced rural people to move into manufacturing wage labor; a recent study of textile factory towns in southern Massachusetts cites unease with factories and rural fears of dependence as an important factor in tightening local labor markets.[24] One solution, adopted by shoemakers and some clothing manufacturers, was to establish rural networks of female outworkers, letting women and girls toil at home. Other entrepreneurs, like Slater and the Boston Associates, adapted their schemes to substitute for the crumbling patriarchal farmstead, by reconstituting the household sexual division of labor and adapting established domestic codes to new uses.[25] The wage work of women and children was central to all these strategies. In 1840, half the manufacturing work force in the United States, and an even higher percentage in the New England factory trades, was female. Children under sixteen constituted between one-third and one-half of the New England labor force in the 1820s and 1830s. Quite possibly, the majority of native Massachusetts girls who reached late adolescence in the 1830s and 1840s spent at least some portion of their lives working in manufacturing.[26]

We know most about the girls in the dormitory Waltham-Lowell mills. To overcome Yankee suspicions, the Waltham-style mill owners promised high wages and independence from family authority, mixed with a regular, benevolent guardianship—a chance for young farm girls to enlarge their experiences and get paid for their labors before leaving the mill to set up families on their own. "As long as high wages and a benevolent paternalism provided a comfortable haven," one historian has written, "the mill girls' dignity remained intact."[27] The Slater mills took different measures to refashion customary patterns: management tried hard to retain family members during economic downturns, provided cottages in which family members could live together, transferred children's wages directly to their parents, and always paid fathers more than any of their sons and daughters.[28] Employers could not, however, sustain such "benevolence" under either of the prevailing factory systems. Intensified competition, coupled with maturing bank debts for overhead costs, forced mill owners to speed production and cut their wage bills, at the same time that they tightened restrictions on leisure time and daily life in the mills. Dissatisfaction among the mill hands led to a rapid increase in turnover rates and fresh complaints from owners about labor shortages; in one of the premier Lowell mills, 25.7 percent of those on the payroll either left or entered employment over a single five-week period in 1836.[29] Those Lowell girls who stuck out the usual two or three annual stints, and those families that stayed in the Slater mills, expressed their grievances differently, emboldened by a sense of gender and family solidarity developed on the job. In 1824, women and men in Slater's Pawtucket mills struck after a cut in wage rates. Over the next twelve years, factory workers struck (among other places) the mills at Dover, New Hampshire, and Lowell itself. Other turnouts hit the embryonic New England shoemaking industry in the mid-1830s.[30]

Mechanization, factory production and unrest were not confined to New England. In the middle states, satellite industrial towns and cities—like Paterson, New Jersey—grew up in the immediate hinterland of the established seaports and drew their work force from both natives and the continuing waves of British and Irish immigrants who arrived in the ports. The Delaware Valley, from Philadelphia to Wilmington, became a hub of these enterprises; in Philadelphia's Manayunk district, a major concentration of textile mills earned notoriety as "the Manchester of America." If anything, the middle-state operatives—thrust on a burgeoning labor market, with employers who made little pretence to paternalism—faced even harsher conditions than the New Englanders. Fortified by the British operatives, many of whom had had experience with industrial conflict and radical ideas back home, they quickly undertook strikes and local political actions. Paterson's workers—first the skilled spinners, later the women and children operatives—fought running battles with the mill owners and city officials in the late 1820s and 1830s. The Manayunk operatives' activities culminated in a series of tumultuous walkouts in 1833 and 1834, which helped galvanize the rest of Philadelphia's workers.[31]

The awakening militancy of the mills and central shops indicated how far working-class formation had begun to spread since Jefferson's presidency, yet it represented only part of the labor movement of the 1820s and 1830s. Just as turbulent was the renewed agitation in the major northern seaports and the new inland commercial cities like Cincinnati. Fed by streams of migrants from the countryside as well as from abroad, these cities grew enormously through the 1840s. With this expanding labor supply, the bastardization of the local crafts—and the tempo of labor protest—

quickened. Available strike figures, although incomplete, confirm the accelerating pace of protest and the gradual spread of labor unrest along the pathways carved out by the transportation revolution.[32] Just as significant as the strikes and protests were the important institutional innovations undertaken by organized workers—the first city central unions, a loosely confederated National Trades' Union—and the first tentative instances of cooperation across the lines of skill and gender. Although their movements were small in comparison with those of the Gilded Age, and still a far cry from nationwide working-class presence, the urban unionists and strikers generated a consciousness of class that cut across craft lines and sharpened fresh critiques of capitalist wage labor, combining democratic-republican ideals with various radical interpretations of the labor theory of value.[33]

Three distinct groups of workers (apart from the mill workers in the major cities) participated. The craft journeymen have received the most attention, for these men established the city central unions and the National Trades' Union as well as the most energetic cooperatives and other conspicuous working-class institutions. As in the Jeffersonian period, the journeymen's organization reflected the uneven pattern of urban seaboard industrialization: tailors, shoemakers, furniture workers, and others who faced the swiftest transformation of craft labor relations were at the forefront. These trades also bore the brunt of what appears to have been a decline in real earnings and opportunities for advancement for most urban craft workers, particularly in the seaboard cities. Their organized activities began in the late 1820s (in alliance with radical small producers and other sympathizers) in the short-lived radical Working Men's movements of Philadelphia and New York. After the deflection and disruption of the "Workies," journeymen turned to more coercive forms of union organization, both to combat declining real wages and the rearrangement of workshop labor and press for political reforms while preserving strict party neutrality.[34]

Women workers faced greater difficulties in organizing on their own behalf. Apart from a relatively small number of black workers at the very bottom of the occupational hierarchy, the growing numbers of white women wage earners were by every account the most miserable of all in the major northern Jacksonian cities. The largest women's occupation, domestic service, drew on a particular pool of unmarried young women and placed them in a unique (and by no means comfortable) set of work conditions that inhibited formal collective action.[35] Most other women worked in the consumer finishing trades, as well as in specific branches of other, predominantly men's trades like bookbinding. The numbers of "sweated" women craft workers expanded steadily in the 1820s and 1830s. Their experiences underscored the complex relations among class formation, family authority, and gender.[36]

Roughly half of the women in the trades were the daughters and wives of craft workers and common laborers, whose earnings were indispensable for the sustenance of their families. The rest—widows, abandoned wives and daughters, single girls new to the city—eked out a living either by banding together or sending children out to work.[37] Within this double split labor market, divided by women's relations to men as well as by gender itself, women wage earners at once endured special forms of subordination to men employers and foremen and found special sources of independent solidarity. Their sweated piece wages were the lowest in urban manufacturing, from one-third to one-half those paid to men in some trades; their tasks, like shirtmaking, were the most wearisome of all. Still subject to a plebeian republican domestic code—one that dictated that women's labor, in the words of one N.T.U. Commitee, "should be only of a domestic nature"—they were not admitted to the journeymen's unions. Although the journeymen did not actively oppose women wage earners as they had in the Jeffersonian period and although they occasionally voiced their support, the unions argued that the best way to end sweatshop "slavery" was to raise their own wages to allow them to keep their women at home—an argument that would appear and reappear in labor movements throughout the industrializing world.[38]

The consequences were ambiguous: whereas the fight for a family wage became a focus of conflict (and provided, at least in theory, for women in families with men workers), the plebeian cult of domesticity also distanced all women from the labor movement. Left to their own devices, most women remained unorganized. Those women seamstresses, bookbinders, shoe binders, and umbrella makers who did organize did so independently of workingmen, sometimes winning as much or more sympathy from concerned middle-class reformers as from the labor press. When allied with middle-class reformers, the women occasionally borrowed from evangelical rhetoric to portray their plight as a consequence of the sinful greed and coercion of their employers. More often, the women adapted the republican arguments of men unionists, stressing their rights, as the "daughters of freemen," to workshop justice. A curious mixture emerged, of trade unionism and a gender consciousness that occasionally bordered on feminism—an outlook well beyond the normal limits of masculine republican discourse.[39]

Recent scholarship has told us less about the third group of urban workers, the common laborers, including mariners, building laborers, stevedores, and dock laborers. Because these men lacked the highly prized skills of the craft workers, they usually faced condescension (and sometimes contempt) from unionists. Yet their importance should not be minimized. Certainly, their numbers and proportions in the urban work force expanded in the first half of the nineteenth century. And certainly native-born laborers, black and white, had their own traditions of sometimes riotous political engagement and sporadic strike activity—at times uniting workers across racial and national lines—dating back to the Revolution and before. To these, British and Irish immigrants added a great deal. British workers brought their experience with industrial conflict; the Irish and rural British brought their own techniques of agrarian intimidation and the rougher forms of collective bargaining. What we have just begun to discover is the sophistication and influence of common laborers in the urban class conflicts of the Jacksonian years (as well as outside the cities, on the canals and in the early mines), despite their political distance from the journeymen unionists. In Philadelphia, a strike by local coal heavers in 1835 sparked that city's general strike for the ten-hour workday (in which cordwainers took up the chant: "We are all day laborers"). Soon after, the laborers secured formal admission to Philadelphia's General Trades' Union. In New York, turnouts by dock workers and building laborers prompted an official show of force that intensified a climactic strike wave in 1836 and brought tentative moves toward a journeyman-laborer alliance.[40]

A fourth sub-group of workers—free blacks—had a far more troubled relation to the urban upsurge. Small communities of urban freedmen heroically consolidated something of a successful stratum of professionals and skilled artisans. Most African-Americans, however, were trapped in unskilled or menial occupations. Men worked as laborers, mariners, servants, waiters, coachmen, stevedores, and hod carriers; women as dressmakers, seamstresses, cooks, and washerwomen. If anything, the situation for free black workers worsened in this period, as newly arrived immigrants (particularly the Irish) began to crowd them out of certain occupations, notably domestic service. Despised as a preternaturally dependent inferior group, black workers won minimal sympathy from the labor movement, and even less from the mass of white workers. Sporadic efforts by blacks to organize on their own—either on an ad hoc basis or in short-lived groups like the American League of Colored Laborers—came to little or nothing. It would be a mistake to see the racial divide as unbridgable; some white labor leaders, like New York's John Commerford, were also outspoken abolitionists and friends of equal rights. Far more striking, however, were the signs of everyday strife between blacks and whites—strife that, on occasion, turned into full-scale assaults on black neighborhoods by white workers, most notably during the New York City antiabolition riots of 1835.[41]

Yet the hard facts of white racism should not obscure how the urban labor movements, along with the flare-ups in the mill towns, signaled a deepening of class divisions and identities in the Northeast. At no point did this translate into a movement of a sharply calibrated, united class of wage earners. Important divisions remained: between skilled and unskilled, blacks and whites, immigrants and native-borns, and between men and women—the last being particularly important, given that the expansion of capitalist wage relations brought with it a feminization of wage labor. Untold numbers of wage-earners, in highly skilled positions or in trades that thrived with the quickening economic tempo, had no use for the labor movement. What was extraordinary, however, was the extent to which thousands of workers in different sectors and strata of the wage-labor force began to think and act in class ways, at least with respect to their employers and the issues that divided their workshops.

There were other signs of class division as well, quite distinct from the realm of work. By 1840 (and in some cities long before then), separate zones of workers' and marginal small producers' housing and leisure had emerged in the seaports and the most rapidly growing manufacturing towns of the hinterland. The widening social distance between Broadway and the Bowery in New York City, the great emblem of the urban divide, was renowned by the early 1840s. In newer cities like Rochester, New York, businessmen and their families huddled in respectable enclaves within earshot of early slums and working-class resorts.[42] A complex, at times contradictory working-class culture arose in these zones. This culture included the instrumental radicalism of the labor reformers and trade unionists, with their newspapers, meeting halls, and parades. But it also encompassed far more: the early popular theaters (mingling Shakespeare with "Jim Crow" Rice), the taverns and working-class boulevards, ethnic, racial, and antiabolitionist rioting, eroticized terrains of sexual bargaining, plebeian evangelical churches, fire companies, gangs, and the sensational penny press.[43]

Social historians have begun to describe the rougher side of early working-class life, but it still needs far closer analysis. It should not be romanticized; there was nothing pretty about white working-class racism and misogyny or the violence it provoked. "Working-class" culture was not simply an autonomous creation of urban workers: much of it, like the penny press and the theaters, arose in part from the self-conscious efforts of this country's first purveyors of commercial culture. Nor can "working-class" culture be taken simply as a "traditionalist" *survivance* from earlier days: fire companies, minstrel shows, the working-class boulevards, all were very new forms of lower-class sociability, that took shape only as respectable fears of the "dangerous classes" began to darken. Not all workers shared in this culture; many—the upright Methodist churchgoer, the ambitious and thrifty clerk—scrupulously avoided most "working-class" haunts. And the supposedly uplifting "rebel" culture of the trade unions certainly overlapped with the world of the roughs, with its celebration of manly independence, republican antielitism, and (at times) white supremacy. Above all, we need to know far more about the production and transmission of early working-class cultural life and the tensions within it—tensions of sex and gender, as well as the more familiar tensions between blacks and whites and between immigrants and native-born.[44] What is clear is that by the age of Jackson, a new lower-class milieu had emerged in the nation's northern cities, one that would provide the impetus (and in large measure the audience) for much of what we take to be "urban" culture, from popular melodrama to the crude realism of *The Police Gazette*—a culture that was beginning to unnerve urban entrepreneurs and their families.

No account of early American labor is complete without a closer look at these entrepreneurs: working-class formation was inextricably bound up with changes in the emerging American bourgeoisie. Merchant capital, we have been told, was a parasitic, Janus-faced creature that adapted to existing forms of politics and labor while it revolutionized marketing, transportation, and finance, and established the preconditions for industrial capitalist accumulation.[45] The image is appropriate to early national and Jacksonian America, where aggressive merchants and financiers, building on their late eighteenth century achievements, coordinated a mixture of several different labor systems—including, in the North, a bastardized form of artisan production, and in the South various forms of chattel slavery. "Liberal" in their ideas about commerce and finance, American merchant capitalists were generally committed to social hierarchy, tradition, and order, at least through the Era of Good Feelings. Although the Quakers and many New England Federalists expressed strong antislavery views, a coherent American ideology of free labor only began to emerge after 1830 and then mainly among a newer breed of entrepreneurs. Key northern merchant capitalists—the commercial captains of New York City, the most prominent New England lords of the loom—considered the political economy of venturous conservatism both personally rewarding and a self-evident national good long after 1840; among other things, it would lead them to take a conciliatory attitude toward the slave South even as the Union began to fall apart.[46]

Yet the merchant capitalists' innovations in transport and finance also encouraged social and ideological transformations that would, in time, undermine the existing order. Most pertinent here, the commercialization of northeastern manufacturing and northern agriculture brought with it the rise of a large new middle class without parallel (at least with respect to relative size) in other industrializing countries—a loose configuration of younger and local merchants, manufacturers, and small capitalist farmers. The formation of this Yankee bourgeoisie—dedicated to the theory and practice of free labor, social mobility, and self-ownership as well as democratic politics—eventually culminated in an irrepressible national conflict over labor, liberty, and the nation's destiny. In the 1830s and 1840s, it pitted urban entrepreneurs against workers in local struggles for power and legitimacy.

We know most about the northern middle-class formation in the rapidly developing areas of western New York in the 1820s and 1830s, although similar transformations have been detected in other parts of the North.[47] The family was a crucial locus of these changes. By the 1830s, the commercialization of both city and countryside had removed the women of the new middle class from the production of goods, including goods strictly for household use. As a result, the world of the propertied began to separate into two spheres—a men's public sphere of politics, business, and the market, and a women's private sphere of domestic duties and child rearing. In place of older, more coercive forms of direct paternal control, a new domestic ethos, encouraged and in part formulated by women, recast fatherly obligations and prerogatives. At home, men were expected to be temperate, genteel husbands and fathers, responsible for their actions, respectful of the moral autonomy (and, to some writers, the moral superiority) of women.[48] It was an image of family life and domestic responsibility wholly at odds with the necessities of the laboring poor—a class distinction that became charged when middle-class reformers tried to interfere in working-class homes and offer them spiritual and material regeneration.[48]

In a parallel way, the erosion of an idealized mutuality between employers and employees fostered a new code of personal responsibility and moral autonomy at work. Only by taking responsibility for their own actions and by cultivating regular, temperate habits (middle-class publicists explained) could either entrepreneurs or workingmen ever achieve their competency. Together, these public and private ideals formed what one writer has called the "moral imperative" around which the Jacksonian northern middle class began to cohere as a class. That imperative gained explicit expression in the Finneyite evangelical revivals of the Second Great Awakening but was hardly limited to them. What Carl Schurz would later recall as his strongest first impression of the United States—seeing "what I might call the middle-class culture in process of formation"—could be observed well before 1840, in the temperance and sabbatarian movements, in common school reform, in abolitionism, and in most of the other humanitarian crusades of the Jacksonian era.[49]

Outside of the world of reform, legitimations of free wage labor—and an updated image of America as a classless utopia—began to appear in textbooks of political economy and in less polished speeches presented in lyceums and on the political stump. In part, the reformulation of American political economy involved a distancing of American entrepreneurs from some of the harsher prejudices of the eighteenth century against banks, corporations, and the mercantile elite. Above all, the idea that wage labor itself was a commodity, to be bought by entrepreneurs as the labor market dictated, cohered among northerners in the 1820s and 1830s, in part as a result of the period's labor struggles. By the 1830s, manufacturing employers, while still claiming the republican mantle of independence and commonwealth, did not have to waste much time explaining why the unions were selfish and tyrannical; they had only to point out the self-evident truth that "labour, like every other commodity, will seek its own level, and its true value, in an open and unfettered market."[50] Between 1815 and 1848, these ideas came to set off the labor movement's version of the republican heritage from the first assumptions of the emerging republican middle class.

They also increasingly set the North apart from the South. Historians have tended to overlook class formation in the South before 1865, presumably because the southern economy was based on a "backward," non-capitalist labor system. It is, by now, almost traditional to view southern history from 1815 to the Civil War as a bloc, thereby blurring important regional variations and the dynamic aspects of southern economics, politics, and social relations.[51] These variations and dynamics, to be sure, never upended the slaveholders' regime or the political power enjoyed by the wealthiest planters—and therein lies one of the keys to early nineteenth century American history. But to view the South as a static region makes inexplicable certain well-known facts of southern political and social history—and ultimately makes it hard to explain the outbreak of the Civil War. What set the South on a course in conflict with the free labor North was not a lack of economic change or class formation, but rather the ways in which slavery shaped southern change and class formation, binding the South's political leadership to increasingly strident defenses of the peculiar institution.

The main lines of southern economic change—the incipient crisis of the eastern economies in the 1780s and 1790s, followed by the rise of the cotton kingdom—require no extended rehearsal here. After 1815, the South's economy grew rapidly, generating (on average) relatively high incomes for slaveholders and other whites; in the 1840s, per capita income in the South (including the slaves) began to increase more rapidly than that of the nation as a whole. Productive as it was, southern agriculture faced serious obstacles to long-term development, chiefly the lack of an extensive domestic market or of any spur for technical improvements. These factors, combined with the ready availability of land, only committed the South more deeply to slave labor. Land and slaves remained the chief forms of investment. Slavery permitted the larger planters to impose strict labor controls on their farms and plantations, in a regimen as intricate—if far more brutal—as the more advanced of the northern mills. Under these conditions, the slaves, like northern workers, did what they could to resist. But the terms of class formation and conflict in the South, for blacks and whites, were wholly different than those in the North.[52]

The history of southern class relations before 1848 can be viewed from three angles, the most familiar being the relations between masters and slaves.[53] Slavery was no monolith; the character of master-slave relations was subject to important differences related to product, subregion, and scale of enterprise. Inevitably, however, slavery rested on different justifications and antagonisms than those typical in the North. Although few masters could have held any illusions about the slaves being a source of profit—"the planter," as Eugene Genovese has written, "was no less acquisitive than the bourgeois"—their sense of moral imperatives vis-à-vis the slaves could not rest on an appeal to the abstract justice of the labor market or to the moral autonomy of the slaves.[54] Nor could racial ideology alone—in America the main line of argument concerning the "otherness" of the enslaved—fully justify bondage in a system where the slaves' humanity continually intruded on plantation operations. Out of their struggles to contain the slaves and legitimize their own authority, masters combined, in varying degrees, Christian doctrines of stewardship, paternalistic images of black-white mutuality, and hard-nosed commercial realism into a distinctly American organic world view, at odds with the atomistic liberalism that was coming to dominate life in the North. As these ideas were tested—in part by northern antislavery agitation, more importantly by the slaves themselves—the legitimations hardened into a defense of slavery as a positive good.[55]

The slaves, meanwhile, did not need to be told that a true paternalist did not break up slave families and sell off his "children" (sometimes, quite literally, *his* children). Nor did it take the slaves long to realize that the Bible had two testaments, one of which was an allegory of endurance and deliverance. To these understandings, they added their own self-evident labor theory of value—"We bake de bread / Dey gib us de crust," ran the old slave song—and an awareness of proclaimed American democratic rights, to form a powerful sense of themselves as a people and a class. Occasionally, slaves seized upon their ideas and visions in dramatic and ultimately disastrous uprisings. Far more commonly, conflicts worked themselves out in acts of day-to-day resistance. No one of these acts was calculated to undo slavery; cumulatively, however, they helped establish the limits of the master's will and define the terrain of class antagonism. Every runaway slave, every feigned pregnancy, every piece of "accidentally" broken equipment sharpened the contradictions of bondage, even as they pushed slaveholders further along in declaring their social benevolence and obedience to God.[56]

Off the plantations, class antagonisms also divided southern white society—the second vantage point for viewing class relations. This process should not be confused with northern class formation. In the North, the transportation revolution unleashed the growth of capitalist agriculture and manufacturing wage labor; merchant capitalist innovation in the South remained an adjunct to the expansion of slavery and to the further acquisition of land and slaves. Capitalist wage relations did arise in the major southern cities, which would lead to the emergence of a mainly immigrant urban white working class and the decline of urban slavery over the decade before

the Civil War. Scattered across the countryside, a handful of southern entrepreneurs built ironworks, tobacco mills, and textile factories and tried to
adapt Yankee forms of free-labor paternalism—none more famously than
William Gregg at his Graniteville textile operation in South Carolina. The
South's own transportation and financial improvements nurtured a local
commercial bourgeoisie, which provided the region with canals, railroads,
credit, and a banking system. But southern capitalists operated mainly at
the convenience of southern slaveholders, to enable them to hold their own
against intraregional competitors, and did not challenge the power or the
authority of the slaveholding minority. Nor did these capitalists, any more
than the slaveholders, appear to fancy the creation of a large-scale white
working class. Some free white labor was clearly necessary and welcome,
to dig the canals and perform all sorts of skilled, specialized tasks on the
farms and plantations and in the towns. More than that would have undermined the masters' rationale for slavery and created a potentially explosive
propertyless political strata, far more dangerous than the already troublesome free blacks. Poor whites, for their part, proved if anything more recalcitrant than their Northern counterparts when it came to adapting to the
factory regime.[57] Rather, class formation among whites pitted slaveholders
(and especially the conservative wealthier planters and their commercial re-
tainers) against propertied, mostly nonslaveholding whites—the yeomanry.

The planter-yeoman division had arisen in the upper South long before
the rise of the cotton kingdom, but it replicated itself with extraordinary
sharpness as the line of settlement moved southwestward. The uneven development of the southern "dual economy" split some newer states like Mississippi in two, leaving a plantation black belt along the richer lands (allied
to the wealthier towns and cities) and a poorer "piney woods" backcountry
populated mainly by yeomen and their families. As several recent studies
have shown, this division marked off two different social worlds. The yeomanry, unlike the planters and small farmers of the black belt, subordinated
staple production to quasi self-sufficiency for their households. Yeomen
households in turn established a dense network of barter-based exchange,
domestic manufacture, and common rights—a form of simple commodity
production on the periphery of the market not unlike the "household mode
of production" that had begun to crumble in the rural Northeast at the end
of the eighteenth century.[58]

There were ample grounds for discord and distrust between the preten-
tious acquisitive slaveholders of the black belt and towns and the upcountry
small producers. The rapid development of the staple-export areas in the
1820s and 1830s, followed by a push for a sound banking system and internal improvements, had exacerbated the conflict, particularly in those areas
where the expansion of the market began to destabilize the yeoman economy. Not all of the destabilization came from outside the yeoman communi-

ties; throughout the yeoman South (as, earlier, in the rural Northeast) some farmers welcomed what they saw as new commercial opportunities, withdrew from strictly local exchange networks, and undermined the simple commodity regime. Nor is it likely that the southern yeomanry could have escaped forever the fate of most northeastern household rural producers; even before the Civil War, yeoman areas untouched by commercial penetration showed signs of difficulty from overpopulation coupled with limited natural and technological resources.[59] But large sectors of the yeomanry (especially in the Southwest and lower South) resisted the political supremacy of the black belt and the incursions of commerce into the back country. They brought the battle directly into politics, in controversies over suffrage reform, apportionment, the location of state capitals, banking charters, taxation, and internal improvements. It is almost impossible to read the annals of southern state politics after the Panic of 1819 and not be struck by a sense of pervasive class conflict.[60]

Ultimately, however, the slaveholders held the balance of power, mainly because the yeomen's protests never extended into an attack on slavery, the foundation of the black belt's power. Despite their local clashes, planters and yeoman shared some wide areas of political agreement about the importance of states' rights and inexpensive government; underlying these agreements was an increasingly broad consensus about slavery. Slaveholders and their allies never failed to point out how slavery served the interests of poorer whites: because of slavery, propertyless whites received more for their labor; because the elite invested in slaves as well as land, land ownership was more equitably distributed; because the yeomen grew nonstaple crops, they did not have to compete with the planters. Having been born in a nation that condoned slavery and exhibited a cultural obsessiveness about race, the yeomanry saw blacks as abject dependents, whose subjugation protected their own economic independence and democratic rights. The Georgia upcountry politician Joseph Brown put the matter bluntly: "Slavery is the poor man's best government."[61] No amount of political friction could destroy the racist foundation of planter-yeoman unity. Ultimately, this fact could help consolidate the planters' positive-good arguments and reinforce southern white solidarity against the Yankees. In the 1830s and 1840s, it helped keep the upcountry's often intense class battles within the plantation belt from turning into even more subversive affairs.

A third perspective on southern class relations encompasses the deteriorating condition of free black workers. Most free blacks held marginal positions in the southern economy, working as common laborers and domestics. Singular exceptions were the relatively high numbers of skilled free black mechanics in the port cities of the lower South. In Charleston, South Carolina, black artisans controlled a large share of the work in some leading trades and actually dominated in others. In the upper South, significant numbers of free blacks labored as factory hands and teamsters. Where they gained a foothold, however, free blacks came under increasing attack from white master and journeymen craftsmen, who called for all sorts of public measures to restrict or eliminate black competition. Where political action failed, white workers resorted to intimidation and violence, forcing skilled blacks to find more menial work. After the beginnings of immigration to the urban South late in the period, free blacks faced the additional problems of being squeezed out of familiar lowly positions—as hod carriers, waiters, and haulers—by newly arrived Irishmen. A tiny proportion of the free black population managed to slip through the net of discrimination, work at lucrative trades, participate in the white economy, and accumulate property. Most remained consigned to the most menial of laboring tasks or (if lucky) to one of the stigmatized, so-called "nigger work" trades: barbering, carpentering, plastering, blacksmithing, bricklaying, and shoemaking. Their experience only underscored how the strenghthening bonds of white supremacy helped obscure the very real class divisions within white society.[63]

Taken together, then, northern and southern economic change involved the deepening of class divisions within each section, as well as the emergence of two distinct political economies, northern capitalism and southern slavery, tied together by the political and economic networks of the nation's merchant capitalists. This hybrid process reached an important passage in the 1830s. In the North, labor organizing hit almost every variety of urban manufacturing setting, from the Lowell factories to the sweatshops of the seaboard cities. Ideas were as much a material part of the struggle as the changing relations of production. Organized workers, schooled in radical interpretations of the labor theory of value and the natural rights of free-born Americans, refined a working-class critique of their employers' republican capitalism. The struggle reached its peak in 1835 and 1836, when trades' unionists and their supporters defied a legal counteroffensive by their employers and weighed in with strikes, cooperatives experiments, and (in some places) tentative talk of forming a labor party. The old "mechanics' interest," with its ideology of artisan republicanism, had divided into opposing class interests, each with its own interpretations of what the artisan republican legacy was; women craft workers, mill hands, and unskilled laborers seized their own radical and republican ideals to defend their movements.[63]

The South also had its share of alarms in the 1830s, on and off the plantations. The spreading labor agitation of the North struck a chord among the comparatively smaller southern free working class. City central unions, much like the New York and Philadelphia G.T.U.s, appeared in Baltimore, Washington, D.C., and Savannah, Georgia; a spotty labor press cropped up in the border states and upper South.[64] Even more significant were the popular movements for democratic reform, which succeeded in eliminating prop-

erty qualifications for voting and office-holding in most southern states before the decade's end—although agitation against free black workers
undercut class alignments.[65] On the plantations, meanwhile, Nat Turner's
rebellion in 1831 wonderfully concentrated the slaveholders' minds about
what their "children" might do to them if given the chance. The ensuing
Great Reaction, a virtual reign of terror launched against criticism of slavery, at once ratified the sanctity of slaveholding and set down some clear
rules about southern class confrontation. Slaveholders might be willing to
compromise about democracy for white men (indeed, might embrace it), but
nothing would be allowed to threaten slavery.[66]

Looking back, we can detect in these developments the social origins of
the sectional bloodbath that lay ahead. As the class conflicts of the urban
North helped sharpen the justification for free labor, so the slaveholders'
struggle to contain the yeomen, the slaves, and the free wage-earners sharpened their justification for slavery. The rise of immediatist abolition reform
in the North and militant states'-rights proslavery in the South forecast the
coming struggle, as, briefly, did the nullification crisis of 1832–1833. Yet
the immediate political outcome of the 1830s was not national disunion but
the consolidation of a new intersectional party system.

It has become fashionable to interpret the party politics of the 1830s and
1840s as divorced from class formation (indeed, from any meaningful social
or ideological conflict)—"the mass, non-ideological politics of the Jackson
era," one historian had called them.[67] Such claims stand up only if we assume either that "genuine" ideological conflict turned exclusively on slavery, or that "class" politics would have necessitated some sharply drawn
battle between opposing parties of the propertied and the propertyless. In
fact, Jacksonian politics were inflamed by social and ideological passions,
mainly over issues concerning merchant capitalist expansion, North and
South. And although both of the major parties were elite-led, cross-class coalitions, unwilling to disturb the legitimacy of either northern capitalism or
southern slavery, their respective mass constituencies reflected the social divisions being thrown up by northern and southern economic change.

Much still remains to be learned about the social and political origins
of the Jacksonian party system—the combination of democratization and
professionalization that widened the franchise in key states like New York
and broke the Jeffersonian gentry's grip on politics. Without question, the
move into politics of self-made lawyers, newspaper editors, and other ambitious professional men ventilated the political system and opened it up to
increased participation from below.[68] Simultaneously, the Jeffersonians'
crablike movement toward accepting revised nationalizing vehicles of regulated merchant capitalist growth set up the possibility for new battles over
the issues of political economy joined in the 1780s and 1790s.

Only after Andrew Jackson's elevation to the White House, however, did the new party system begin to fall into place. Certain essentials were clear as early as 1828: most important, any successful national party would have to remain impervious to sectional prejudices; somehow, politicians would have to broker the nation's distinct (and increasingly contradictory) regional interests. But it took the Bank War and the nullification crisis for Jackson and his party to elaborate something approaching a coherent ideological appeal; not until 1834–1835 did a national opposition party begin to take shape. Against the backdrop of local and regional class antagonisms, rival politicians began to tap some of the deepest fears and aspirations of the white male citizenry. By 1840, following Van Buren's insistent (and politically disastrous) turn to the left, two truly national political organizations were in competition, offering contrasting views of political economy and the benefits of commercial expansion.[69]

In general, the Democrats appealed to those who felt cut off from or injured by the continuing transformation of market relations. This by no means restricted their following to peripheral areas or the lower classes: disgruntled local bankers, free-trade merchants, and upstart slaveholders claimed the key positions in the party hierarchy and kept more radical insurgencies like the Working Men's movements in line. The Democrats' mass base, however, tended to come from northern rural areas well removed from transportation lanes, from white workers in proletarianized trades and industries, and from the southern yeomanry. The Whigs, meanwhile, captured their major support from the most rapidly commercializing northern and western rural areas, from "mutualist" Protestant workers (many evangelicals among them) in skilled trades and tariff-protected industries, from manufacturers and successful merchants, and from the southern black belt. The pattern became ever clearer during Van Buren's presidency, when his "Loco Foco" advocacy of an Independent Treasury sent conservative northern bankers and southern planters (at least temporarily) into the Whigs' ranks. Overall, party alignments tended to divide the upper strata of workers from the lower; while colored by class passions, they also gave workers strong political identities that superseded class and marginalized radical movements like the Working Men.[70]

By 1840, party politics reflected the intraregional conflicts generated by merchant capitalist expansion, even as the national and local political leaders kept these conflicts from challenging the existing social order. Over the next eight years, party imagery established the Democrats as the party of the common producers and the Whigs as the party of the respectables—constituencies broad enough to bring spirited, closely fought national elections. Over the same period, meanwhile, some of the more dramatic social conflicts that had helped shape the Democratic-Whig division began to simmer down, reducing possible challenges to party elites from below.

In the northern cities, the Panic of 1837 crushed the union offensive (a sign of the fragility of the workers' organizations). Some individual unions struggled on and survived; when the depression lifted in middecade, labor movements in New England, New York, and Pennsylvania organized strikes and political action, seeking reforms like the ten-hour workday. Yet the 1840s were also very different for northern workers from the decade that preceded it. In the years after the Panic, with unemployment soaring and the unions in retreat, workers looked for new ways to preserve their self-respect. A wave of lower-class religious revivalism, yet to be studied closely, brought workers and small producers into Methodist and Baptist churches as never before, as well as into more exotic enthusiasms like the Millerite movement. Some of this fervor eventually fueled a distinctly working-class evangelicalism, with anticapitalist as well as antiemployer overtones. But the chiliasm of despair took other forms as well—forms that often exacerbated divisions within the emerging working class. Along with plebeian Washingtonian temperance, the first powerful insurgence of local nativist politics engaged Protestant workers resentful of the growing deference of professional politicians toward "unrepublican" Catholic immigrants. An entire generation of young, usually poorly trained urban workers suffered marginality and took courage in a boisterous street culture epitomized by the true-life Bowery Boy and Bowery Gal. Local urban politics temporarily entered a period of status conflict; at the state level, Whig and Democratic leaders softened some of their harsher "class" rhetoric, and started to reach compromises on outstanding economic issues.[71]

In the South, meanwhile, the recovery from the panic helped calm class resentments in politics. The collapse of credit and banking after 1837 brought a strong backlash against commercial expansion and internal improvement; in some southern states not a bank could be found in the mid-1840s. By the end of the decade, though, as the South's more gradual recovery commenced, slaveholders and their urban allies from both parties began working out compromises on state-sponsored banking and internal improvements schemes. Tensions between upcountry and black belt did not disappear and could, at any moment, break into fresh political battles. But the semblance of a modus vivendi also fell in place, backed by local political elites and sealed by a cross-class loyalty to the peculiar institution.[72]

By the mid-1840s, the nation seemed poised for a period of extraordinary prosperity. Only isolated voices in the North challenged the free labor regime; few in the South who harshly criticized slavery stayed in the South for long. The two national parties could count on reliable followings and stood a reasonable chance of taking national office. Yet, these appearances were deceiving. The maturation of northern capitalism and southern slavery may have temporarily quieted intraregional class conflicts; it also started to raise issues that the best efforts of Whigs and Democrats could not eliminate by compromise. The logic of the Jacksonian party system had been to build national coalitions out of the conflicts that divided northerners against northerners, southerners against southerners. Now, however, politicians began to fight on sectional grounds, as the drive to control newly settled western territories sent free labor and slavery on a collision course.

As early as 1842, only two years after the founding of the antislavery Liberty Party, a small coterie of antislavery activists, coming mainly from the evangelized districts of the Old Northwest, had secured places in Congress. Two years later, the southern mavericks John C. Calhoun and John Tyler and their proslavery associates effectively controlled the national Democratic party and torpedoed the expected renomination of ex-president Martin Van Buren. The rashness of Tyler's successor, James K. Polk, in pursuing a manufactured war with Mexico only seemed to prove that the party of Jackson had become the party of the South. Although it would take nearly a decade of further struggle before the existing party lines finally collapsed, the reorientation of national politics away from issues of economic development and toward slavery and free labor was all too apparent during the slavery extension debates of 1846 and 1847. Van Buren's presidential candidacy on the sectional Free Soil party ticket in 1848 was a fitting emblem of how badly merchant capitalist politics had broken down; the annexation of Texas, that same year, announced a troubling conclusion to the southwest expansion, begun in the wake of Jackson's victory at New Orleans in 1815.[73]

With these events, American politics entered a new phase. So did the history of American capitalism and the working class. The previous seventy years had witnessed extraordinary economic expansion throughout the country. In the Northeast and a few southern cities, a working class had formed with its most vocal leaders and unions declaring ideas about the republic at odds with the prevailing wisdom of their employers. In certain places, notably the seaboard cities, a diverse set of working-class cultures and political currents emerged that would endure, through many changes, over the rest of the century. Yet it was still too early, in the mid-1840s, to speak reasonably about a national working class. Most Americans worked in agricultural pursuits, as something other than wage laborers. More important, over 2 million American working people were enslaved. Only after momentous political struggles would the United States acquire a national working-class presence. Foremost among these was the destruction of slavery and the vindication of free labor.

As early as 1850, some astute observers were well aware of the impulses that were propelling the merchant capitalist republic to its ruin; among them was Herman Melville. Melville had been born to a family of merchant traders with Jacksonian affinities and associations. While composing *Moby Dick*, he intended no simple allegory of American politics or of his personal breaks with his family, but his writing was deeply attuned to the destructive elements that were overtaking the country. He could still find something of the old democratic republican utopianism—a "just Spirit of Equality" and "democratic dignity"—among ordinary Americans, a cosmopolitan multi-racial crew of the "meanest mariners, and renegades and castaways." Now, though, the American ship of state was on a diabolical course of vengeful destiny, commanded by a madman and his compliant officers. Ahab, like Andrew Jackson, had been "picked from the pebbles" and then thundered "higher than a throne"; like the slaveholding democrats and their merchant capitalist allies, he derived his authority from the appropriated power of the Pequod's black and brown harpooners. His quest, though, negated the orderly hunt for raw commodities; he waged no crusade for popular sovereignty but an unholy kind of war, securing men's loyalties with the promise of an Equadoran doubloon of virgin gold. "He would be a democrat to all above; look how he lords it over all below," the Yankee Quaker Starbuck says of his captain. Like the Pequod, merchant capitalist America, guided by Young Hickory Polk, his successors and their abettors, headed south-westerly, only to be swallowed up in its own vortex.[74]

As Melville sensed, it would take the destruction of the existing order in a bloody civil war to settle the national political crisis. Yet out of the war came a new order, which Melville could not foresee. In combination with other decisive developments that began in the late 1840s and 1850s, that new order would give birth to a national working class—and with it the start of a furious struggle over the meaning of free labor in a rapidly industrializing republic.

WORKING-CLASS DEVELOPMENT IN THE AGE OF CAPITAL, 1848–1877

The third quarter of the nineteenth century, the American age of capital, witnessed the great breakthrough of industrial capitalism in the United States. The mid-century crisis and the disintegration of merchant capitalist comity, foreshadowed in the sectional battles of the late 1840s, led to secession and civil war; the war brought the social revolution of emancipation and a restructuring of the national political economy. By the mid-1870s, industrial capitalists had affirmed their dominant position in the reconstructed nation-state and completed extraordinary feats of entrepreneurial expansion. Meanwhile, a new ethnic and immigrant working class, though divided socially and politically in numerous ways, began to cohere in a national labor movement, capable of pressing its own political claims. Working-class development proceeded unevenly; in the South, for example, the proletarianization of the freedmen and yeomen whites was only beginning in the late 1860s and 1870s. Working-class politics and culture varied in different kinds of industrial sites. Yet with the Great Depression of 1873–1878, a common reference point and structure of feeling could be detected among workers around the country. Out of that depression, and the growing working-class unrest at industrial capital's triumph, would come the great upheavals of the 1880s and 1890s.

1848–1865

The mid-century crisis, best known as a political turning point, actually involved a conjuncture of several important economic, demographic, and political changes. First, the mass immigration from Ireland and Germany, peaking during the period 1845–1855, sharpened the differences between North and South and fundamentally changed the social texture of emerging class relations in the urban North. The numbers of new arrivals was staggering, even in comparison to the mounting figures of the 1830s and early 1840s; in all, more than 3.1 million persons arrived between 1845 and 1855. As they settled, mainly in northern cities and towns, the immigrants very quickly entered an already fractured manufacturing economy. Nativist charges that these immigrants *caused* the debasement of manufacturing labor were as exaggerated as they were misplaced. As we have seen, capitalist transformations had overtaken the republican workshop and the Yankee paternalist mill well before the greatest waves of immigrants arrived. But there is no question that the sudden influx of a fresh supply of surplus labor greatly accelerated the growth of northern manufacturing. By the mid-1840s, Irish immigrants had replaced Yankee women as the mainstay of the New England textile workforce—a shift that marked the final collapse of the old paternalism. Ten years later, immigrants, along with a still-small proportion of northern blacks, literally became the working class in the seaports and in smaller cities, leaving a relatively small number of native-born white Protestant wage earners in more privileged skilled occupations and in trades still largely unaffected by early industrialization.[75]

Some long-standing academic myths about the antebellum immigrants have been dispelled over the last fifteen years. Few of the newcomers matched the image of the benighted, deferential, conservative peasantry presented in the pioneering studies of America's "uprooted." The Germans tended to come mainly from the middling strata of urban artisans and rural small producers; the Irish, though overwhelmingly from rural areas, included small farmers, sharecroppers, agricultural laborers, marginal tenants, and seasonal workers. Both groups brought with them bitter experiences with employers, tax-collectors, and absentee landlords, which would serve them well in their struggles with American employers. Although the Irish, in particular, made the antebellum immigration a heavily Catholic one (leading to a fivefold increase in the number of American Catholics between 1840 and 1860), theirs was not the reactionary, ultramontane Catholicism of France or Spain but a deeply antimonarchical, often prorepublican Catholic way of life of the colonized lay poor and the hedgerow priests—a viewpoint not wholly antithetical to the American working-class republicanism of the 1830s and 1840s. Above all, there is substantial evidence that the renowned "breakdown" of immigrant culture and family life that supposedly preceded immigrant assimilation to Yankee "middle-class" norms did not, in fact, occur.[76]

The terms of immigrant adaptation varied. German workers, with their craft skills and Jacobin traditions, tended to be more receptive to reform politics and trade unionism than others; a large proportion of them would wind up in the Republican party. The Irish, by contrast, faced tougher circumstances. Arriving in America often desperately poor, consigned to the lowest levels of a casualized labor force, and settling in amid waves of militant Protestant revivals and nativist outbursts, the Irish had ample reasons to band together against the rest of the world. Not surprisingly, they tended to abhor Whiggish, Anglo-American reformers and fought hard to protect their own cultural territory from the intrusions of middle-class temperance advocates and evangelicals. The Irish immigrants' search for dignity led to sometimes murderous expressions of ethnic solidarity and white supremacy in the rough-and-tumble world of the gangs. These class and cultural resentments usually led, in turn, to the Democratic party, whose leaders in some of the bigger cities tapped Irish prejudices and aspirations in order to establish the first local political machines. Yet this world also had its complexities. A variety of radical and democratic ideas—republican nationalism, O'Connellism, militant trade unionism—survived the Atlantic crossing from Ireland and came to exist side-by-side with an assimilationist church and the Democratic party. Along with the legacy of racism and opposition to Yankee reform, these survivals would prove to be of increasing importance to the rise of a national labor movement over the next twenty years.[77]

As the immigrants arrived, the American economy entered a period of sustained growth that would last, despite fluctuations and periodic slumps, until the Panic of 1873. In the South, the cotton boom of the 1850s brought spiralling profits, a pressure for territorial expansion, rapid construction of railroads and other internal improvements, and a further movement of the yeomanry into staple production; in addition, a mainly immigrant working class grew up in the leading southern cities. Agriculture on the old northwest frontier experienced rapid commercialization of production and capitalization of production techniques, which spread to the more recently settled areas of the Midwest in the 1850s. These developments, coupled with increased European demand for American foodstuffs, dramatically shifted the center of northern agriculture westward and secured the political alliance between Northeast and Northwest.[78]

Northern industry, meanwhile, expanded both qualitatively and quantitatively. Although W. W. Rostow's metaphor of the "take-off" is inadequate to describe the unevenness of industrial development and although the impressive figures on rising per capita income after 1839 hide deep inequalities, there is no question that American industry entered a new period of self-generating growth in the third quarter of the nineteenth century. The turning point came roughly between 1847 and 1854, when the introduction of steam-powered machinery in key sectors (notably shoemaking), facilitated by the arrival of the railroad, the telegraph, and the steamship, opened the way for what one historian has called "the flowering of the industrial economy."[79]

Together, the mass immigration and the quickening of economic development helped force the basic political issues over slavery and the nation's destiny. The strengthening links between the industrializing North and the commercializing West, along with the northern population boom, held out to southern slaveholders the dangerous prospect of an irreversible marginalization in national politics, precisely when pressure for the territorial expansion for slavery was mounting. Having secured the political initiative over the yeomanry, the slaveholders steadily moved away from compromise, first to demand the end of federal restrictions on slavery in the territories and ultimately to demand federal protection of slavery.

To northerners of every variety, the specter of an untrammeled, expansionist slave South now began to threaten their own way of life. To be sure, only a minority of northerners—least of all the poorest Irish immigrants and loyal Democrats—shared in the sense of racial equality that drove the most zealous abolitionists. Nor did most northerners, including the leading antislavery congressmen, imagine that resistance to the South would lead to immediate emancipation. But by the late 1850s, the slaveholders' political belligerence and successful transgressions against northern rights and liberties (emblematized in the struggle over fugitive slaves and the personal liberty laws) appeared to a growing majority of northerners as a threat to American democracy and their own personal independence. Although party continued to divide Americans across class lines, the old center of national politics, commanded by Stephen A. Douglas and the partisans of "popular sovereignty" and by a dwindling band of southern unionist Whigs, fell apart. By 1860, the election of Abraham Lincoln, hardly the most outspoken antislavery politician, was enough to trigger southern secession.[80]

As the Jacksonian party system cracked at the seams, the terms of debate over American republicanism and the legacy of the Revolution changed. Try as they might, centrist politicians like Douglas could not patch up the polity by reviving the old issues of economic development and intersectional comity. In the South, republicanism came to be equated with states' rights, white equality, resistance to moralistic Yankee authority, and protection of property in slaves. In the North, republicanism became the namesake for a new political party, dedicated to resisting the Slave Power and its supposedly aristocratic leaders and thereby protecting self-ownership, the dignity of independent free labor, and ultimately democracy and the Union.

These political and ideological shifts, especially the rise of the Republican party, had enormous implications for the emerging working class. Contrary to old economic determinist accounts, the advent of the Republicans did not represent a clear-cut coming to power of a new "industrial" bourgeoisie; the fight for "free labor" was not, at least in the short run, a mere cover for industrialist power. To be sure, the Republican notion of "free labor" had nothing to do with the collective rights of wage earners; by locating the primary threat to northern liberties outside the North and projecting Yankee cultural assumptions, the party repelled some of the poorest sectors of the northern working class, especially the Irish. But the free labor attack on the Slave Power also expressed cherished notions of independence and nationalism shared by northern union leaders, native-born and German craft workers, and Democrats (including the Irish). These notions would come to the fore during the secession crisis, when even anti-Republican workers joined the army to help save the Union. In a similar way, western and rural antislavery embraced far more than the evangelical and entrepreneurial passions of Yankee capitalists. The Republicanism of Lincoln, for example, was certainly rooted in Whiggish precepts of state-aided economic expansion and social harmony—but Lincoln also held to older petty-producer ideals of freedom based on personal economic independence and access to the full fruits of one's labor. Above all, by breaking decisively with the norms of merchant capitalist politics, the Republicans raised the issues of slavery, freedom, and labor in ways that would unite the North in the wake of secession but that would also help create a context for fresh struggles within the North over the proper form of American labor relations.[81]

It took the slaveholders' rebellion and the revolution that followed to establish fully that new context. The Civil War was a central event—if not *the* central event—in the lives of all who lived through it. Viewed as part of working-class history, the war marked a point of no return in two all-important matters.

The abolition of slavery was, of course, the most wrenching change in the entire history of nineteenth century labor relations. It was not, however, an inevitability or a necessary outgrowth of northern victory. Certainly Abraham Lincoln, whatever his deep antislavery convictions and speculations about slavery's future, entered the conflict with no intention of turning the war for the Union into a war of liberation. It took, instead, the actions of rebellious slaves—in particular the runaways to the Union lines—to force the matter, pushing northern generals, congressmen, and finally Lincoln himself to recognize the military (as well as the political) necessity of emancipation. Lincoln's proclamation of 1863, though limited to areas outside Union control, was greeted by slaves in large areas of the Confederacy as a declaration of their freedom. Hundreds of thousands struck off the plantations once the Yankees reached within a safe distance. Safe behind the lines, they pressed for admission into the army; the subsequent enlistment of over 150,000 ex-slaves gave important aid to the Union cause. By war's end, Lincoln, the cautious emancipator, was pressing for passage of the Thirteenth Amendment; once ratified, that amendment destroyed the foundations of antebellum southern society and began a new struggle to determine what kind of society would take slavery's place.[82]

The Civil War also brought with it the creation of a state unlike any the American people had ever known. Had Thomas Jefferson lived to see 1865, slavery's demise would have surprised him far less than the size and scope of centralized power behind the war effort. More than 2 million men served in the Union army alone; that army and its Confederate foe killed well over half a million Americans. To finance the war, the North established a national taxation system and a national debt. With only token opposition, Lincoln declared martial law in large areas of the country, suspended habeas corpus, and arrested spokesmen suspected of disloyalty. With considerably more opposition, especially from the immigrant poor of New York City, the Union relied on conscription to reinforce the ranks as the war dragged on and enlistment fell. The parallel sometimes drawn between Lincoln and Bismarck, in this respect, is not completely fanciful; like his German counterpart, Lincoln oversaw not simply the preservation of the American union but the birth of a single nation out of what had been a testy compact of American states. What remained to be seen after 1865 was what would become of this American state amid the social conflicts to come.[83]

Northern workers, like the southern freedmen, had a particularly deep interest in this last matter. Northern class divisions were certainly complicated by the midcentury immigration wave; the ensuing national crisis, though it exacerbated class tensions over issues like conscription, also joined northerners across class lines against a common enemy. Yet the Civil War era hardly eradicated the emerging class identities of the Jacksonian era, or sidetracked labor radicalism. Indeed, the economic boom of the 1850s, and the workers' experience of the war actually helped consolidate what one early labor historian described as the first "modern" American labor movement.[84]

After the failures of the Ten Hours' movements of the 1840s and the urban labor reform congresses of 1850–1851, a new order of labor organizations came to the fore in the early 1850s, centered in the skilled and semiskilled trades and intent on securing both adequate wages and work rules. The workers' main weapon was the strike. Skilled workers, best able to organize unions, would set a rule (or union rate) below which no union man would work; strikes against noncomplying employers, so-called rat shops, would continue until all union men were paid according to the rule or until the union gave up. As David Montgomery has noted, such tactics—a far cry from later methods of collective bargaining—were "peculiarly appropriate" for workers "who had progressed but part way down the path from journeyman artisan to factory wage-laborer."[85] For all their rigidity, they proved effective in bringing the nation's mostly small and medium-sized firms to terms, without creating an elaborate union bureaucracy to threaten workers' sense of themselves as independent citizens. Unskilled workers, meanwhile, were less well-placed to organize unions and resorted to a different kind of strike, the spontaneous "turn out" in which workers simply walked off their jobs (and appealed to others to do so) until their grievances were attended to.[86]

At the peak of labor activity in 1853–1854, more than 400 union strikes were recorded in the largest American states, a quantum leap from the figures of the 1830s and 1840s; the greatest single strike in pre-Civil War America virtually closed down the New England shoemaking industry in 1860. Many more spontaneous stoppages occurred on a daily basis. Having stepped back from the more overtly "political" labor movements of the 1830s and 1840s, the trade unionists dug in for a protracted economic struggle with employers. Their outlooks, however, hardly conformed to the "pure-and-simple" economism ascribed to them by later historians. Although some organized workers, especially in the mechanized trades, came to recognize that their labor had been transformed into a market commodity, trade union manifestos bristled with attacks on "the wages system"— and not simply inadequate wages—as the source of their plight, a threat to their republican citizenship.[87]

Apart from its militance, one of the more interesting—and as yet largely unexplored—aspects of antebellum unionism was its ability to attract immigrant support and occasionally bridge deep ethnic divisions. To be sure, ethnic antagonisms were explosive in the mid-1850s. These divisions were reproduced in party politics before and after the Know-Nothing upsurge, as the emerging Republican party tended to attract propertied and Protestant workers and exclude the poorer immigrant Catholics. One study of Newark workers has shown that the 1850s witnessed both a hardening of class lines and a conflagration of ethnic conflict that left the city's working class bitterly divided. But the impact of these divisions needs to be understood in the context of uneven economic development and not as a given of social life. First, ethnic divisions among workers were usually closely related to the internal stratification of the emerging working class, setting a relatively small group of skilled native Protestants against the masses of proletarianized im-migrants. In many places, especially the eastern cities, "ethnic" divisions did not cut across the working class as a whole, but bespoke divisions between a minority upper stratum of wage earners and the bulk of the working class.[88] Second, the immigrants' participation in trade unions, sometimes in collaboration (cautious as it must have been) with native workers, began almost immediately after their arrival. As early as 1850, Irish and German workers had helped to organize unions and assumed leadership positions. The surviving records of New York's Amalgamated Trades' Convention of 1853–1854 depict an interesting sight: among the trade union delegates sat the representatives of the city's Hibernian United Benevolent Society. Given the large numbers and proportion of immigrant workers as early as 1855, in organized "sweated" trades and factories as well as in day labor and do-mestic service, it seems improbable that the immigrant presence in the dec-ade's strike waves was not pronounced. Although our knowledge of ante-bellum unionism is still meager, it is likely that, even before the Civil War, trade unions had begun to familiarize new arrivals with American labor or-ganizing and even mitigate "ethnocultural" conflict among workers.[89]

Other factors did more than ethnic discord to hinder the revived labor movement. Hit hard by the recession of 1854–1855 (and even more by the devastating depression of 1857–1859), caught up in the secession crisis and nationalist upsurge of 1860–1861, the unions foundered. Those that did not dissolve before the Civil War found their ranks depleted by army enlistment and later the draft; as soon as the war came, the Philadelphia bookmakers voted to disband in order "to enlist with uncle Sam," adjourning "until ei-ther the Union is safe or we are whipped." Those workers who stayed be-hind, however, remained touchy about wages and hours, and struck to offset the wartime inflation. Over the last eighteen months of the conflict, a renais-sance of trade union organizing increased the number of locals by more than threefold. By 1865, more than a dozen national trade unions existed.[90]

From these modest beginnings, skilled and semiskilled workers took to the offensive, in politics as well as strikes. Although political and racial ani-mosities persisted—with grisly consequences, as in New York's draft riots in 1863—and although nativism lasted in the eastern cities, the experience of warfare and nationalist sacrifice helped break down ethnic and religious barriers. Events abroad—Fenianism and agrarian disturbances in Ireland, Lassallean agitation in Germany—interjected radical ideas into ethnic American workers' communities just after the war's close.[91] As the federal government emerged, briefly, as the fulcrum of Reconstruction reform and as southern state governments began feeling the effects of the newly enfran-chised freedmen, a reforming labor movement began to press its own politi-cal claims.

The northern labor movement would, of course, be only one factor in the political conflicts that followed Appomattox. Freedmen, reformers, merchants, planters, and industrialists, as well as workers, would all have a hand in the process of national reconstruction. Out of this many-sided struggle, would eventually come a momentous triumph for the nation's industrial capitalists. Out of it as well would come the shape of a national working class.

1865–1877

Shortly after he was elected president, Abraham Lincoln spoke in New Haven, offering some reflections about the great strike that had gripped the shoemaking cities of New England. The "true system" of labor, Lincoln explained, allowed all men an equal chance in "the race of life," to "hope to be a hired laborer this year and the next, work for himself afterward, and finally hire men to work for him!" In such quasi-artisanal relations, without any fixed condition of labor, wage earners were "not obliged to work under all circumstances," and strikes were permissible: "*I am glad to see that a system prevails in New England under which laborers CAN strike* when they want to." Lincoln barely understood the significance of organized labor; his conception of a "strike" essentially meant the right to leave one's job and seek another one. One wonders if he would have remained so sanguine about strikes and the "true system" of labor had he lived to see the great railroad rebellion of 1877. We do know what his private secretary and adviser John Hay made of these later events: "The prospects of labor and capital both seem gloomy enough. The very devil seems to have entered into the lower classes of working men, and there are plenty of scoundrels to encourage them to all lengths." Hay urged a military buildup to repress such outrages.[92]

A burst of industrial capitalist development separates Lincoln's observations from Hay's, one that brought the decay of the Republican's early free-labor optimism and a deepening of class antagonisms throughout the reunited nation. The acceleration was temporarily halted by the bitter depression of 1873–1878; in the great upheaval that soon followed, the realities of class conflict shattered the mythic harmony of the free-labor republic.

It is important not to caricature the immensity of industrial expansion after 1865. Although manufacturing output registered impressive gains over the thirty years following 1849, overall nonagricultural productivity rose only marginally from 1860 to 1880. The celebrated fall in industrial prices between 1860 and 1880 came only after the Civil War inflation ended and was especially marked after the onset of depression in 1873—and, thus, indicated little about changing industrial capacity. Individual firms remained generally of small to moderate size, especially in the most dynamic regions of development outside New England. Manufacturing of all kinds was dispersed in small towns and cities; American capitalism had not yet "ruralized" the countryside into an adjunct of urban industry. It remained possible for at least some talented mechanics to succeed as industrial entrepreneurs, giving an aura of truth to the "rags-to-riches" fictions of the day. These entrepreneurs, as well as those born to wealth, only began to experiment with the use of limited liability stock companies and primitive forms of horizontal integration; most remained attached to the individual firm or simple partnership—"the family business"—with its crude, often idiosyncratic accounting methods. The American factory of the 1880s, in one historian's words, remained "a congeries of craftsmen's shops rather than an integrated plant." Intense competition drove prices down, while transportation and material costs stayed relatively stable. Manufacturers responded by cutting wage costs rather than by reorganizing their businesses. Even then, the near-anarchy of entrepreneurialism took its toll in bankruptcies and lagging profits.[93]

Within these limits, industrial capital made major advances. Critical industrial sectors—especially iron, coal, and the railways—enjoyed rising productivity, largely as a sustained outgrowth of the railway booms of the 1850s. Two regions, the Ohio River Valley between Pittsburgh and Louisville and the lower Great Lakes from Buffalo to Milwaukee, experienced exceptionally rapid growth in mining, iron, glass, oil refining, and railroads. Those firms that survived the competitive chaos concentrated the work force into larger units; the average number of workers per firm in manufacturing rose by roughly one-fourth in the troubled 1870s. In some metropolitan trades, above all printing and food processing, factory production expanded rapidly; in other major trades previously unaffected by metropolitan industrialization, cigarmaking being the classic case, simple technological advances opened the way for sweatshop production. Use of the McKay stitcher completed the shift of shoemaking into factories. Protective tariffs, liberalized land policies, immigration law reform, rationalization of a national currency and banking system, all initiated while the South was out of the Union, enhanced industrial capitalists' political position. In conjunction with the wartime inflation, these policy changes helped entrepreneurs break free of their dependence on merchant capital. Less reputable forms of persuasion accompanied the usual lobbying, turning Congress and state legislatures into faro-halls of bribery, speculation, and preferential treatment. Still portraying themselves as "producers," the enemies of parasitic commercial capitalists, the industrial entrepreneurs of the 1860s and 1870s found in Congress and state legislatures instruments to help them preserve and expand the family firm and consolidate their political power.[94]

Workers also began, during the age of capital, to approach the government to secure *their* interests. They fared very differently. The Civil War had held out hopes to northern workers and southern freedmen that the vindication of free labor could be carried further, to ensure that all Americans would secure the full fruits of their labor. Instead, a combination of rapid industrial development, sharpening economic fluctuations, and elite political compromise widened the gaps between classes and initiated new and increasingly violent class conflicts throughout the nation.

The outstanding structural feature of the postbellum industrial work force was its largely immigrant and ethnic composition. What remained of the mostly Yankee working class that had formed in the 1830s and 1840s was largely supplanted by newcomers and their children. Immigration remained a primary source of urban population growth well after the famine immigration and the hiatus of the Civil War years; in all, 5.1 million immigrants, mainly from Ireland, Germany, and Britain, arrived from 1861 through 1880. In 1870, one-third of the nation's industrial workers were immigrants; the figures were far higher in the major commercial-manufacturing centers. Of the nation's six largest cities, only Philadelphia had more native-born workers than immigrants in manufacturing; elsewhere, the ratio of immigrants to native-born ranged as high as two to one. The figures are even more striking if the sons and daughters of immigrants (listed in the census as "native-born") are distinguished from the children of native-born Americans. By disaggregating the manuscript census, Herbert Gutman found that the vast majority of workers outside the building trades in 1880 were either first- or second-generation immigrants or blacks, in major cities and smaller towns alike; in some places, the figures ranged as high as 90 percent. Alongside the thousands of newcomers whose experiences bridged the Old World and the New, a new generation of ethnic American workers came of age after the Civil War, whose entire lives had been spent in industrializing America.[95]

The Irish, along with the Germans and the British still one of the three major immigrant groups, offer the clearest example of the intergenerational dynamics at work within the immigrant-ethnic working class. During the Famine immigration, the Irish tended to cluster in the commercial-manufacturing ports and factory towns and occupied the bottom of the occupational scale, in domestic service, day labor, and the most debased, sweated branches of manufacturing and the building trades. A less spectacular but still formidable Irish migration replenished the ranks of domestic servant girls and laborers in the 1860s and 1870s. At the same time, however, a significant portion of the Irish-American working class, especially of the second-generation "natives," began moving incrementally into skilled and semiskilled positions (iron molding, steamfitting, masonry) as well as into petty retailing. From their ranks would come politicians, editors, trade unionists, and informal community leaders of wideranging views, who were fully at home in America but still sensitive to the travails of their poorer countrymen. They, along with their counterparts of other nationalities, would prove central figures in the consolidation of both ethnic and class solidarities in the 1870s and 1880s.[96]

A very different process unfolded in the conquered South. As in other postemancipation societies, the politics of southern Reconstruction turned, as Christopher Memminger predicted in 1865, on "the decision which shall be made upon the mode of organizing the labor of the African race." The ex-slaves had no intention of remaining within the purview of their former masters. Nor did they show any inclination for the "freedom"" of rural wage labor. They wanted what they thought was theirs. "We has a right to the land where we are located," one freedman proclaimed; "For why? I tell you. Our wives, our children, our husbands has been sold over and over again to purchase the land we now locates upon; for that reason we have a divine right to the land." For a moment, the freedmen reached for that "divine right," by getting and protecting a piece of land, electing all-important legislators and local officials, pressing for state-funded schools and other reform programs, and helping to beat back the Black Codes, passed in 1865 and 1866. Sharecropping represented, at least initially, something of a compromise between the planters' drive for subjugation short of slavery and the freedmen's resistance to both wage labor and the plantation.[97]

It took what W. E. B. Du Bois described fifty years ago as a "counterrevolution of property" in the 1870s, undertaken by southern merchant-planters and abetted by northern Republicans veering ever rightward, to foreclose the freedmen's near future. The famous compromise of 1877, which brought Reconstruction to an end, marked the political ratification of this revolution. With a startling quickness (considering the devastation of the war), a new southern ruling class began to climb out of the ashes of the Confederacy. As early as 1870, these incipient "new" southerners had helped begin to rebuild the South's railway lines: the next twenty years would bring a commercialization of the southern economy that shifted the center of economic activity away from the black belt to the upcountry and the towns and swept impoverished blacks and petty-producing whites into the vortex of the cotton economy—yet left the South an underdeveloped sectional colony, ruled by an American planter capitalist elite. The hopes of Reconstruction were not suddenly forgotten, as some black activists, North and South, would prove in local labor struggles in the 1880s and 1890s. But these hopes would be measured against the depressing realities of resubjugation, recurring resurgencies of racial politics, and in time, an institutionalization of the American version of the highest stage of white supremacy.[98]

Most of the resubjugated black working class and the newly subjugated whites worked on the land, as tenant farmers, sharecroppers, and agricultural wage laborers. The primary setting for class conflicts in the emerging New South was hence the countryside, where impoverished would-be small producers fought to preserve customary land use rights and built new collective institutions. These efforts would eventually culminate in the Farmers' Alliance and the People's party, the most extraordinary democratic popular uprising of the late nineteenth century.[99] At the same time, the first industrial stirrings of the postwar era promised to enlarge the South's tiny industrial working class. The region's major commercial cities, like New Orleans and Richmond, already had a sizable immigrant working class, which continued to grow in the postwar era. By the 1880s, southern and northern investors were poised to begin the first large-scale wave of southern textile-mill construction. Continued southern railroad construction further stimulated industrial working-class formation. A great deal was left to come before industrial capitalism would thoroughly transform the South; still, as early as the 1870s, the seeds of industrial unrest were being planted alongside those of agrarian revolt.[100]

As black resistance to proletarianization was crushed and as the southern white yeomanry reached its last great struggle, a combination of necessity and technological innovation led northern women and children to take up wage labor, contrary to middle-class domestic norms. The labor shortages of the Civil War temporarily pulled as many as 300,000 women who might otherwise never have sought jobs into the labor market. Thereafter, new jobs opened for women in some trades, notably cigarmaking and printing, while in others, above all ready-made garment production, continued subdivision and subcontracting degraded standards still further and opened opportunities—if that is the word—for the women and children in the work force.[101] Women's entry into wage labor was uneven and segmented. Overall, for example, black women seem to have been more likely to secure paid work outside the household over the decade of 1870–1880.[102] The great majority of women manufacturing workers remained in those sectors already opened before the war—the needle trades, shoemaking, textile production. Still, in one form or another, women's paid work (to say nothing of their unpaid work) proved vital for the lower ranks of the working class. So did child labor. In 1870, children under sixteen years of age made up 13 percent of the labor force in the Massachusetts mills, 21.8 percent in the Pennsylvania mills, and 29 percent in the South Carolina mills. In the well-studied textile town of Cohoes, New York, two-thirds of the total population of native-, Irish-, English-, and French Canadian-born children between 15 and 19 worked in the textile factories in 1860; children from age 10 to 19 made up about half of the city's textile labor force.[103] In the old metropolitan centers, children worked in all sorts of casual jobs as well as in the factories, in a real-life world of Ragged Dick that Horatio Alger portrayed at its most picaresque and other writers at its most lurid.[104]

Working-class demographics and family life reflected the harsh necessities of the family economy. The cliché that urbanization and industrialization led to a dramatic decrease in fertility and family size probably held true for only a minority of the urban work force in the third quarter of the nineteenth century. In the households of skilled, relatively well-paid men wage earners, there seems to have been a noticeable decline in fertility from 1850 on. In laborers' households, however, and particularly among the poorer immigrants, the period 1855 to 1900 seems to have brought a dramatic *increase* in fertility ratios, as high as 13.5 percent according to the best local study of the subject.[105] For those families whose men could reasonably set their sights on earning a "family wage," the "normal," purposeful reduction of family size seems to have made sense; for tens of thousands of others, it did not. Indeed, though we should be cautious about reading too much about motivations, sexuality, and "reproductive strategies" from statistics, it would appear that a logic of increased family size may have held—out of some configuration of necessity and family politics—for the mass of immigrant and unskilled and semiskilled.

Underlying these figures were the hard material conditions endured by American workers. Statistics on American incomes seem to belie these difficult conditions; overall, real wages rose by about 50 percent between 1860 and 1890, by far the highest improvement of the century. Yet these numbers misled, because they masked growing inequalities within the working class. A privileged group of skilled workers centered in the metal, printing, and construction trades earned more than enough to support a family in comfort. The vast majority of the semiskilled and unskilled workforce had to struggle to make ends meet amid the brutal Civil War inflation and the rapid contraction of the 1870s. One scholar has estimated that, by 1880, 40 percent of the nation's industrial labor force lived at or below the poverty level, and that 25 percent lived in real destitution.[106]

Perhaps the most severe hardship affecting working families after 1865 was the expectancy of unemployment. The problem had arisen in New England and the middle states as early as the 1830s, but was mitigated by the ease with which Yankee workers could move into farming or temporary work. By the 1870s, however, the mass of immigrant and ethnic workers was thoroughly dependent on the wage-labor market. Periodic slumps or local recessions meant acute distress for workers' families already on the edge of poverty. More important, the intensely competitive entrepreneurial strategies of the postwar period led employers to keep their hiring and firing practices as flexible as possible. The result, as Alexander Keyssar has demonstrated for the key state of Massachusetts, was the emergence of a reserve army of labor at every level of the postwar industrial working class. Up to half of all blue-collar workers, skilled and unskilled, could expect to be out of work up to three months out of the year. The pressure on family budgets led to chronic impoverishment for many, and a hard scrabble existence for many more—and forced parents to send their able-bodied children to work, keeping their families firmly in the ranks of the working class.[107]

The class divergencies in demographics, unemployment, domestic expectations, and gender roles sharpened class awareness after 1865, in and out of the workplace. In part, the struggle focused (as before, though in new ways) on efforts by middle-class uplifters to reform the laboring poor in their own image. Less driven by evangelical zeal but fortified by the cult of domesticity and environmentalist theories about the etiology of poverty, a new generation of urban missionaries found in the ungenteel domestic arrangements of the laboring poor a shocking mixture of shiftlessness, motherly indifference, and familial anarchy. Though not insensitive to economic hardship, reformers latched on to these seeming irregularities as the root of poverty. Quite simply, one historian has pointed out, the poor "had no *homes*" in the reformer's eyes: "Middle-class people valued family privacy and intimacy: among the poor, they saw a promiscuous sociability, and 'almost fabulous gregariousness.'" Their response was to clear the streets of promiscuous public display, including the ragtag armies of juvenile workers and scavengers, and shore up the working-class home with industrial schools and lodging houses.[108]

More broadly, middle-class reform efforts began to supplement and sometimes counter workers' own formal and informal cultural institutions. The scope of working-class associational life widened rapidly after the Civil War, as urban ethnic communities stabilized and grew. Along with the antebellum pillars of lower-class sociability—taverns, fire companies, and political parties—scores of fraternal orders, benevolent societies, church-sponsored auxiliaries, cooperatives, and sporting clubs won the attention of men and women, preserved standards of mutuality at odds with middle-class norms, and sometimes battled for the right to exist. The transformation of leisure from an everyday communal prerogative into a working-class right—symbolized in the short-hour slogan, "eight hours for work, eight hours for rest, eight hours for what we will"—linked leisure time to industrial politics. Outside of work-related conflicts, efforts by local middle and upper classes to reform, reshape, and restrict working-class recreation brought continual battles over civil service reform, saloons and licensing laws, parks and recreational space, municipal property rights, public ceremonies—even popular fiction. "The resulting conflicts," one writer has observed, "made leisure time and space into arenas where workers and industrialists struggled over the values, world-view, and culture that would dominate working-class life."[109]

There were, of course, abundant ambiguities in the politics of working-class culture. Antidrunk crusades, for example, could divide workers along religious, ethnic, and gender lines, reinforcing the intraclass tensions and cross-class ethnic solidarities that dominated national party politics and voting. The close associations between saloon keepers and political machines could at once give workers a measure of political leverage and feedback into local politics and tie them to established political parties outside of their control. Although labor historians have yet to explore the matter, the robust culture of the saloon was also shot through with an anomie, rage, and misogyny that took its toll in barroom bathos, alcoholism, battered wives, and broken lives. On the other hand, native and ethnic workingmen's clubs could help provide members with a sphere of "self-will"—what the Germans called *eigensinn*—to distance themselves from the harsher realities of urban industrial life.[110] Some of the clubs with political allegiances or overtones—notably, among the Irish, the Fenian Brotherhood, the Ancient Order of Hibernians, and, in the 1870s, various Land League support groups—had the dual effect of supporting nationalist and other radical causes in the Old World and pulling ethnic workers closer to the American labor movement. Other groups of skilled natives, ethnic workers, and immigrants alike would help facilitate working-class organization by mobilizing support in local communities or by serving themselves as the mainsprings of collective action. Among the latter would be a secret benevolent society founded in 1869, the Knights of Labor.

The character and extent of working-class organization varied according to the different kinds of working-class communities that spread across industrializing America. In smaller single-industry cities and mining towns, divisions between workers and the independent middle classes tended to be less sharp than in larger cities. Continually, in times of duress and turmoil, workers in these smaller places received the support of their fellow townspeople, including (in times of labor conflict) support against "the company." By the same token, workers' community ties in small cities and towns tended to blur ethnic and religious differences. Wherever a few companies employed all or most of a town's workers, the entire work force would feel the impact of any attack on wages and conditions. The overwhelmingly working-class composition of the different ethnic communities in these places made it difficult for the tiny ethnic middle class to escape identification—and self-identification—with local workers. As a result, ethnic organizations had a pronounced working-class character; local community life and politics afforded workers real opportunities to exert power and influence.[111]

In major cities, interclass divisions ran far deeper, as did ethnic and religious differences among workers. Segmented by neighborhood residence, ethnic background, and income, big city workers showed far less capacity to join together as a single body of "producers"; when they did, at various flashpoints of industrial conflict, that unity proved difficult to sustain for very long. The social divide between big city workers and the growing ranks of the professional and white-collar middle class posed even more formidable problems. Middle-class sympathy for employers, and middle-class self-identification as distinct from workers, allowed large municipal governments to take action against workers' organizations with political impunity. Moreover, ethnic organizations in the larger cities, including radical groups like the Irish Land League, tended to fall under the control of the ethnic middle class, muffling the power of ethnic workers. Of course, these obstacles did not prevent big-city workers from organizing all sorts of groups, including the largest labor unions in the country. But, whereas small city workers tended to draw together across barriers of craft and ethnicity, the ethnic craft union tended to be the focus of workers' organization in the larger cities.[112]

Whatever the site, meanwhile, workers were hardly united in their opposition to middle-class acquisitive individualism or in their attachment to collective action. Enough opportunities remained for some ambitious workers to set up on their own—as small shopkeepers, artisans, or subcontractors—or to advance through the ranks as foremen and managers. One study of Detroit estimates that as many as one-third of the city's skilled workers and one-fourth of its unskilled workers climbed out of the working class in the late nineteenth century. Many more workers could harbor hopes for such advancement, either for themselves or for their children. Under the circumstances, the ideal of self-improvement—an ideal central to the labor movement—could easily be turned toward improving one's individual situation, at the expense of collective action. And at the other end of the scale, the reserve industrial army moved constantly in a search for work; if their experiences rarely reconciled them to middle-class individualism, it remained exceedingly difficult for them and their families even to consider uniting with other workers.[113]

Along with these community and intraclass variations, the troubled state of American politics shaped workers' responses to their situation. The Civil War had shattered the old national political alliances; for the first few years after Appomattox, it remained unclear what new coalitions might replace them. National politics turned on the implications of the war. The issues of freedmen's rights and southern reinstatement, along with the currency and tariff issues, divided Democrats and Republicans much as sectional matters had divided them before the war. With the Union preserved, the normal cross-class coalitions of national politics slowly fell back into place, dividing ethnic Catholic Democratic workers against native Protestants. The emotions generated by Republicans waving the bloody shirt and Democratic denunciations of the Radical dictatorship deepened the partisan loyalties of the electorate. Down to the 1890s, the war's legacy basically established national voting patterns, making it virtually impossible for labor to act as a unified political class in national affairs.[114] Yet the political disarray caused by the war's outcome and the postwar splits among the nation's elites did briefly open up possibilities for working-class political action on the local and state level.

Such action concerned the larger meaning of Reconstruction. For workers, the Radical Republicans' attacks on the ex-slaveholders' property and political power could easily be turned around, into demands that similar measures be taken against northern industrialists. "So too must our dinner tables be reconstructed," The Boston Labor Reform Association resolved immediately after the war's close, "[and] our dress, manners, education, morals, dwellings, and the whole Social System."[115] At the same time, Democratic workers could seize upon their party's attack on the Republicans as a prelude to a thorough overhaul of government policy. In the late 1860s and 1870s, as freedmen, displaced yeomen, and a reconstituted labor movement took up their demands, northern industrialists and southern planters began to notice that they faced a potentially hazardous challenge from below.

On several fronts, organized workers pressed their claims for power. The number of national craft unions almost tripled from 1865 to 1879; alongside these appeared a plethora of Eight Hour Leagues, workingmen's benevolent associations, the Knights of St. Crispin and other protective orders, the National Labor Union, and locally based craft unions. Strikes remained the workers' most immediately effective weapon, but they had others. Iron molders, coopers, and others formed producer cooperatives, in an attempt to free themselves altogether from "wage-slavery." The boycott, a form of action pioneered in Ireland, was adapted to industrializing America as a means to supplement strikes and gather support. Consumer cooperatives, mutual-aid societies, and fraternal groups—organized along class and ethnic lines—sprang up across the country.[116]

This loose, amorphous labor movement also entered politics. Momentous reform campaigns for the eight-hour workday hit New York, Massachusetts, and several other states in 1867–1868, with surprising effectiveness. Where labor's appeal for the enforcement of new laws fell short, strikes and demonstrations followed, capped by the partially successful walkout of 100,000 workers in New York City in 1872. In 1869, the Knights of St. Crispin elected two dozen state legislators in Massachusetts on their own party line; nine years later, the Greenback-Labor party won local offices in Pennsylvania and New York. Without managing to sever most workers' allegiances with the major parties, various labor reform associations showed that, at least in the leading northeastern industrial states, workers were beginning to find a collective political voice.[117]

By the early 1870s, the labor movement had consolidated a local and national leadership and enunciated a distinctive producer ideology. Although they had little direct connection to the Jacksonian labor movement, ethnic and immigrant workers retrieved the established republican values of "independence" and commonwealth and the radical distinction between producers and nonproducers. To these core ideals, workers of various backgrounds brought to bear numerous strains of dissent: radical Irish nationalism and agrarianism, German Marxism and Lassallean socialism, English and American working-class evangelicalism (with its stress on free-agency, self-help, and temperance). A kind of working-class ethnic assimilation came to a head, in which workers combined the democratic and nationalist idealism of the war with their own political traditions to form a world view at odds with native middle-class assumptions.[118]

The molder's leader and N.L.U. president William Sylvis expressed the "reform syndrome" of the movement's mainstream. In 1865, Sylvis saw America as a nation whose "toiling masses" had crushed armed rebellion by "the proud and opulent of the land"—but was, nevertheless, on the verge of convulsive class warfare:

> What would it profit us, as a nation, were we to preserve our institutions and destroy the morals of the people; save our Constitution and sink the masses into hopeless ignorance, poverty, and crime; all the forms of our republican institutions to remain on the statute books, and a great body of the people sunk so low as to be incapable of comprehending their most simple and essential principles?

Only the self-directed actions of the workers themselves toward cooperative production, Sylvis argued, could end this degradation, vindicate republican institutions, and make the United States "a nation of employers—the employers of our own labor." As the "first step toward competence and independence," Sylvis looked toward union organizing, to secure for labor "a right to a voice in the fixing" of its just share of the national wealth.[119]

For all its militance, the labor movement's ideology and program contained its own unresolved contradictions through the early 1870s. The old producerist language of social conflict sometimes obscured the lines of class at a time when manufacturers, many of them having risen through their trades, still thought of themselves as "producers" pitted against "capital." Both the self-improvement ethos of the labor movement and its commitment to a society open to upward mobility based on talent struck a chord with middle-class free-labor Radical Republicans, some of whom warmly welcomed the labor movement.[120]

Above all, in ideology, membership, action, and intent, the postbellum labor movement was geared almost entirely to those white skilled and semiskilled industrial workingmen who could still aspire to a "manly" independence and inflict considerable immediate damage upon employers. Although the proportion of industrial workers who enrolled in the labor and trade

unions of the early 1870s was, perhaps, the highest of any time in the nineteenth century, roughly 85 percent of the industrial work force was not unionized. A significant number of women organized petition campaigns, cooperatives, and trade unions (including the Daughters of St. Crispin and the
Troy [N.Y.] Laundry Union and Cooperative Collar Company), but the
movement meant little to the masses of sweated seamstresses and factory
hands—and vice versa. The same was true for thousands of immigrant laborers, for whom the promise of a competence seemed a will-o'-the-wisp
and the ethos of temperate self-help a curiosity at best. Only tentative
thought was given to how the movement of industrial workers might also
embrace the plight of rural small producers, ex-slaves, and sharecroppers.
And for the many nonwhites and newcomers whom the labor movement
despised as "intruders" and inferiors—the Chinese "coolie" laborers of the
West Coast were an especially stark example—organized labor offered more
threats than promises.[121]

The turmoil of the 1870s began to resolve some of these ambiguities. The
misbegotten courtship of free-labor Radical Republicans by working-class
reformers during the late 1860s broke down amid middle-class resistance
to agitation for shorter hours and the elaboration of a more class-conscious
trade unionism by theorists like Ira Steward. Just as the Radical Republican
bloc lost its revolutionary zeal and turned toward Liberal Republicanism,
Jay Cooke's brokerage house failed, sparking a financial crash and severe industrial depression that would not lift until 1878. The United States joined
the rest of the world in an economic catastrophe that, as E. J. Hobsbawm
has noted, would have seemed absurd in 1870.[122]

The depression's impact was profound and lasting. A spiral of business
failures ruined hundreds of industrialist entrepreneurs and spelled the end
of the old "family business" order. Those who survived the great crash—
including such industrial leaders as Andrew Carnegie, Thomas A. Scott, and
Gustavus Swift—would pioneer new, more concentrated institutional forms
of production, marketing, and finance in the 1880s and 1890s. The crash
also wiped out the advances and experiments of the labor movement. There
were so many workers who sought jobs on any terms that unions could not
enforce their own rules; secret societies sometimes replaced the unions
themselves. With trade unionists on the defensive and unemployment soaring beyond the limited capacities of public and private charities, some of
the gaps that had separated various levels of the working class began to narrow. "Among all classes," one reporter said of a premier industrial city in
1873, "there is a feeling of gloom and intense anxiety in regard to the future." The situation worsened over the next five years.[123]

The importance of the depression also extended far beyond exclusively
economic facts. The social, economic, and political changes of two
decades—the spread of entrepreneurial industry, the consolidation of local

ethnic communities, the gradual emergence in smaller cities of a strata of skilled workers and nonindustrial property owners with close links to lower working-class strata—were all tested by grave economic difficulty. Unions would be of less importance here than those less formal structures of solidarity that touched skilled and unskilled workers alike and reached outside the ranks of wage earners to join petty proprietors, workers, and often city officials against local industrialists. The flashpoint of conflict came, typically, when hard-pressed employers attempted to impose severe wage cuts in order to save their faltering enterprises. Throughout industrializing America, a pattern of reaction recurred, particularly in the smaller towns and cities. With surprising strength and tenacity, unorganized or poorly organized workers mounted strikes and other forms of industrial action. In the resulting stalemate, industrialists looked elsewhere—the state government, the National Guard, private police forces—to bolster their authority. Steadily, often violently, a national working-class presence, rooted in local circumstances and united across ethnic and religious lines, began to emerge. What was left of the postbellum promise of "free labor" disintegrated.[124]

To forestall this threat—and the spectre of agrarian unrest and black political power in the South—the nation's economic and political elites began to reconsolidate. The backlash would not begin to reach its full fury until the 1880s, when state and federal courts, backed by business trade associations, cut down those reforms the labor movement managed to win.[125] Before then, national leaders of both major parties looked for compromises that might finally end the violence of formal political conflict. Without abandoning all their differences, Republicans and Democrats softened their positions on southern reinstatement, freedmen's rights, and the currency and tariff issues. As the reform passions of the 1860s ebbed, party leaders resettled the balance of power along a new axis of merchant-planter and industrialist control and comity. Federal abandonment of the freedmen, completed in the compromise of 1877, was the most dramatic immediate outcome of the Reconstruction settlement. So, too, came a hardening of the line against the nation's organized workers. Where possible, legislators and officials made concessions to organized labor, as in the establishment of state bureaus of labor statistics. For the most part, no moves were taken to suppress strikes, boycotts, or unions. But once labor activity spilled out of the workplaces into community resistance, reaction came swiftly.[126]

The fateful year for the labor movement (as for the freedmen) was 1877, but the process of confrontation had begun well before then. Trouble started on the railroads, the vanguard of *national* class formation, in 1873–1874, when workers on the Pennsylvania system and at least seventeen other lines, most of them not unionized, struck unsuccessfully to protest wage cuts, blacklisting, and the use of iron-clad contracts. Middecade saw the "long strike" in the Pennsylvania anthracite fields, the breaking of the multiethnic

Workingmen's Benevolent Association, the underground Molly Maguire agitation, and a string of strikes and protests in factories and mines all across industrializing America.[127] By July 1877, when the Baltimore and Ohio Railroad announced an additional 10 percent wage cut, local brush fires of class conflict had been burning on and off for three and one-half years. Over the next two months, these fires burst into a national conflagration that aroused the commitment of workers and their sympathizers across the country in small towns and major cities alike—prompting military intervention on an unprecedented scale to protect industrial capital's rights of property.[128]

For months after the Great Strike was extinguished, industrialists and their supporters—particularly the interlocking directorate of railroad executives, politicians, and military officers—spoke gravely about how European communism had finally taken root among the rabble of republican America. Only the creation of a large standing army, they insisted, could ward off a more successful insurrection, along the lines of the Paris Commune of 1871, and keep America a democratic republic. These analyses were as inaccurate as they were self-contradictory; the strikes, as one Pittsburgh newspaper reminded its readers, "originated in well ascertained grievances," based on a variety of distinct (though related) local situations.[129] But the worried reactions of the new industrial elite point out the major significance of 1877. There was nothing in the industrialists' free-labor republicanism that could allow them to understand the uprising as anything *but* an anti-American conspiracy or an eruption of the dependent rabble. Some of their supporters knew better; President Rutherford B. Hayes, after authorizing the necessary violence to crush the strikes, confided in his diary that "The railroad strikers as a rule are good men, sober, intelligent and industrious."[130] But Hayes was left befuddled about what had led upright American workingmen to virtual insurrection and how to prevent such outbursts in the future. Beginning in the 1830s, and even more since the 1850s, men and women like Hayes had come to believe that for the industrious, virtuous, and self-disciplined, wage work was but a prelude to individual independence; capitalist wage labor was, as they saw it, a harmonious reciprocal arrangement between employer and employee, one that, if properly regulated by the natural market, would promote individual well-being and national wealth. The railroad strikes made no sense in this mystified world of republican capitalist equality. Hayes remained confused, though he stifled his doubts in public. Others drew more clear-cut lessons: the only way to ensure the survival of the republic, they agreed, was to buttress the rights of property through federal assistance, moral and educational reform of the workingman, and the raising of a well-drilled national army.[131]

To the largely ethnic working class and its supporters, such outcries, like the display of military force during the strikes, denied all that the Great Republic of the West was supposed to be and all but confirmed that American free labor was to be little more than American wage slavery. They seized upon the same republican rhetoric and ideals proclaimed by their mostly Anglo-American predecessors of the 1830s and 1840s to test whether the nation—in many cases the workers' adopted nation—would abandon its entire political culture in order to secure what one class deemed to be natural property rights. Capital, and not labor, they proclaimed, was at war with republican political values and relations. Proposals for a national army and such, declared the prolabor *New York Sun*, amounted to "nothing less than a radical revolution of our whole republican system of government."[132] And in a more pervasive way, the events of 1877, set against the long depression, again raised those doubts voiced by the Jacksonian journeymen, about whether the American political system had been so corrupted and the "wages system" become so entrenched that a new oligarchy of capital had usurped the liberties and independence of American citizens. The Irish-American socialist J. P. McDonnell, though hardly a typical labor leader, gave voice to typical sentiments when he surveyed industrializing America for his Paterson, New Jersey, readership in 1879: "After a century of Political independence, we find that our social system is not better than that of Europe and that labor in this Republic is not better than that of Europe, and that labor in this Republic, as in the European monarchies, is the slave of capitalism, instead of being the master of its own products."[133] Two years earlier, in the immediate aftermath of the railroad strike, a Pittsburgh paper reported that the troubles had "given a great impetus to the growth of secret labor organizations and workingmen by the hundreds are paying their necessary dues and taking strange oaths—but all in secrecy."[134] Shortly thereafter, one of these organizations, the Noble and Holy Order of the Knights of Labor, established its first permanent national organization, dropped its secrecy in deference to Roman Catholics, and began its effort to organize workers regardless of sex, skill, race, or national origin. From these united efforts to resolve what the Knights called an "inevitable and irresistible conflict between the wage-system of labor and republican system of government," would come the first national rising of the American working class.[135]

CONCLUSION: TOWARD THE GREAT UPHEAVAL

As the United States entered its second century, it also entered its age of empire and modern industry. Between 1880 and 1900, the number of nonagricultural workers more than doubled and rose proportionally from 48.4 percent of the nation's gainfully employed to 59.6 percent.[136] Rapid technological changes and mechanization of steel, food processing, machine production, and other major industries increased overall per capita productivity and broke down remaining craft skills. The entrepreneurial industrialism of the age of capital gave way to new oligopolistic experiments in corporate forms and financing. The new immigration from southern and eastern Europe began to send tens of thousands of workers into the sweatshops, mines, and mills. Accompanying (and sometimes prompting) these changes was a protracted period of working-class unrest and employer repression, beginning with the Great Upheaval of 1884–1886.

In back of these developments was a century of American working-class formation and development. Compared with the other major industrializing nations, the process had moved forward with extraordinary rapidity in the United States. In 1776, it had seemed reasonable to assume that this country might escape, or at least delay, the massive social transformations that were overtaking large portions of the Old World, creating new forms of monied power and new classes of proprietors and propertyless workers. America, lacking the remnants of feudalism, offered abundant land and opportunities for would-be independent producers, just as these seemed to be disappearing in Britain and on the Continent. Merchant capital, though critical to the economy and politics of the port cities, clung to the seaboard and mainly acted as a conduit for regional and international commerce in agricultural goods, with little expressed interest in developing the continent before it. Where labor shortages developed, Americans mostly relied not on dispossessed free persons but on chattel slaves stolen from Africa and unfree white indentured servants.

Yet, only a century later, the social structure and class relations of Revolutionary America had been virtually destroyed and replaced by an aggressive American capitalism. The fundamental element in this transition was the demise of unfree labor and the emergence of capitalist labor markets— steadily and with little outward disturbance in the North in the late eighteenth and early nineteenth centuries, suddenly and violently in the South in the 1860s. Accompanying these changes was the disruption of petty production, urban and rural, that came with rapid internal commercial development after 1815. Although the final debacle of the American yeomanry would not arrive until the 1890s, capitalist agriculture had clearly overtaken independent rural production in large areas of the countryside by the late 1870s. Although skilled craftsmen remained essential to industrial production, even in the factories of the Gilded Age, the old artisanal system of production, governed by customary notions of workshop justice and mutuality, was all but dead.

The rise of the American working class out of all these changes was never a smooth and even process. At almost every point before the mid-1870s, the growing numbers of American wage earners were divided by ethnicity, skill, region, religion, race, and sex. Although able to organize politically at the local and state levels, labor failed to build a unified force in national politics. Given the staggered pace of capitalist development, it may even make sense to talk of the rise of two successive working classes between 1776 and 1877. The first working class emerged before 1848, primarily in New England and the middle states, and was dominated by native Yankee men and women and British immigrants; a second working class emerged after 1848 and consisted mainly of Irish and German immigrants (and their children) and free blacks. The discontinuities in this successive reformation should not be underestimated. From the beginning, as Herbert Gutman pointed out, American labor history involved not a linear progression of class formation and development but an unceasing construction and reconstruction of the working class, drawn from new groups of rural people in this country and immigrants from around the globe.[137]

And yet, despite the divisions and discontinuities, a certain logic united the history of American workers in the nation's first century. In 1776, Americans, striking for their political independence, proclaimed a set of natural rights to equality and personal autonomy that were supposed to be universal. Not long after the Revolution, urban craft workers began to organize and complain that the realities of the new labor market amounted to a desecration of these natural rights and a threat to all that the Revolution was supposed to have won. So, over the next hundred years, various groups of Americans who were swept into the wage-labor force—Yankee farm women, displaced yeomen, Irish and German immigrants, southern freedmen—reshaped this critique and railed against the disparities between the "wages system" and America's professed political and social ideals. Each group of workers had to confront this contradiction for itself; when it did, not all workers came to the same conclusions about how best to better their individual and collective lot; a significant portion of the working class reconciled itself to the new regime. Yet, in a cyclical pattern of ever increasing intensity, large numbers of American workers drew together—in their neighborhoods as well as in their workshops, in organized and informal movements—to combat the decline of democratic republicanism as they understood it. And, in the aftermath of the panic of 1873 and the rebellion of 1877, that drawing together proceeded in unprecedented ways to announce a nationwide working-class presence.

Of course, few Americans in the 1870s had known the popular radicalism and union struggles of the 1830s and 1840s; almost none of the labor movement's leaders had. The arguments of the "first" American working class, since the 1840s, had been leavened by the experiences and ideas of new groups of immigrant and ethnic workers. Yet, one man who did bridge the gap—who had thrilled as a youngster to the firebrand Fanny Wright, written poetry for the Bowery radical Mike Walsh, and lived to witness the

1877 rebellion—caught some of the main issues at stake for the ethnic workers of the Gilded Age, like their Yankee predecessors. Now an elderly cult figure, Walt Whitman refused to take up some of his younger acolytes' enthusiasm for socialism and labor radicalism. He was too old, Whitman explained, to adopt any new politics now. Yet in the 1870s, as he saw tramps and chiffoniers walking bedraggled in these states, Whitman wrote darkly of what America had become and what it might become. His imagery was ambivalent, at times unflattering when it came to the working poor, but his sense of the contradictions at hand was sure: "If the United States, like the countries of the Old World, are able to grow vast crops of poor, desperate, dissatisfied, nomadic, miserably-waged populations, such as we see looming upon us of late years— . . . then our republican experiment, notwithstanding all its surface successes, is at heart an unhealthy failure."[138] Over the next twenty years, American workers would take it as a matter of patriotic duty as well as of self-interest to see that the experiment would not fail.

NOTES

Acknowledgments: Many colleagues and friends have helped improve this essay with their criticism and support. Comments, impromptu and otherwise, from the participants at the DeKalb conference (where an earlier version was first delivered) were extremely helpful. I am particularly grateful to Gary B. Nash and Alfred F. Young. Subsequently, the members of the Princeton Americanist colloquium scrutinized the essay closely and offered more helpful suggestions. Finally, Paul Berman, Eric Foner, Alice Kessler-Harris, and J. Carroll Moody read a revised draft and forced me to rethink a great deal. All of these scholars are well aware just how provisional this survey is—and I thank them for reminding me of that. Special thanks to Carroll Moody for his editorial patience with a trying author.

1. For estimates on the eighteenth century wage labor force, see Jackson Turner Main, *The Social Structure of Revolutionary America* (Princeton, NJ, 1965), pp. 271–76; Marcus Rediker, *Between the Devil and the Deep Blue Sea: Merchant Seamen, Pirates, and the Anglo-American Maritime World* (New York, 1987), p. 296. On the 1870s, see David Montgomery, *Beyond Equality: Labor and the Radical Republicans* (New York, 1967), pp. 25–32, 448–51; Daniel T. Rodgers, *The Work Ethic in Industrial America* (Chicago, 1978), pp. 36–37.

2. For an elaboration of this point, see Sean Wilentz, "Against Exceptionalism: Class Consciousness and the American Labor Movement, 1790–1920," *International Labor and Working Class History* 26 (1984): 1–24.

3. Important recent synthetic treatments of American labor history include David Gordon, Richard Edwards, and Michael Reich, *Segmented Work, Divided Workers: The Historical Transformation of Labor in the United States* (Cambridge, MA, 1982); and Bryan D. Palmer, "Social Formation and Class Formation in North America, 1800–1900," in David Levine, ed., *Proletarianization and Family History*

(New York, 1984). On "primitive accumulation" and the era before 1776, see Peter Linebaugh, "All the Atlantic Mountains Shook," *Labour/Le Travailleur* 10 (1982): 87–121; and Marcus Rediker, "Good Hands, Stout Heart, and Fast Feet: The History and Culture of Working People in Early America," in Geoff Eley and William Hunt, eds., *Reviving the English Revolution: Reflections and Elaborations on the Work of Christopher Hill* (London, 1986). On the era after 1877, see Martin Shefter, "Trade Unions and Political Machines: The Organization and Disorganization of the American Working Class in the Late Nineteenth Century," in Ira Katznelson and Aristide R. Zolberg, eds., *Working-Class Formation: Nineteenth-Century Patterns in Western Europe and the United States* (Princeton, NJ, 1986). On gender and working-class formation, see Alice Kessler-Harris, *Out to Work: A History of Wage-Earning Women in the United States* (New York, 1982); Jacqueline Jones, *Labor of Love, Labor of Sorrow: Black Women, Work, and the Family from Slavery to the Present* (New York, 1985).

4. Rediker, "Good Hands," includes a useful typology of the prevailing labor systems in colonial America. See also Richard S. Dunn's important essay, "Servants and Slaves: The Recruitment and Employment of Labor in Colonial America," in Jack P. Greene and J. R. Pole, eds., *Colonial British America: Essays in the New History of the Early Modern Era* (Baltimore, 1984). Both essays also serve as guides to the growing literature on colonial labor history. On indentured servitude, Abbot Emerson Smith's pioneering work should now be read alongside David W. Galenson, *White Servitude in Colonial America: An Economic Analysis* (New York, 1981).

5. On stratification, see Jeffrey Williamson and Peter Lindert, *American Inequality: A Microeconomic History* (New York, 1980), pp. 14–30; Darrett B. Rutman and Anita H. Rutman, *A Place in Time: Middlesex County, Virginia, 1650–1750* (New York, 1984); James T. Lemon and Gary B. Nash, "The Distribution of Wealth in Eighteenth-Century America: A Century of Changes in Chester County, Pennsylvania," *Journal of Social History* 2 (1968): 1–24; Edward M. Cook, Jr., *The Fathers of the Towns: Leadership and Community Structure in Eighteenth-Century New England* (Baltimore, 1976); James A. Henretta, "Economic Development and Social Structure in Colonial Boston," *William & Mary Quarterly* 22 (1965): 75–92; Allan Kulikoff, "The Progress of Inequality in Revolutionary Boston," *William & Mary Quarterly* 28 (1971): 375–412; Gary B. Nash, *The Urban Crucible: Social Change, Political Consciousness, and the Origins of the American Revolution* (Cambridge, MA, 1979); Billy G. Smith, "The Material Lives of Laboring Philadelphians, 1750–1880," *William & Mary Quarterly* 38 (1981): 163–202. On domestic work, see Kessler-Harris, *Out to Work*, chapters 1 and 2. On urban wage work, see above all Richard B. Morris, *Government and Labor in Early America* (New York, 1946), chapters 1, 2, 4, and passim. On rural wage labor, see Main, *Social Structure*, pp. 61–62; James A. Henretta, "Familes and Farms: Mentalité in Pre-Industrial America," *William & Mary Quarterly* 35 (1978): 3–32; and on rural developments generally Allan Kulikoff's forthcoming "The Rise and Destruction of the American Yeoman Classes, 1600–1900." I am grateful to Kulikoff for showing me an advance version of this work. On wage labor in a relatively isolated seventeenth-century patron-client community, see Steven Innes, *Labor in a New Land: Economy and Society in Seventeenth-Century Springfield* (Princeton, NJ,

1983). And on wage labor generally, see also Eric Guest Nellis, "Communities of Workers: Free Labor in Provincial Massachusetts, 1690–1765" (Ph.D. diss., University of British Columbia, 1979); Daniel F. Vickers, "Maritime Labor in Colonial Massachusetts: A Case Study of the Essex County Cod Fishery and the Whaling Industry of Nantucket, 1630–1775" (Ph.D. diss., Princeton University, 1981); and Rediker, *Between the Devil and the Deep Blue Sea.*

6. Main, *Social Structure*, p. 272; Henretta, "Economic Development"; Nash, *Urban Crucible*; Smith, "Material Lives."

7. Sharon V. Salinger, "Artisans, Journeymen, and the Transformation of Labor in Late Eighteenth-Century Philadelphia," *William and Mary Quarterly* 40 (1983): 69.

8. Sharon V. Salinger, "Colonial Labor in Transition: The Decline of Indentured Servitude in Late Eighteenth-Century Philadelphia," *Labor History* 22 (1981): 165–91; idem., "Artisans," pp. 62–84; Jacob Price, "Economic Function and the Growth of American Port Towns," *Perspectives in American History*, no. 8 (1974): 123–86; Nash, *Urban Crucible*, 312–38.

9. David Montgomery, "The Working Classes of the Pre-Industrial City, 1780–1830," *Labor History* 9 (1968): 1–22; Smith, "Material Lives"; Salinger, "Artisans"; Charles G. Steffen, *The Mechanics of Baltimore: Workers and Politics in the Age of Revolution, 1763–1812* (Urbana, IL, 1984), pp. 27–50; Howard B. Rock, *Artisans of the New Republic: The Tradesmen of New York City in the Age of Jefferson* (New York, 1979), pp. 237–322. On the decline of customary wage arrangements in an important urban craft, see Henry P. Rosemont, "Benjamin Franklin and the Philadelphia Typographical Strikers of 1786," *Labor History* 22 (1981): 398–429.

10. *New York Journal* (April 7, 1768), quoted in Morris, *Government and Labor*, p. 196.

11. On artisan politics before the 1770s, see Nash, *Urban Crucible*, esp. pp. 144–48, 362–74. Artisan movements in revolutionary New York have received especially detailed treatment, mainly in response to the controversies first touched off by Carl Becker. See Carl Lotus Becker, *The History of Political Parties in the Province of New York, 1760–1776* (1909; reprint, Madison, WI, 1960), Chapters 2 and 3; Staughton Lynd, "The Mechanics in New York City Politics, 1774–1785," *Labor History* 5 (1964): 225–46; Roger Champagne, "Liberty Boys and Mechanics in New York City, 1764–1774," *Labor History* 8 (1967): 115–35; Edward Countryman, *A People in Revolution: The American Revolution and Political Society in New York, 1760–1790* (Baltimore, 1981), pp. 124–25, 162–65; as well as the numerous works cited in these accounts.

12. Alfred F. Young has examined the origins and early development of artisan republicanism in a number of essays; see, for example, "George Robert Twelves Hewes: A Boston Shoemaker and the Memory of the American Revolution," *William and Mary Quarterly* 38 (1981): 561–623; and "English Plebeian Culture and Eighteenth-Century American Radicalism," in Margaret Jacob and John Jacob, eds., *The Origins of Anglo-American Radicalism* (London, 1984). See also Eric Foner, *Tom Paine and Revolutionary America* (New York, 1976); Steven Rosswurm, *Arms, Country, and Class: The Philadelphia Militia and the "Lower Sort" during the*

American Revolution (New Brunswick, NJ, 1987); Steffen, *Mechanics,* pp. 53–80; Sean Wilentz, *Chants Democratic: New York City and the Rise of the American Working Class, 1788–1850* (New York, 1984), pp. 63–66, 87–97; Ronald Douglas Schultz, "Thoughts among the People: Popular Thought, Radical Politics, and the Making of Philadelphia's Working Class, 1765–1828" (Ph.D. diss., University of California at Los Angeles, 1985). On the English background, see above all Christopher Hill, "Pottage for Freeborn Englishmen: Attitudes to Wage Labour," in his *Change and Continuity in Seventeenth-Century England* (Cambridge, MA, 1979).

13. Morris, *Government and Labor,* pp. 198–207; Steffen, *Mechanics,* pp. 102–20, 209–27; Rock, *Artisans,* pp. 264–94; Wilentz, *Chants Democratic,* pp. 56–60; idem., "Power, Conspiracy, and the Early Labor Movement: *The People v. James Melvin,* 1811," *Labor History* 24 (1983): 572–79; Paul A. Gilje, "Mobocracy: Popular Disturbances in Post-Revolutionary New York City, 1780–1829" (Ph.D. diss., Brown University, 1980), p. 272; Leonard Bernstein, "The Working People of Philadelphia from Colonial Times to the General Strike of 1835," *Pennsylvania Magazine of History and Biography* 74 (1950): 322–39; Gary J. Kornblith, "From Artisans to Businessmen: Master Mechanics in New England, 1789–1850" (Ph.D. diss., Princeton University, 1983).

14. Wilentz, *Chants Democratic,* pp. 58–59, 97–100; Kornblith, "Artisans to Businessmen," pp. 132–160; Steffen, *Mechanics.* On those ambiguities in Adam Smith that could be seized upon by early workers' organizations, see E. G. West, "The Political Economy of Alienation: Karl Marx and Adam Smith," *Oxford Economic Papers* 21 (1969): 1–23; Donald Winch, *Adam Smith's Politics: An Essay in Historiographic Revision* (Cambridge, England, 1978).

15. Rock, *Artisans,* p. 277: Wilentz, *Chants Democratic,* pp. 59–60.

16. The issues arising out of the Constitution and the Jeffersonian settlement have been subjected to intense debate of late. See Lance Banning, *The Jeffersonian Persuasion: The Evolution of a Party Ideology* (Ithaca, NY, 1978); Drew R. McCoy, *The Elusive Republic: Political Economy in Jeffersonian America* (Chapel Hill, NC, 1980); Joyce O. Appleby, *Capitalism and a New Social Order* (New York, 1984); Richard K. Matthews, *The Radical Politics of Thomas Jefferson: A Revisionist View* (Lawrence, KA, 1984); Forrest McDonald, *Novus Ordo Seclorum: The Intellectual Origins of the Constitution* (Lawrence, KA, 1985); John R. Nelson, *Liberty and Property: Political Economy and Policymaking in the New Nation, 1789–1812* (Baltimore, 1987). On artisans and politics after 1787, the best studies are Alfred F. Young, *The Democratic Republicans of New York: The Origins, 1763–1797* (Chapel Hill, NC, 1967); and Eugene Perry Link, *The Democratic-Republican Societies, 1790–1800* (New York, 1945). On Jeffersonian hostility to trade unionism, see Richard J. Twomey, "Jacobins and Jeffersonians: Anglo-American Radicalism in the United States" (Ph.D. diss., Northern Illinois University, 1974).

17. David Szatmary, *Shays' Rebellion: The Making of an Insurrection* (Amherst, MA, 1980); Thomas P. Slaughter, *The Whiskey Rebellion: Frontier Epilogue to the American Revolution* (New York, 1986).

18. George Rogers Taylor, *The Transportation Revolution, 1815–1860* (New York, 1951).

19. See for example Allen R. Pred, "Manufacturing in the Mercantile City, 1800–1840," *Annals of the Society of American Geographers* 56 (1966): 307–35; Richard B. Stott, "The Worker in the Metropolis: New York City, 1820–1860" (Ph.D. diss., Cornell University, 1983), pp. 168–292. See also Raphael Samuel, "The Workshop of the World: Steam Power and Hand Technology in Mid-Victorian Britain," *History Workshop*, no. 3 (1977): 6–72.

20. On the rise of New England textile factories, a voluminous early literature must be supplemented with Thomas Dublin, *Women at Work: The Transformation of Work and Community in Lowell, Massachusetts, 1826–1860* (New York, 1979); Gary Kulik, "The Beginnings of the Industrial Revolution in America: Pawtucket, Rhode Island, 1672–1829," (Ph.D. diss., Brown University, 1980); Jonathan Prude, *The Coming of Industrial Order: Town and Factory Life in Rural Massachusetts, 1810–1860* (New York, 1983); Barbara Tucker, *Samuel Slater and the Origins of the American Textile Industry, 1790–1860* (Ithaca, NY, 1984). On textile production outside New England, see Anthony F. C. Wallace, *Rockdale: The Growth of an American Village in the Early Industrial Revolution* (New York, 1978); Philip Scranton, *Proprietary Capitalism: The Textile Manufacture at Philadelphia, 1800–1885* (New York, 1983), pp. 3–176; Cynthia J. Shelton, *The Mills of Manayunk: Industrialization and Social Conflict in the Philadelphia Region, 1787–1837* (Baltimore, 1986). On shoemaking, the classic work of John R. Commons has now been surpassed by Alan Dawley, *Class and Community: The Industrial Revolution in Lynn* (Cambridge, MA, 1976); Paul G. Faler, *Mechanics and Manufacturers in the Early Industrial Revolution, 1780–1860* (Albany, NY, 1981); Mary H. Blewett, *Men, Women, and Work: Class, Gender, and Protest in the New England Shoe Industry, 1780–1910* (Urbana, IL, 1988).

21. On the transformation of the countryside, see Clarence Danhof, *Change in Agriculture: The Northern United States, 1820–1870* (Cambridge, MA, 1969), Chapter 1; Michael Merrill, "Cash Is Good to Eat: Self-Sufficiency and Exchange in the Rural United States, 1750–1850," *Radical History Review* 15 (1977): 42–71; Robert E. Mutch, "Yeoman and Merchant in Pre-Industrial America: Eighteenth-Century Massachusetts as a Case Study," *Societas* 7 (1977): 279–302; Christopher Clark, "The Household Economy, Market Exchange, and the Rise of Capitalism in the Connecticut Valley, 1800–1860," *Journal of Social History* 13 (1979): 169–90; Richard L. Bushman, "Family Security in the Transition from Farm to City, 1750–1850," *Journal of Family History* 6 (1981): 238–56; Prude, *Coming*, pp. 3–33; Philip L. White, *Beekmantown, New York: Forest Frontier to Farm Community* (Austin, TX, 1979); Robert A. Gross, "Culture and Cultivation: Agriculture and Society in Thoreau's Concord," *Journal of American History* 69 (1982): 42–61; Hal S. Barron, *Those Who Stayed Behind: Rural Society in Nineteenth-Century New England* (New York, 1984). See also Kulikoff, "Rise and Fall," as well as the classic works of Percy W. Bidwell and Paul Wallace Gates. Cf. Joyce O. Appleby, "Commercial Farming and the 'Agrarian Myth' in the Early Republic," *Journal of American History* 68 (1982): 833–49. On legal issues and implications, see Morton Horwitz, *The Transformation of American Law, 1780–1860* (Cambridge, MA, 1977). On fertility, see Richard A. Easterlin, "Factors in the Decline of Farm Fertility in the United States: Some Preliminary Research Results," *Journal of American His-*

tory 63 (1976): 600–14; Robert V. Wells, *Revolutions in Americans' Lives: A Demographic Perspective on the History of Americans, Their Families, and Their Society* (Westport, CT, 1982), and the literature cited therein. A spirited, at times polemical debate is underway on the "household mode of production," a concept introduced by Merrill in "Cash Is Good to Eat." In addition to Merrill's published replies to his critics [in *Radical History Review*, no. 18 (1978): 166–71; no. 22 (1979–1980): 129–46], see Winifred B. Rothenberg, "The Market and Massachusetts Farmers, 1750–1855," *Journal of Economic History* 41 (1981): 283–314; Rona S. Weiss, "The Market and Massachusetts Farmers, 1750–1850: A Comment," and Rothenberg's reply, ibid., 43 (1983): 475–80; Michael A. Bernstein and Sean Wilentz, "Marketing, Commerce, and Capitalism in Rural Massachusetts," and Rothenberg's reply, ibid., 44 (1984): 171–79. See also Michael Merrill, "The Ghost of Karl Polanyi" (unpublished paper, 1984).

22. Paul E. Johnson, "The Modernization of Mayo Greenleaf Patch: Land, Family, and Marginality in New England, 1766–1818," *New England Quarterly* 55 (1982): 488–516.

23. Nancy F. Cott, *Bonds of Womanhood: "Woman's Sphere" in New England, 1780–1830* (New Haven, CT, 1977); Mary Beth Norton, *Liberty's Daughters: The Revolutionary Experience of American Women, 1750–1800* (Boston, 1980); idem., "The Evolution of White Women's Experience in Early America," *American Historical Review* 82 (1984): 593–619, and literature cited therein. See also Mary P. Ryan, *Cradle of the Middle Class: The Family in Oneida County, New York, 1790–1865* (New York, 1981).

24. Prude, *Coming*, p. 45.

25. Dublin, *Women at Work*, pp. 23–57; Prude, *Coming*, pp. 116–20; Dawley, *Class*, pp. 47–50; Kessler-Harris, *Out to Work*, pp. 28–38; Thomas Dublin, "Women and Outwork in a Nineteenth-Century New England Town: Fitzwilliam, New Hampshire, 1830–1850," in Steven Hahn and Jonathan Prude, eds., *The Countryside in the Age of Capitalist Transformation* (New York, 1985).

26. Kessler-Harris, *Out to Work*, pp. 70–72; Claudia Goldin and Kenneth Sokoloff, "Women, Children, and Industrialization in the Early Republic: Evidence from the Manufacturing Census," *Journal of Economic History* 42 (1982): 741–74.

27. Kessler-Harris, *Out to Work*, p. 38.

28. Prude, *Coming*, pp. 116–17. On Pawtucket, see Kulik, "Beginnings"; and "Pawtucket Village and the Strike of 1824: The Origins of Class Conflict in Rhode Island," *Radical History Review*, no. 17 (1978): 5–37.

29. Dublin, *Women at Work*, pp. 68, 89. See also Prude, *Coming*, pp. 144–50.

30. Kulik, "Pawtucket"; Dublin, *Women at Work*, pp. 86–107; Dawley, *Class*, p. 62.

31. Shelton, *Manayunk*, pp. 54–155; Howard Harris, "The Transformation of Ideology in the Early Industrial Revolution: Paterson, New Jersey, 1820–1840" (Ph.D. diss., City University of New York, 1985). See also Wallace, *Rockdale*.

32. John R. Commons et al., *History of Labour in the United States* (New York, 1918), vol. 1, pp. 478–84. These figures should be handled cautiously. As

Walter Sullivan showed and Paul Gilje confirms in his forthcoming book on popular violence in New York, Commons and his associates undercounted the numbers of strikes in both the entrepôts and smaller cities. The undercount is probably at least as severe for the period before 1833, when the new labor press began extensive coverage of strike activity around the country. Nevertheless, the figures probably accurately reflect the pace of strikes after 1833 and the primacy of the seaports. See Walter A. Sullivan, *The Industrial Worker in Pennsylvania, 1800–1840* (Harrisburg, PA, 1955).

33. On the size of unions, see Maurice Neufeld, "The Size of the Jacksonian Labor Movement: A Cautionary Note," *Labor History* 23 (1982): 599–607. Neufeld shows that standard estimates of membership size have been greatly exaggerated; and that the union movement, nationwide, claimed in the neighborhood of 30,000 members in the 1830s. The proportion of wage earners who enrolled in the unions remains, nevertheless, impressive, particularly in the seaports.

34. Bruce Laurie, *Working People of Philadelphia, 1800–1850* (Philadelphia, 1980), pp. 85–104; Wilentz, *Chants Democratic*, pp. 172–216; Susan E. Hirsch, *Roots of the American Working Class: The Industrialization of Crafts in Newark, 1800–1860* (Philadelphia, 1978), pp. 84–88, 109–15; Steven J. Ross, *Workers on the Edge: Work, Leisure, and Politics in Industrializing Cincinnati* (New York, 1985), pp. 42–63; Louis Arky, "The Mechanics' Union of Trade Associations and the Formation of the Philadelphia Workingmen's Movement," *Pennsylvania Magazine of History and Biography* 76 (1952): 142–76; Edward Pessen, *Most Uncommon Jacksonians: Radical Leaders of the Early Labor Movement* (Albany, NY, 1967). Cf. Walter Hugins, *Jacksonian Democracy and the Working Class: A Study of the New York Workingmen's Movement, 1829–1837* (Stanford, CA, 1960).

35. Kessler-Harris, *Out to Work*, pp. 65–66; Christine Stansell, *City of Women: Sex and Class in New York, 1789–1860* (New York, 1986), pp. 155–68; Carol Lasser, "'The World's Dread Laugh': Singlehood and Service in Nineteenth-Century Boston," in Herbert G. Gutman and Donald H. Bell, eds., *The New England Working Class and the New Labor History* (Urbana, IL, 1987).

36. Stansell, *City*, pp. 103–29; Kessler-Harris, *Out to Work*, pp. 54–55; Carol Groneman, "'She Earns as a Child—She Pays as a Man': Women Workers in a Mid-Nineteenth-Century New York Community," in Richard L. Erlich, ed., *Immigrants in Industrial America* (Charlottesville, NC, 1977), pp. 33–46.

37. Statistics on primary and secondary women wage earners appeared only in the mid-1850s. These estimates are based on those presented in Stott, "Worker."

38. Stansell, *City*, pp. 130–54; Kessler-Harris, *Out to Work*, pp. 68–70; Wilentz, *Chants Democratic*, pp. 248–50.

39. The importance of the family wage as an issue of class conflict is emphasized in Jane Humphries, "Class Struggle and the Persistence of the Working-Class Family," *Cambridge Journal of Economics* 1 (1977): 241–58. For a critique, see Gita Serr, "The Sexual Division of Labor and the Working Class Family," *Review of Radical Political Economics* 12 (1980): 78–89. See also the works by Stansell and Kessler-Harris already cited.

40. Jesse Lemisch, "Jack Tar in the Streets: Merchant Seamen in the Politics of Revolutionary America," *William and Mary Quarterly* 25 (1968): 371–407; Gilje, "Mobocracy," pp. 177–80; Laurie, *Working People*, pp. 90–91; Wilentz, *Chants Democratic*, pp. 250–51, 288–89.

41. Much more work is needed on the Afro-American working class in these years; for good starting points, see Gary B. Nash, "Forging Freedom: The Emancipation Experience in the Northern Seaport Cities, 1775–1820," in Ira Berlin and Ronald Hoffman, eds., *Slavery and Freedom in the Age of Revolution* (Urbana, IL, 1986); and Leonard Curry, *The Free Black in Urban America, 1800–1850: The Shadow of the Dream* (Chicago, 1981).

42. Wilentz, *Chants Democratic*, pp. 257–58; Paul E. Johnson, *A Shopkeeper's Millennium: Society and Revivals in Rochester, New York, 1815–1837* (New York, 1978), pp. 48–55; Elizabeth Strother Blackmar, "Housing and Property Relations in New York City, 1780–1850" (Ph.D. diss., Harvard University, 1980).

43. Wilentz, *Chants Democratic*, pp. 258–71; Laurie, *Working People*, pp. 53–66; Leonard L. Richards, '*Gentlemen of Property and Standing': Anti-Abolition Mobs in Jacksonian America* (New York, 1970); Alexander Saxton, "Blackface Minstrely and Jacksonian Ideology," *American Quarterly* 27 (1975): 3–28; Lawrence Levine, "William Shakespeare and the American People: A Study in Cultural Transformation," *American Historical Review* 89 (1984): 34–66; Dan Schiller, *Objectivity and the News* (Philadelphia, 1981); Susan G. Davis, *Parades and Power: Street Theatre in Nineteenth-Century Philadelphia* (Philadelphia, 1986); Stansell, *City*, pp. 76–101; 171–92; Ross, *Workers*, pp. 164–79; Eliot Gorn, "Good-Bye, Boys, I Die a True American: Homicide, Nativism, and Working-Class Culture in Antebellum New York City," *Journal of American History* 74 (1987): 388–410.

44. I have adopted the term *commercial culture* from William R. Taylor, in preference to the overused *mass culture*, a term that lumps together nineteenth and twentieth century developments that were quite distinct. See William R. Taylor, "The Launching of a Commercial Culture: New York City, 1860–1930" (unpublished paper, 1984), pp. 1–2. For critiques of the concept of working class "traditionalism," see Freidrich Langer, "Class, Culture, and Class Consciousness in Antebellum Lynn: A Critique of Alan Dawley and Paul Faler," *Social History* 6 (1981): 317–22; Bryan D. Palmer, "Classifying Culture," *Labour/Le Travailleur* 8–9 (1981–1982): 160–62. On the production and distribution of urban commercial culture, see Schiller, *Objectivity*; and Peter G. Buckley, "To the Opera House: Culture and Society in New York City, 1820–1860" (Ph.D. diss., State University of New York, 1984).

45. On merchant capital, see Elizabeth Fox Genovese and Eugene D. Genovese, *Fruits of Merchant Capital: Slavery and Bourgeois Property in the Rise and Expansion of Capitalism* (New York, 1983), as well as Maurice Dobb, *Studies in the Development of Capitalism* (New York, 1973). See also Palmer, "Social Formation".

46. Philip S. Foner, *Business and Slavery: The New York Merchants and the Irrepressible Conflict* (Chapel Hill, NC, 1941); Thomas H. O'Connor, *Lords of the Loom: The Cotton Whigs and the Coming of the Civil War* (New York, 1968).

47. Johnson, *Shopkeeper's Millennium*; Ryan, *Cradle*, are the key works, but see also the suggestive material in Wallace, *Rockdale*; Carroll Smith-Rosenberg, *Religion and the Rise of the American City: The New York City Mission Movement, 1817–1870* (Ithaca, NY, 1970); Nancy A. Hewitt, *Women's Activism and Social Change: Rochester, New York, 1822–1872* (Ithaca, NY, 1984).

48. Ryan, *Cradle*, pp. 60–104; Carroll Smith-Rosenberg, "Sex as Symbol in Victorian Purity," in John Demos and Sarane Spence Boocock, eds., *Turning Points: Historical and Sociological Essays on the Family* (Chicago, 1978), as well as the now formidable literature on the cult of domesticity cited therein.

49. Johnson, *Shopkeeper's Millennium*, pp. 8, 121–28; Wallace, *Rockdale*, pp. 269–321; Wilentz, *Chants Democratic*, pp. 145–53; Stansell, *City*, pp. 63–75; Carl Schurz, *The Reminiscences of Carl Schurz* (New York, 1907–1908), vol. 2, p. 158, quoted in Eric Foner, *Free Soil, Free Labor, Free Men: The Ideology of the Republican Party before the Civil War* (New York, 1970), p. 18. The recent literature on American reform is ably summarized in Ronald Walters, *American Reformers, 1815–1850* (New York, 1978). See also David Brion Davis, *The Problem of Slavery in the Age of Revolution, 1770–1823* (Ithaca, NY, 1975); Johnson, *Shopkeeper's Millennium*.

50. Paul E. Conkin, *Prophets of Prosperity: America's First Political Economists* (Bloomington, IN, 1980), pp. 11–34, 171–99; Samuel Rezneck, "The Rise and Early Development of Industrial Consciousness in the United States, 1760–1830," *Journal of Business and Economic History*, supplement, 4 (1932): 784–811; Kornblith, "Artisans to Businessmen," sections 1 and 3; Wilentz, *Chants Democratic*, p. 284.

51. For a corrective of this tendency, see Ira Berlin, "Time, Space, and the Evolution of Afro-American Society in British Mainland North America," *American Historical Review* 85 (1980): 44–78.

52. A good introduction to the antebellum southern economy is Gavin Wright, *The Political Economy of the Cotton South: Households, Markets, and Wealth in the Nineteenth Century* (New York, 1978). Still of importance, despite some of its more questionable neoclassical assertions, is Robert W. Fogel and Stanley Engerman, *Time on the Cross: The Economics of American Negro Slavery*, 2 vols. (Boston, 1974). For an important corrective on occupations, mobility, and master-slave relations, see Michael P. Johnson, "Work, Culture, and the Slave Community: Slave Occupations in the Cotton Belt in 1860," *Labor History* 27 (1986): 325–55. On slavery as a labor system, Kenneth Stampp, *The Peculiar Institution: Slavery in the Ante-Bellum South* (New York, 1956), is indispensible.

53. Limits of space prevent a closer look at the origins of southern master-slave relations. The places to start include Peter H. Wood, *Black Majority: Negroes in Colonial South Carolina from 1670 through the Stono Rebellion* (New York, 1974); Edmund S. Morgan, *American Slavery, American Freedom: The Ordeal of Colonial Virginia* (New York, 1975); Allan Kulikoff, *Tobacco and Slaves: The Development of Southern Cultures in the Chesapeake, 1680–1800* (Chapel Hill, NC, 1986). Likewise, I have had to gloss over certain intraregional differences in slavery and class formation after 1815, especially between the upper and deep South. On

these, see Ira Berlin, *Slaves without Masters: The Free Negro in the Antebellum South* (New York, 1974); Barbara Jeanne Fields, *Slavery and Freedom on the Middle Ground: Maryland during the Nineteenth Century* (New Haven, CT, 1985).

54. Eugene D. Genovese, *The Political Economy of Slavery* (New York, 1965), p. 28.

55. On slaveholders' ideology, Eugene D. Genovese, *Roll, Jordan, Roll: The World the Slaves Made* (New York, 1975); Drew Gilpin Faust, *James Henry Hammond and the Old South: A Design for Mastery* (Baton Rouge, LA, 1982), are especially insightful.

56. John Blassingame, *The Slave Community*, 2d ed. (New York, 1979); Herbert G. Gutman, *The Black Family in Slavery and Freedom, 1750–1920* (New York, 1976); Nathan I. Huggins, *Black Odyssey: The Afro-American Ordeal in Slavery* (New York, 1977) are but a few of the relevant titles. Genovese, *Roll, Jordan, Roll*. More recently, Elizabeth Fox-Genovese has modified earlier work on slave families while probing the primacy of class and color in *Within the Plantation Household: Black and White Women of the Old South* (Chapel Hill, 1988). For a beautiful ethnographic evocation of slave culture, see Charles Joyner, *Down By the Riverside: A South Carolina Slave Community* (Urbana, IL, 1984).

57. Barbara J. Fields makes this point well, concerning a part of the South where the press of free labor was more urgent than elsewhere *(Slavery and Freedom*, Chapter 1). On industrial stirrings in the Old South, see Ernest M. Lander, Jr., *The Textile Industry in Antebellum South Carolina* (Baton Rouge, 1969); David C. Ward, "Industrial Workers in the Mid-19th Century South: Family and Labor in the Graniteville (SC) Textile Mill, 1845–1880," *Labor History* 28 (1978): 328–48. On the use of slaves in industrial settings, see Robert Starobin, *Industrial Slavery in the Old South* (New York, 1970). On free labor in the cities, see Ira Berlin and Herbert G. Gutman, "Natives and Immigrants, Free Men and Slaves: Urban Workingmen in the Antebellum South," *American Historical Review* 88 (1983): 1175–1200. Immigrant displacement of blacks was to cause a political crisis in the more industrialized areas of the South in the 1850s, precisely because the enfranchised immigrants threatened to bring class issues into politics, as the disenfranchised blacks could not. See Fred Siegel, "Artisans and Immigrants in the Politics of Late Antebellum Georgia," *Civil War History* 27 (1981): 221–231.

58. Important recent work on the yeomanry includes Eugene D. Geovese, "Yeoman Farmers in a Slaveholders' Democracy," in Fox-Genovese and Genovese, *Fruits of Merchant Capital*; Steven Hahn, *Roots of Southern Populism: Yeoman Farmers and the Transformation of the Georgia Upcountry, 1850–1890* (New York, 1983); David Freeman Weiman, "Petty Commodity Production in the Cotton South: Upcountry Farmers in the Georgia Cotton Economy, 1840 to 1880" (Ph.D. diss., Stanford University, 1983); Lacey K. Ford, Jr., "Social Origins of a New South Carolina: The Upcountry in the Early Nineteenth Century" (Ph.D. diss., University of South Carolina, 1983); John T. Schlotterbeck, "Plantation and Farm: Social and Economic Change in Orange and Greene Counties, Virginia, 1716 to 1860" (Ph.D. diss., Johns Hopkins University, 1980). The literature is nicely summarized and discussed in Harry L. Watson, "Conflict and Collaboration: Yeomen, Slaveholders, and

Politics in Antebellum South," *Social History* 10 (1985): 273–98. On the "dual economy," see Morton Rothstein, "The Antebellum South as a Dual Economy: A Tentative Hypothesis," *Agricultural History* 41 (1967): 373–82.

59. On this point, see especially Weiman, "Petty Commodity Production," pp. 51–119.

60. Genovese, "Yeomen Farmers."

61. Brown quoted in Hahn, *Roots*, 86.

62. On free black workers, Berlin, *Slaves Without Masters*, pp. 217–49, is the place to start. See also Fields, *Slavery and Freedom*; and Berlin and Gutman, "Natives and Immigrants."

63. See the works cited in notes 30 and 33.

64. The history of antebellum southern labor activism and trade unionism— and, generally, of southern free labor—still need far more attention from historians. But see Commons, *History of Labour*, vol. 1, pp. 287–90, 297, 352, 443–52; Herbert Aptheker, *The Labor Movement in the South during Slavery* (New York, n.d. [1954]).

65. The classic works are Fletcher M. Green, *Constitutional Development in the South Atlantic States, 1776–1860: A Study in the Evolution of Democracy* (Chapel Hill, NC, 1930); and idem., "Democracy in the Old South," *Journal of Southern History* 12 (1946): 3–23.

66. Eric Foner, *Nat Turner* (New York, 1972), presents relevant documents and commentary on the rebellion; cf. Eugene D. Genovese, *From Rebellion to Revolution: Afro-American Slave Revolts in the Making of the Modern World* (Baton Rouge, LA, 1979). On the Great Reaction, Clement Eaton, *Freedom of Thought in the Old South* (Durham, NC, 1940), remains the best overview, although cf., Carl N. Degler, *The Other South: Southern Dissenters in the Nineteenth Century* (New York, 1974).

67. Eric Foner, *Politics and Ideology in the Age of the Civil War* (New York, 1980), p. 39.

68. On the ideological origins and consequences of these changes, see Richard Hofstadter, *The Idea of a Party System: The Rise of Legitimate Opposition in the United States, 1780–1840* (Berkeley, CA, 1969).

69. On these contrasting visions, see John Ashworth, *"Agrarians" and "Aristocrats": Party Political Ideology in the United States, 1837–1846* (London, 1983); and Daniel Walker Howe, *The Political Culture of the American Whigs* (Chicago, 1979).

70. Amy Bridges, *A City in the Republic: Antebellum New York and the Origins of Machine Politics* (New York, 1984); Ronald P. Formisano, *The Transformation of Political Culture: Massachusetts Parties, 1790s–1840s* (New York, 1983); William G. Shade, *Banks or No Banks: The Money Issue in Western Politics, 1832–1865* (Detroit, 1972); James Roger Sharp, *The Jacksonians versus the Banks: Politics in the States after the Panic of 1837* (New York, 1970); Harry L. Watson, *Jacksonian Politics and Community Conflict: The Emergence of the Second Party System in Cumberland County, North Carolina* (Baton Rouge, LA, 1981).

71. Norman Ware, *The Industrial Worker, 1840–1860* (Boston, 1924), pp. 125–227; Laurie, *Working People*, pp. 115–24; 140–47; 167–97; Wilentz, *Chants*

Democratic, pp. 300, 306–25, 363–89; Dublin, *Women at Work*, pp. 108–31; Johnson, *Shopkeeper's Millennium*, p. 202, n. 4; Dawley, *Class*, p. 58; Ian R. Tyrell, *Sobering Up: From Temperance to Prohibition in Antebellum America, 1800–1860* (Westport, CT, 1979), pp. 159–224; David Montgomery, "The Shuttle and the Cross: Weavers and Artisans in the Kensington Riots of 1844," *Journal of Social History* 5 (1972): 411–46; Michael Feldberg, *The Philadelphia Riots of 1844: A Study in Ethnic Conflict* (Westport, CT, 1975). Wallace, *Rockdale*, pp. 322–446, argues, unconvincingly, that an "evangelical counterattack" from above crushed freethinking labor radicalism, and joined employers and workers in an ideology of harmonious Christian industrialism.

72. See above all J. Mills Thornton, III, *Politics and Power in a Slave Society: Alabama, 1800–1860* (Baton Rouge, LA, 1978), pp. 267–342; Marc W. Kruman, *North Carolina Parties and Politics, 1836–1865* (Baton Rouge, LA, 1982), pp. 140–58; Watson, "Conflict and Collaboration," pp. 294–96.

73. A fine summary of these events appears in Eric Foner, "Politics, Ideology, and the Origins of the American Civil War," in his *Politics and Ideology*.

74. Herman Melville, *Moby-Dick; or, The Whale* [1851] (New York, 1950), p. 135. For insightful readings, see Michael Paul Rogin, *Subversive Geneaology: The Politics and Art of Herman Melville* (New York, 1983); Ann Douglas, *The Feminization of American Culture* (New York, 1977); C. L. R. James, *Mariners, Renegades, and Castaways* (New York, 1953).

75. United States Bureau of the Census, *Historical Statistics of the United States, Colonial Times to 1970* (Washington, DC, 1975), vol. 1, pp. 23, 106; Bruce Laurie et al., "Immigrants and Industry: The Philadelphia Experience, 1850–1880," *Journal of Social History* 9 (1979): 219–48; Theodore Hershberg et al., "Occupation and Ethnicity in Five Nineteenth-Century Cities," *Historical Methods Newsletter* 7 (1974): 174–216; Hirsch, *Roots*, pp. 32–51; Howard M. Gitelman, "The Waltham System and the Coming of the Irish," *Labor History* 8 (1967): 227–53; Robert Ernst, *Immigrant Life in New York City, 1825–1863* (New York, 1949); Oscar Handlin, *Boston's Immigrants: A Study in Acculturation*, 2d ed. (Boston, 1959).

76. Oscar Handlin, *The Uprooted* (Boston, 1951); and Stanley Aronowitz, *False Promises: The Shaping of American Working Class Consciousness* (New York, 1973), offer the conventional wisdom, albeit from very different points of view; cf. Mack Walker, *Germany and the Emigration, 1816–1885* (Cambridge, MA, 1964); Carol Groneman (Pernicone), "The 'Bloody Ould Sixth': A Social Analysis of a New York Working-Class Community in the Mid-Nineteenth Century" (Ph.D. diss., University of Rochester, 1974); Kathleen Conzen, *Immigrant Milwaukee, 1836–1860: Accommodation and Community in a Frontier City* (Cambridge, MA, 1976); Clyde Griffen and Sally Griffen, *Natives and Newcomers: The Ordering of Opportunity in Mid-Nineteenth Century Poughkeepsie* (Cambridge, MA, 1978); Stanley Nadel, "Kleindeutschland: New York City's Germans, 1845–1880" (Ph.D. diss., Columbia University, 1981); Bruce C. Levine, "Free Soil, Free Labor, and *Freimanner*: German Chicago in the Civil War Era," in Hartmut Keil and John Jentz, eds., *German Workers in Industrial Chicago* (DeKalb, IL, 1983); Kerby A. Miller, *Emigrants and Exiles: Ireland and the Irish Exodus to North America* (New York, 1985), esp. pp. 280–344, among a proliferation of fine studies.

77. Theodore S. Hamerow, *Restoration, Revolution, and Reaction: Economics and Politics in Germany, 1815–1871* (Princeton, NJ, 1967); Oliver MacDonagh, "The Irish Famine Emigration to the United States," *Perspectives in American History*, no. 10 (1976): 373–91; T. Desmond Williams, ed., *The Secret Societies in Ireland* (Dublin, 1973); Miller, *Emigrants*; Emmet Larkin, "The Devotional Revolution in Ireland, 1850–1875," *American Historical Review* 77 (1972): 625–52; Jay P. Dolan, *The Immigrant Church: New York's Irish and German Catholics, 1815–1865* (Baltimore, 1975), pp. 56–57 and passim; Bruce C. Levine, "In the Heat of Two Revolutions: The Forging of German-American Radicalism" in Dirk Hoerder, ed., *Struggle a Hard Battle: Essays on Working-Class Immigrants* (DeKalb, IL, 1986). Gilbert Osofsky traced the tortuous relations between the Irish repeal movement and American abolitionists in "Abolitionists, Irish Immigrants, and the Dilemmas of Romantic Nationalism," *American Historical Review* 80 (1975): 889–912. On early Irish trade unionism, see Ernst, *Immigrant Life*; Wilentz, *Chants Democratic*, pp. 351–53, 363–89. On class, ethnicity, and ties to the Democratic party, see above all Bridges, *City in the Republic*, pp. 83–102.

78. Lewis C. Gray, *History of Agriculture in the Southern States to 1860* (Washington, DC, 1935), vol. 2; Fogel and Engerman, *Time on the Cross*, vol. 1, pp. 86–106; Genovese, *Political Economy*, pp. 243–74; Ira Berlin and Herbert G. Gutman, "Natives and Immigrants, Free Men and Slaves: Urban Workingmen in the Antebellum South," *American Historical Review* 88 (1983): 1175–1200. On the transformations in western agriculture, see Danhof, *Change*; Paul W. Gates, *The Farmer's Age, 1815–1860* (New York, 1952); idem, *History of Public Land Law Development* (Washington, DC, 1968); Alan G. Bogue, *From Prairie to Corn Belt: Farming on the Illinois and Iowa Prairies in the Nineteenth Century* (Chicago, 1963); Margaret Beattie Bogue, *Patterns from the Sod: Land Use and Tenure in the Great Prairie, 1850–1900* (Springfield, IL, 1959); John Mack Faragher, *Women and Men on the Overland Trail* (New Haven, CT, 1979); idem., *Sugar Creek: Life on the Illinois Prairie* (New Haven, CT, 1986).

79. Montgomery, *Beyond Equality*, p. 4.

80. Foner, *Free Soil;* Bruce Collins, "The Ideology of the Ante-Bellum Northern Democracy," *Journal of American Studies* 11 (1977): 103–21.

81. Foner, *Free Soil*; Gabor S. Borrit, *Lincoln and the Economics of the American Dream* (Memphis, TN, 1978); Howe, *Political Culture*, pp. 263–98.

82. On the importance of the slaves in the coming of emancipation, see above all the continuing work of the Freedmen and Southern Society Project, including Ira Berlin et al., eds., *Freedom: A Documentary History of Emancipation, 1861–1867*, series 1, vol. 1, *The Destruction of Slavery* (New York, 1985); series 2, *The Black Military Experience* (New York, 1982).

83. For a comprehensive, readable treatment, see James M. McPherson, *The Battle Cry of Freedom* (New York, 1988). On conscription, see Adrian Cook, *The Armies of the Streets: The New York City Draft Riots of 1863* (Lexington, KY, 1974); and Iver Bernstein, "The New York City Draft Riots and Class Relations on the Eve of Industrial Capitalism" (Ph.D. diss., Yale University, 1985).

84. George A. Stevens, *Typographical Union No. 6: A Study of a Modern Trade Union and Its Predecessors* (Albany, NY, 1913).

85. Montgomery, *Beyond Equality*, p. 143. See also idem., "Strikes in Nineteenth-Century America," *Social Science History* 4 (1980): 81–104, which identifies the 1850s as the critical turning point in strike activity in the nineteenth century.

86. Montgomery, *Beyond Equality*, pp. 135–60 passim.

87. Montgomery, "Strikes"; Ware, *Industrial Worker*, pp. 227–40; Hirsch, *Roots*, pp. 119–20; Ross, *Workers*, pp. 141–62; Stott, "Worker," pp. 271–90; Carl Neumann Degler, "Labor in the Economy and Politics of New York City, 1850–1860: A Study of the Impact of Early Industrialism" (Ph.D. diss., Columbia University, 1952), pp. 258–68; Daniel J. Walkowitz, *Worker City, Company Town: Iron and Cotton-Worker Protest in Troy and Cohoes, New York, 1855–84* (Urbana, IL, 1978), pp. 81–88; Brian Greenberg, *Worker and Community: Response to Industrialization in a Nineteenth-Century City, Albany, New York, 1850–1884* (Albany, NY, 1985), pp. 25–41.

88. Hirsch, *Roots*, pp. 106–107, 120–23; Laurie, *Working People*, pp. 197–203; Montgomery, *Beyond Equality*, p. 120; Bridges, *City*, pp. 39–60.

89. John R. Commons et al., *Documentary History of American Industrial Society* (Cleveland, 1910–1911), vol. 8, pp. 331–34, 336–55.

90. Montgomery, *Beyond Equality*, pp. 93, 96–101; Commons, *History of Labour*, vol. 2, pp. 13–41.

91. Montgomery, *Beyond Equality*, pp. 126–34 passim., 165–66.

92. Roy B. Basler, ed., *The Collected Works of Abraham Lincoln* (New Brunswick, NJ, 1953), vol. 4, pp. 24–25; William Roscoe Thayer, *The Life and Letters of John Hay* (Boston, 1908), vol. 2, p. 5.

93. Robert Gallman, "Commodity Output, 1839–1899," in Conference on Research in Income and Wealth, *Trends in the American Economy in the Nineteenth Century* (Princeton, NJ, 1960), pp. 13–67; Harold G. Vatter, *The Drive to Industrial Maturity: The U.S. Economy, 1860–1914* (Westport, CT, 1975), pp. 184, 243–51; Montgomery, *Beyond Equality*, pp. 6–25, 27, 34–35; Scranton, *Proprietary Capitalism*, pp. 177–352; Ross, *Workers*, pp. 94–140; Daniel Nelson, *Managers and Workers: The Origins of the New Factory System in the United States, 1880–1920* (Madison, WI, 1975), p. 4.

94. Montgomery, *Beyond Equality*, pp. 5–6, 14–25; Bruce Laurie and Mark Schmitz, "Manufacture and Productivity: The Making of an Industrial Base, Philadelphia, 1850–1880," in Theodore Hershberg et al., eds., *Philadelphia: Work, Space, Family, and Group Experience in the Nineteenth Century* (New York, 1981); Dawley, *Class*, pp. 76–78. For witty, devastating accounts of the era's politics, see Matthew Josephson, *The Politicos, 1865–1896* (New York, 1938); Richard Hofstadter, *The American Poliltical Tradition* (New York, 1948), Chapter 6. Above all, see C. Vann Woodward, *Reunion and Reaction: The Compromise of 1877 and the End of Reconstruction* (Boston, 1951).

95. *Historical Statistics*, vol. 1, p. 106; Montgomery, *Beyond Equality*, pp. 35–37; Ira Berlin and Herbert Gutman, "Class Composition and the Development

of the American Working Class, 1840–1890: Immigrants and Their Children as Wage Earners," in Ira Berlin, ed., *Power and Culture: Herbert G. Gutman and the American Working Class* (New York, 1987).

96. Ernst, *Immigrant Life*, pp. 214–17; Pernicone, "'Bloody Ould Sixth'"; Handlin, *Boston's Immigrants*; David N. Doyle, "The Irish and American Labor, 1880–1920," *An Saothar: Journal of the Irish Labor History Society* 1 (1975): 45–53; Sean Wilentz, "Industrializing America and the Irish: Towards the New Departure," *Labor History* 20 (1979): 579–95; David Montgomery, "The Irish and the American Labor Movement," in David N. Doyle and Owen Dudley Edwards, eds., *America and Ireland, 1776–1976* (Westport, CT, 1980); Hasia Diner, *Erin's Daughters in America: Irish Immigrant Women in the Nineteenth Century* (Baltimore, 1983); Miller, *Emigrants*, pp. 345–555 passim.

97. Eric Foner, *Nothing but Freedom: Emancipation and Its Legacy* (Baton Rouge, LA, 1983), quotations on pp. 44, 56.

98. W. E. B. Du Bois, *Black Reconstruction in America, 1860–1880* [1935] (Cleveland, 1964); Leon Litwack, *Been in the Storm So Long: The Aftermath of Slavery* (New York, 1980); Hahn, *Roots*; Gutman, *Work, Culture, and Society*, pp. 137–208; Sterling D. Spero and Abram L. Harris, *The Black Worker: The Negro and the Labor Movement* (New York, 1968); Leon Fink, *Workingmen's Democracy: The Knights of Labor in American Politics* (Urbana, IL, 1983), Chapters 5 and 6. The political economy of black proletarianization has recently received excellent treatment in Gerald David Jaynes, *Branches without Roots: Genesis of the Black Working Class in the American South, 1862–1882* (New York, 1986). Eric Foner, *Reconstruction: America's Unfinished Revolution* (New York, 1988) appeared too late for me to incorporate, but should be consulted by anyone interested in a synthetic view of this period.

99. Hahn, *Roots*; Lawrence Goodwyn, *Democratic Promise: The Populist Moment in America* (New York, 1976).

100. C. Vann Woodward, *Origins of the New South, 1877–1913* (Baton Rouge, 1951), pp. 107–141; Broadus Mitchell, *The Rise of Cotton Mills in the South* (Baltimore, 1921); and Ben F. Lemert, *The Cotton Textile Industry of the Southern Apalachian Piedmont* (Chapel Hill, NC, 1933), remain classic works; see also David L. Carlton, *Mill and Town in South Carolina, 1880–1920* (Baton Rouge, LA, 1982); Jacquelyn Dowd Hall, Robert Korstad, and James Leloudis, "Cotton Mill People: Work, Community, and Protest in the Textile South, 1880–1940," *American Historical Review*, 91 (1986): 245–86. On labor in an important southern city, see Peter Jay Rachleff, "Blue, White, and Gray: Working-Class Activism in Richmond, Virginia, 1865–1900" (Ph.D. diss., University of Pittsburgh, 1981); and *Black Labor in the South: Richmond, Virginia, 1865–1890* (Philadelphia, 1984).

101. Kessler-Harris, *Out to Work*, p. 76.

102. Claudia Goldin, "Female Labor Participation: The Origins of Black and White Differences," *Journal of Economic History* 37 (1979): 87–108.

103. Montgomery, *Beyond Equality*, pp. 33–44; Walkowitz, *Worker City*, pp. 62–63.

104. See above all Paul Boyer, *Urban Masses and Moral Order in America,*

1820–1920 (Cambridge, MA, 1978), pp. 85–107, 123–31; David Nasaw, *Children of the City: At Work and at Play* (New York, 1985).

105. Kessler-Harris, *Out to Work*, pp. 110–11; Hirsch, *Roots*, pp. 53–76; Michael B. Katz and Mark J. Stern, "Fertility, Class, and Industrial Capitalism: Erie County, New York, 1855–1915," *American Quarterly* 33 (1981): 63–92.

106. David Montgomery, "Labor in the Industrial Era," in Richard B. Morris, ed., *A History of the American Worker*, 2d ed. (Princeton, NJ, 1983), pp. 96–97.

107. Alexander Keyssar, *Out of Work: The First Century of Unemployment in Massachusetts* (Cambridge, MA, 1986).

108. Christine Stansell, "Women, Children, and the Uses of the Streets: Class and Gender Conflict in New York City, 1850–1860," *Feminist Studies* 8 (1982): 309–35, quotation on p. 325; Boyer, *Urban Masses*.

109. Roy Rosenzweig, *Eight Hours for What We Will: Workers and Leisure in an Industrial City, 1870–1920* (New York, 1983), pp. 94 and passim. On associations, see also Walkowitz, *Worker City*, pp. 121–48, 156–70; Greenberg, *Worker and Community*, pp. 89–101, 119–40. For an insightful reading of a key aspect of working-class culture in these years, see Michael Denning, "Cheap Stories: Notes on Popular Fiction and Working-Class Culture in Nineteenth-Century America," *History Workshop*, no. 22 (1986): 1–17.

110. Rosenzweig, *Eight Hours*, pp. 35–64; 103–26; Alf Lüdtke, "Organizational Order or 'Eigensinn'?: Workers' Privacy and Workers' Politics in Imperial Germany," in Sean Wilentz, ed., *Rites of Power: Symbolism, Ritual, and Politics since the Middle Ages* (Philadelphia, 1985).

111. The distinction between small-town and big-city organizing was drawn most sharply by Herbert G. Gutman; see, especially, "The Workers' Search for Power in the Gilded Age," in H. Wayne Morgan, ed., *The Gilded Age: A Reappraisal* (Syracuse, NY, 1963). See also Shefter, "Trade Unions and Political Machines," pp. 237–42. On working-class and community mobilization in smaller industrial sites, see Victor Greene, *The Slavic Community on Strike: Immigrant Labor in Pennsylvania Anthracite* (Notre Dame, IN, 1968).

112. See, for example, Herbert G. Gutman, "The Tompkins Square 'Riot' in New York City on January 13, 1874: A Re-examination of Its Causes and Its Aftermath," *Labor History* 6 (1965): 44–70; Eric Foner, "Class, Ethnicity, and Radicalism in the Gilded Age: The Land League and Irish America," in Foner, *Politics and Ideology*. On ethnic working-class cultures as "competing cultural systems" in a growing city, see Richard Jules Oestreicher, *Solidarity and Fragmentation: Working People and Class Consciousness in Detroit, 1875–1900* (Urbana, IL, 1986), pp. 30–75.

113. On mobility, see Gutman, *Work, Culture, and Society*, Chapter 4; Oestreicher, *Solidarity*, pp. 13–14. On transients and tramps, see Keyssar, *Out of Work*, pp. 111–42; Patricia Ferguson Clement, "The Transformation of the Wandering Poor in Nineteenth-Century Philadelphia," in Eric H. Monkkonen, ed., *Walking to Work: Tramps in America, 1790–1935* (Lincoln, NE, 1984).

114. On political economy and party politics, see generally Robert Sharkey, *Money, Class, and Party: An Economic Study of the Civil War and Reconstruction* (Baltimore, 1959); Morton Keller, *Affairs of State: Public Life in Late Nineteenth-*

Century America (Cambridge, MA, 1977); Woodward, *Origins*. On voting, see Richard Jensen, *The Winning of the Midwest: Social and Political Conflict, 1888–1896* (Chicago, 1971); Paul Kleppner, *The Cross of Culture: A Social Analysis of Midwestern Politics, 1850–1900* (New York, 1970); Samuel T. McSeveney, *The Politics of Depression: Political Behavior in the Northeast, 1893–1896* (New York, 1972); cf. Richard L. McCormick, *The Party Period and Public Policy: American Politics from the Age of Jackson to the Progressive Era* (New York, 1986), esp. Chapter 1, 2, 5, and 6; Michael McGerr, *The Decline of Popular Politics: The American North, 1865–1928* (New York, 1986).

115. Quoted in Montgomery, *Beyond Equality*, p. ix.

116. Montgomery, *Beyond Equality*, pp. 135–229; Michael Gordon, "The Labor Boycott in New York City," *Labor History* 16 (1975): 184–227.

117. Montgomery, *Beyond Equality*, pp. 231–334; Norman Ware, *The Labor Movement in the United States, 1860–1890: A Study in Democracy* (New York, 1964), pp. 1–54; Dawley, *Class*, pp. 175–88; Walkowitz, *Worker City*, pp. 95–98; Ross, *Workers*, pp. 193–216.

118. Warren Van Tine, *The Making of the Labor Bureaucrat: Union Leadership in the United States, 1870–1920* (Amherst, MA, 1973); Montgomery, *Beyond Equality*, pp. 197–229; Walkowitz, *Worker City*, pp. 170–77; Foner, "Class, Ethnicity, and Radicalism"; David Brundage, "Irish Land and American Workers: Class and Ethnicity in Denver, Colorado," in Hoerder, ed., *Struggle*.

119. Sylvis, quoted in Montgomery, *Beyond Equality*, pp. 228–29.

120. Ibid., esp. pp. 230–31.

121. Kessler-Harris, *Out to Work*, pp. 81–86. The finest study of race, immigration, and the contradictions within the labor movement is Alexander Saxton, *The Indispensible Enemy: Labor and the Anti-Chinese Movement in California* (Berkeley, CA, 1969).

122. Montgomery, *Beyond Equality*, pp. 230–60, 335–86; E. J. Hobsbawn, *The Age of Capital 1848–1875*, paperback ed. (New York, 1979), p. 45.

123. Alfred D. Chandler, Jr., *The Visible Hand: The Managerial Revolution in American Business* (Cambridge, MA, 1977), pp. 145–344 passim; Ware, *Labor Movement*, pp. 25–55; Montgomery, "Labor in the Industrial Era," pp. 105–106. *Chicago Times* (October 31, 1873) [report on Paterson, N.J.], quoted in Gutman, *Work, Culture, and Society*, p. 241. On the variegated impact of the depression on real earnings in two major industries, see Walkowitz, *Worker City*, pp. 145–51.

124. Gutman, *Work, Culture, and Society*, pp. 234–343; idem., "The Buena Vista Affair," *Pennsylvania Magazine of History and Biography* 88 (1964): 252–93; idem., "The Braidwood Lockout of 1874," *Illinois State Historical Society Journal* 53 (1960): pp. 5–28; idem., "An Iron Workers' Strike in the Ohio Valley," *Ohio Historical Quarterly* 58 (1959): 353–70; and, for an overview, idem., "Worker's Search for Power." See also Walkowitz, *Worker City*, pp. 183–218; Ross, *Workers*, pp. 240–69.

125. Arnold Paul, *Conservative Crisis and the Rule of Law* (Ithaca, NY, 1960); Shefter, "Trade Unions and Political Machines," p. 245. Christopher L. Tomlins, *The State and the Unions: Labor Relations, Law, and the Organized Labor Movement in America, 1880–1960).*

126. Woodward, *Reunion*; Shefter, "Trade Unions and Political Machines," p. 248–50.

127. Gutman, "Workers' Search for Power"; Montgomery, "Labor in the Industrial Era"; Wayne G. Broehl, *The Molly Maguires* (Cambridge, MA, 1968).

128. Robert V. Bruce, *1877: Year of Violence* (Indianapolis, 1959); Jeremy Brecher, *Strike!* (San Francisco, 1972), pp. 1–34; Philip S. Foner, *The Great Labor Uprising of 1877* (New York, 1977). On railroads, see Walter Licht, *Working for the Railroad: The Organization of Work in the Nineteenth Century* (Princeton, NJ, 1983).

129. *Pittsburgh Post* (August 5, 1877), quoted in Foner, *Great Labor Uprising*, p. 211.

130. Hayes quoted in ibid., p. 210.

131. Ibid., pp. 213–17.

132. *New York Sun* (August 12, 1877), quoted in ibid., p. 213.

133. McDonnell, quoted in Gutman, *Work, Culture, and Society*, p. 268. For fine accounts of how these sentiments appeared at a local level, see Ronald L. Filipelli, "The Railroad Strike of 1877 in Reading," *Historical Review of Berks County* 17 (1972): 48–72; Nick Salvatore, "Railroad Workers and the Great Strike of 1877: The View from a Small Midwestern City," *Labor History* 21 (1980): 522–45.

134. *Pittsburgh Telegraph* (August 12, 1877), quoted in Foner, *Great Labor Uprising*, p. 229.

135. Fink, *Workingmen's Democracy*, p. 4 and passim.

136. *Historical Statistics*, vol. I, p. 139.

137. See above all Gutman's observations in *Work, Culture, and Society*, Chapter 1; and "Class Composition."

138. Walt Whitman, "The Tramp and Strike Questions" [circa 1879], in Justin Kaplan, ed., *Whitman: Poetry and Prose* (New York, 1982), p. 1065. See also David Montgomery, "Labor and the Republic in Industrial America, 1860–1920," *Le Mouvement Social*, no. 111 (1980): 201–15. Montgomery has greatly expanded on this argument in his *The Fall of the House of Labor: The Workplace, the State, and American Labor Activism, 1865–1920* (New York, 1987).

· A L A N   D A W L E Y ·

Workers, Capital, and the State
in the Twentieth Century

*T*he central argument presented in this essay is that the main features of twentieth century America cannot be understood apart from the relations of force between workers and capital, as governed by the state. To make such a claim in the face of massive reversals since the mid-1970s in trade union strength, worker protection, welfare provisions, and government regulations at first may seem somewhat provocative. But, in fact, the recent crisis itself has disclosed new realms of understanding by making it impossible to continue taking for granted the New Deal and American world predominance.[1]

It is no accident that fresh historical perspectives have come to the fore. These include investigations on subjects that were more or less invisible in the old labor and economic histories—women's paid and unpaid labor, family economy, shop floor struggles, work and leisure, and the place of American workers in the global economy. A new periodization has emerged around the rise and fall of social compromise between workers and their employers. So, as the sun set on the old order, the features of the passing equilibrium, now astonishingly vulnerable, have appeared in unprecedented clarity. The Owl of Minerva has alighted.

This essay seeks to set recent social and labor history in the context of struggles over political power. Three periods stand out for consideration. First, from the 1890s through the 1920s, big business established itself not only as the dominant segment of capital but also as the leading element in society at large at a time when the industrial segment of the working class reached its peak. The problem, then, is to explain how American business managed to establish its leadership without having to reach a compromise with industrial workers. In this respect, the United States differed from most states of western Europe, where historians have identified varieties of "corporatist" compromise underlying the postwar search for stability in the Weimar Republic, France, Italy, and to a lesser extent, Britain.[2] That the United States was different does not make it "exceptional," if by that is meant that its open social order and democratic politics enabled it to escape the larger ramifications of capitalist contradiction. For, despite the weakness of class consciousness among *both* capital and labor, the mainsprings of American politics 1890–1930 lie in the unresolved tension between the real social weight of the industrial working class and the exclusion of wage workers *as workers* from political power.

Second, from the Great Depression to the early 1970s, capital and labor arrived at what may be regarded as a postponed social compromise, with the federal government presiding as chief mediator. Although capital retained those managerial prerogatives most vital to the profit motive, workers for the first time entered a *corporate* existence, enjoying privileges and prerogatives recognized in law (Wagner Act, Social Security, wage and hour laws) and custom. World War II solidified the terms of this compromise, as nationalism promoted an uneasy truce between classes, so that despite postwar differences, the basic agreement remained secure. Not to be overlooked in this equation, support for the expansionist aims of postwar U.S. foreign policy provided an extremely important terrain of agreement, notwithstanding the deafening silence on the subject in monographic research. It should be noted that given the overweening weight of the United States in world affairs, the notion of "American exceptionalism" fades into absurdity, as, more and more, the countries of western Europe felt the gravitational pull of the American system drawing them away from communist or socialist reconstruction after the war. In sum, the question arising from this period is, given the inherited power of big business, what rebalancing of social forces prompted the state to mediate this Great Compromise?

Third, beginning in the early 1970s, the Great Compromise broke down. As the urban poor, working women, blacks, and other groups left out of the original negotiation began demanding their share of the settlement, the price of the truce went up, particularly in terms of the "social wage." For this and other reasons, corporations began demanding concessions of their own in work rules, productivity, the "safety net," environmental regulations, and so on. As the regnant power of the corporations emerged to view, the questions arose, what caused the long-standing social compromise to break down, and further, what are the prospects for a new realignment of forces toward the interests of working people in the future? As in the previous period, the way in which American workers position themselves vis-à-vis foreign labor, especially in Third World havens for corporate flight, will exert a critical influence on the outcome.

Before narrating the events of these three periods, a few brief notations are in order. First of all, it is not as if historians agree on the facts and merely disagree on how to interpret them. This hoary assumption from the age of Ranke and Acton died (or deserved to) in the twentieth century, to be replaced in many quarters by the view that "the historian is engaged on a continuous process of molding his facts to his interpretation and his interpretation to his facts," to quote E. H. Carr's *What Is History?*[3] It will be readily apparent in the following pages that I have relied on methods that derive ultimately from Marx, that I have taken family and gender issues as fundamental points of departure, and that the analysis of "relations of force" owes much to Gramsci's *Modern Prince*. This is not to suggest that only Marxists or feminists know where the true path lies but that, first, historians of all schools ought to make their analytical assumptions explicit and, second, liberal and conservative historians cannot duck questions of systemic social conflict. To borrow a metaphor from E. P. Thompson, there is much to be gained by seeing the social order as a "field of force," with dominant and subordinate groups bound together in polar opposition.[4]

To study social antagonism over time is to study social *transformation*. The question is not just how the future is different from the past but how social conflicts both preserve and alter social hierarchy and under what circumstances these conflicts move in egalitarian directions. The most useful models for understanding social transformation, or the interplay of continuity and change, come from the discipline of history itself. Taking an exemplary work of historical materialism, Eric Hobsbawm's *Age of Revolution*, often praised but rarely imitated, teaches volumes on how a new social order emerges from an older one. It calls up a picture of societies undergoing industrial and political revolution, driven through time by the energy of their own internal contradictions, ever seeking some balance of forces appropriate to a given way of life. The same elegant sense of historical evolution exudes from such Annales school figures as Marc Bloch; from one of the world's pioneer materialist historians, Frederick Jackson Turner; and from Herbert Gutman's studies of the adaptation of immigrant cultures to the hard-driving routines of the factory system.

As a point of departure, then, analysis of social transformation starts with recognition of the nexus of antagonism binding together dominant and subordinate groups. Further, it comes to grips with the ways emerging forces attempt to break free of this field, challenging inherited forms of property, family, and authority in the process. Finally, it examines the role of the state as the arbiter of conflict in the transition from one field of force to another.

CITIZENS OR PARIAHS? 1890–1930

What characterizes the period 1890–1930 is an increasing imbalance between emerging social forces and the state. Inherited structures of power and privilege, such as free contract, laissez-faire, white supremacy, and other features of the liberal state dated from a time of market competition when most Americans were rural Protestants of North European ancestry. However, by the 1920s, big business outweighed small, WASPS were a minority, and industrial workers greatly outnumbered farmers. Indeed, the years immediately after World War I marked the climax of what Lewis Mumford dubbed "carboniferous capitalism"; that is, the nexus of coal, rails, and factories laid down by the Industrial Revolution. Measurements vary, but it is clear that in this moment industrial capitalism peaked— mining and manufacturing accounted for about one-third of GNP, and "industrial" employment (including mining, manufacturing, transportation, and construction) reached 44 percent of the gainfully employed, most of whom were wage earners. The "old working class" of blue-collar manual workers, then, amounted to something more than two-fifths of the work force. It is worth emphasizing that these proportions were the peak for the entire twentieth century. Deindustrialization (at least of the labor force) did not begin in the 1970s but the late 1920s. Indeed, it is startling to recognize that the *absolute* number of miners, railwaymen, and cotton textile operatives in 1920 was greater than ever before, or since![5]

Until the Great Depression spoiled the myth of unqualified success, it was hard to argue with the fact that the United States became successively the world's leading producer of coal and steel, a net exporter of manufactured goods, and finally, from World War I until 1985, a net exporter of capital. The secret of success, as business men and women knew, was "economy" derived from large-scale operations, complex division of labor, and rationalization of the flow of production.[6] One does not have to accept the Marxist categories of absolute and relative surplus value to recognize that both intensified labor (the "drive system," speed-up, "pushers") and more capital-intensive techniques (assembly line, mechanization) also contributed to the bonanza in productivity gains. So did the totalitarian control of the labor process embodied in the schemes of Frederick W. Taylor, Frank Gilbreth, and other "scientific managers," whose time-study, task-and-bonus, and standard-hour systems all had the same objective—raise output while lowering unit labor costs. The fact was that if wages were kept low, or allowed to increase more slowly than productivity, then even narrow profit margins would permit a huge volume of profits. Indeed, allowing for an important role for finance capital, the rise of big business was financed largely by "economy" in the labor process.

Property and Poverty

This transfer of wealth upward was made possible by the shift from family to corporate ownership. This provided the legal framework for the emergence of oligopoly, just as large-scale production provided the technological impetus. Corporate property right, in turn, conferred authority on management to make basic decisions about investment, marketing, and the labor process. Why American executives enjoyed such an unusual degree of unilateral authority in industry by comparison to their European counterparts is not clearly understood. Whether stemming from the unusual degree of oligopolistic concentration or from the opposite tradition of unfettered competition, the fact was that U.S. firms did not implement German-style wage arbitration and social insurance nor accord union recognition to the extent the British did.[7]

That individual firms were free to rationalize production and work discipline did not mean they succeeded in rationalizing the system as a whole. The flaw in their drive for economy lay in the disparity between the capacity to produce and the capacity to consume. Henry Ford stated the problem: "mass production requires mass consumption." The mass media, floating on the rising tide of advertising revenues and the techniques of mass persuasion perfected by the Committee on Public Information in World War I, did their part to bridge this gap. Certainly, the ideology of consumption did much to legitimate big business as the efficient source of an abundant flow of consumer goods.[8]

However, few industrial workers were paid as well as the $5-a-day men at Ford, and one goal of "scientific management" was to keep it that way. The main objective of the new scientific methods of payment was to get workers to produce more for less, so that, as Robert Hoxie's investigations showed, the bonus system became a bonus for management.[9] Now, this was perfectly rational for the individual firm, but it could not help but be counterproductive in the long run. Even if economic growth managed to absorb those who would have been unemployed by increased "economy," the very methods that diverted the bonus to capital helped ensure that domestic consumers would be unable to absorb it, as Ford implied. Mammoth increases in productivity, which doubled in steel 1890–1910, overshot modest gains in wages—20 percent for steelworkers.[10] And further, comparative calculations of wage rates in industry emphasize not so much American prosperity vis-à-vis Europe, of which so much has been made by Werner Sombart and others, but the extreme inequality in U.S. pay scales.[11] In sum, the result was recurrent crises of "overproduction" (1893–1896, 1921–1922, 1929–1939), proof that mass abundance was a built-in requirement of steady prosperity.

The human waste of uncompensated injury, frequent unemployment, and penurious old age made a mockery of the notion of efficiency. In some industries, 15 percent were killed or maimed each year.[12] That posterity knows something of these grim facts is due, in the first place, to contemporary men and women of conscience who set about disclosing them. The Progressive social investigators produced mountains of studies documenting *Poverty, Work Accidents,* and *Adjusting Immigrant and Industry,* plus such pioneering work as the Pittsburgh Survey, John Commons's Bureau of Industrial Research, and the David Saposs interviews of immigrant workers for the Carnegie Commission. In addition, the working-class imprint is obvious in arts (Bellow's "The Cliff Dwellers," Louis Hine's photographs, etc.) and letters (Dreiser's *Sister Carrie,* Dos Passos's *U.S.A.* trilogy, Thomas Bell's *Out of This Furnace,* and Carl Sandburg's "Chicago Poems," to mention a few).[13]

Seeking a measure of social justice, reformers began chipping away at the edifice of laissez-faire. By 1930 most states had enacted some kind of child labor legislation. With Wisconsin's Progressive-Socialist alliance setting the example, a number of states enacted workmen's compensation laws. Accepting the argument of Louis Brandeis and Josephine Goldmark that industrial fatigue sapped the procreative strength of "the mothers of the race," the Supreme Court upheld a ten-hour workday law for women in *Muller vs. Oregon.*[14] Hoping to head off additional restrictions, corporations began to experiment with "welfare capitalism" pioneered by the railroad YMCA and International Harvestor. However, compared to actual need, these were paltry measures. Welfare capitalism extended only to a tiny stratum of labor aristocrats. State welfare was most evident by its absence. And in the last great bastion of the Protestant ethic, private charity for the "deserving poor" failed to fill the breach.[15] In the end, the imbalance between the distributive and judicial structures of the state, on the one side, and the collective existence of the working class, on the other, remained extreme.

The nuclear family provided a weak first line of defense against privation. Only a few of the best-paid men took home the prized "family wage" that enabled dependents to evade paid labor. Otherwise, the family economy depended on wages and in-kind income from wives and children that set working class reality at odds with the regnant ideal of the father as paternalist provider. Margaret Byington's *Homestead* and Edith Abbott's *Women in Industry* disclosed the gap in family budgets between the father's income and the family's needs.[16] Surviving oral testimony adds confirmation to the fact that, in this situation, acquisitive individualism took second place to family security. At the extreme, among the very poor and more generally in hard times, labor exchange, barter, and other precapitalist forms of exchange came into play. Consider the following reminiscence of a Polish woman who as a girl in the Depression lost a father to black lung, worked intermittently as a domestic, and relied on her mother's ability to scrape together a meager living: "But we raised our own food, had our own chickens and ducks. We even tried to make moonshine. We sold a couple of quarts and got a little money that way. My mother was also a midwife for the area. She got paid in food—chickens, ducks."[17]

Sexual Division of Labor

Surviving hard times may have been better accomplished by a more egalitarian division of labor in the home, but as reformers like Charlotte Perkins Gilman argued, that required an industrial system more oriented to human needs, plus social services that the existing state was unwilling to provide. Without these factors, workers relied on the mutual support of the sexual division of labor between husband and wife to get through the dire straits of daily living. The "family values" engendered by this experience, however amenable to distortion, were a humane alternative to the cash values of the marketplace.[18]

Leaving aside the minority of self-supporting women workers, most women who went into paid labor initially pursued family rather than personal goals. This is not surprising, given that most were daughters expecting to contribute to the family economy. Whether remaining at home to do industrial homework or tend boarders or going out to earn a wage, women's "double burden" became painfully apparent in low status jobs, discriminatory wage rates, and their role as a reserve army of labor to be tapped in emergencies like World War I. That was true regardless of whether they exchanged their labor against capital, as in manufacturing, or against a household budget, as in the largest women's occupation, domestic service.[19] The causes and remedies of this dismal situation were in dispute then, as now, with most trade union women arguing for special protective legislation while feminists argued that paternalist protection only wound up as discrimination in the end. Theorists of patriarchy such as Heidi Hartmann must be credited with throwing the burden of proof onto liberal feminists, who have held since the 1920s that removing discrimination through such means as the Equal Rights Amendment would remedy the situation.[20]

Indeed, the whole construction of gender relations around separate "spheres" for men and women purchased esteem for homebound women with the coin of discrimination in the labor market and limited access to the world of affairs. So long as women were regarded as "the mothers of the race," so long would they be second-class citizens in the world at large. That in a nutshell is the chief importance of the main demographic trends leading away from involuntary motherhood toward low birth rates. Rational choice in the matter of procreation proved to be a fundamental threat to male privilege, not just in the family, but in all the places where it was stitched into the fabric of society.

Nevertheless, the force of this argument varies in proportion to the extent of women's labor force participation; that is, the more women contribute income to the family economy, the more burdensome is the sexual division of labor that gives them a "second job" in the home. With participation rates edging up only slightly from 20 percent in 1900 to 24 percent in 1930, we can surmise that the contradiction between the job and the home was great enough to raise the issue of full-scale women's equality, but not so great as to make it as compelling as it became fifty years later.[21] In the meantime, since women's primary concern remained family needs, their need to make do virtually without state support identifies a fundamental imbalance between the collective needs of working people and the structures and policies of the state. Moreover, women's suffrage only highlights the class basis of this gap. Whereas suffrage, presumably, united the interests of middle- and working-class women, welfare issues divided them. With servants to take care of the housework and income sufficient to cover most sickness, retirement, and the rest, middle-class women had less need for state welfare and less reason, therefore, to be unhappy with its absence.

Class and Culture

Kinship obviously played less of a role in structuring modern American life than it did in the small towns of rural America or the peasant villages of Galicia and Abruzzi. It is true that the fragmentation of life in the urban marketplace tore at the kinship networks of these rural migrants, a fact well-developed in the Chicago school sociologists' many studies of social disintegration.[22] Nevertheless, it is equally true that migrants put great reliance on kinship for aid in migration, finding work, and bearing the burdens of survival ("what goes around comes around").[23] In addition, kinship bonds were the stuff of which horizontal solidarities were made, whether among Yankee-Protestant bluestockings or Slavic-Catholic immigrants, as families wove religious and national traditions into the warp and woof of occupational and ethnic cohesion.[24] These larger ethnic networks cushioned the sudden calamities of injury, sickness, and death. Whereas some mutual benefit societies were subsidiary to trade unions like the United Mine Workers, most workers had recourse to the parish church, the national alliance, or the ethnic political club as a second line of defense (after the nuclear family itself) against privation.

To grasp the role of ethnic culture in the transformation of social hierarchy, it is but necessary to find the place of these horizontal solidarities within the nexus of inequality. The arrival of masses of Slavic and Italian immigrants and the great migration of southern blacks did not merely add new groups to an already colorful ethnic mosaic; they rearranged the cultural pecking order, stimulating resurgent nativism, virulent anti-Semitism, and a spate of race riots that peaked around World War I. Notwithstanding the valiant pleas for a tolerant "cultural pluralism," American pluralism was steeped in invidious racial and ethnic intolerance.[25]

Without doubt, this clash of cultures cut across class lines, for example, when Irish and German skilled workers made common cause with Yankee employers or when middle-class Poles rallied with Polish workers around the national flag, rather than class banners.[26] Nonetheless, it is impossible to escape the fact that when racial ideologies sorted cultural groups into "superiors" and "inferiors," they reinforced social hierarchy. It would appear that this invidious "tribalism" not only followed broad class lines but also helped map them out in the supposedly classless American social order.[27] Perhaps, it is so obvious as to be unworthy of mention, but does anyone believe that if by some sudden magic 70 percent of the richest Progressive Era tycoons became Afro-American instead of Anglo-American, white supremacy would have lived another day?[28] Here, at least, would be circumstances in which to conjure with the notion of "reverse racism."

Thus, it is a mistake to construe class and ethnicity as independent "variables," free to wax and wane on their own or ready to be transubstantiated from one to the other by some mysterious alchemy. Likewise, the Weberian trichotomy "class-status-power" is equally misleading in presenting class and status (or ethnicity) as separate, parallel hierarchies. If we wish to grasp the whole process of historical transformation, then we would do better to contemplate not three hierarchies, but one whole social order driven through time by its own internal contradictions, among which is the perpetual conflict between egalitarian and hierarchal forces.

The Workers Movement

The self-conscious workers movement both reflected and affected the process of social transformation. The rise of oligopoly and modern management, the issues of women's labor and social welfare, and the clash of native and immigrant all posed major challenges to the movement now three generations old, yet still in a fight for its very survival. Given the obvious divisions among working people, it seems astounding at first blush that there was enough cohesion to form any kind of movement at all. Thus, it is all the more significant that the level of class conflict as measured by the incidence of strikes and lockouts, the frequency of riot and violence, and the militarization of industrial disputes was higher in these years than at any other period in American history, not excepting the heyday of the Knights of Labor, the birth of the CIO, or the post-World War II offensive.[29] Undeniably, workers shaped the emerging social order not only by their productivity and their welfare needs but by their will to reduce its inequalities of wealth and power.

It is essential to bear in mind that the movement was no monolith but an assortment of competing alternatives, of which the leading force was the craft unionism of the American Federation of Labor. Antiquated before reaching maturity, craft unionism flourished best in industries bypassed by oligopoly, such as construction. Intimidated by the defeat of Eugene Debs's American Railway Union in the Pullman Boycott of 1894, Samuel Gompers drew the grudging conclusion that not even industrial unionism was potent enough to combat the combined strength of wealthy corporations and government injunctions served up by U.S. cavalry. Instead, he paid court to the moguls of the National Civic Federation and appointed himself official labor liaison to the Wilson administration.[30] Gompers personified the pugnacity of the craft unions, timid about infringing upon the rights of property but tough as nails when it came to their own work rules and pay scales. Such union stalwarts showed all workers the way to resist the speed-up, sweating, labor spies, and other assorted tyrannies of the capitalist workplace. Surely, in commanding respect for the dignity of toil from a system that would otherwise have denied it, their influence in this respect undermined the social pyramid.

But before accepting Selig Perlman's elevation of these traits to a theorem about the "job consciousness" of the American labor movement,[31] it is necessary to come to grips with the cultural and gender components of the craft-union mentality. Alongside their manifest resistance to employer tyranny, skilled workers also defended the combined gender and ethnic privileges of men of northern European extraction, fighting to retain what had been one of the defining features of family capitalism. When government regulation served this end, they abandoned "voluntarist" scruples to support it. The AFL signed on to immigration restriction, and Gompers eagerly joined forces with ardent nativist James Davis, Harding's secretary of labor, and Albert Johnson, archenemy of organized labor, after whom the Johnson (National Origins) Act was named. Nativist contempt for unskilled Slavs and Italians led to strikebreaking by skilled steelworkers in 1919, even as the immigrants stuck by the union until the bitter end. Likewise, the AFL supported the regulation of child labor and protective legislation for women in hopes of winning a "family wage" sufficient for a man to support his dependent wife and children.[32] Surely these compromises with gender and cultural inequality explain both why craft unionism found its niche in the competitive sector of the economy and why its narrow definition of the House of Labor was incapable of uplifting the working class as whole.

Meanwhile, industrial unionism suffered a succession of crushing defeats at the hands of big business that prevented it from playing the leading role. Challenging the oligarchs of heavy industry, redoutable organizers repeatedly hurled themselves against the steel trust, the coal barons, and the railroad empires, only to be repulsed. Adapting to the ethnic and cultural diversity of the work force, industrial unions began to break free of nativist and patriarchal assumptions. The United Mine Workers conducted business in three languages; the Amalgamated Clothing and Textile Workers fought for the interests of its women members; the Industrial Workers of the World made racial tolerance and sexual equality cardinal points of its syndicalist philosophy. Both labor socialists and labor progressives like the organizers of the Farmer-Labor party seemed to regard women's protective legislation as the thin edge of the wedge of state paternalist regulation for men as well.[33] Had their organizing campaigns achieved greater success, and if the Left had enjoyed greater influence, there is little doubt that capital would have been forced into significant compromise with workers long before the New Deal.

State Mediation and Repression

As it was, the state intervened to guide the process of social transformation away from a more egalitarian equilibrium of forces. Given the enormous social weight of the working class—its size, its key role in creating wealth, its manifest welfare needs, its cultural estrangement, its conscious struggle for power—it is hard to imagine how the new nexus of inequality could have come into being without the exertion of the "outside" force of state power. If the state is the sum total of collective wills to power, then the key fact in this period is the weakness of workers' collective will, a fact all the more puzzling in light of America's democratic traditions. How could American workingmen be political pariahs when, for so long, they had been full-fledged citizens?

This puzzle can be solved if the state is seen not as a neutral arbiter holding society together against anarchy, but as a power holding a social hierarchy together against its own egalitarian contradictions. In this regard, America's laissez-faire democracy of the late nineteenth century was no less a state than its Czarist contemporary. It is not necessary to describe here the exclusion of women and blacks, the mediating institutions of parties and legislatures, or the coercive role of courts, police, and prisons. Clearly, the urban political machine buffered cultural conflicts between native and immigrant, fostering the Americanization of the immigrant worker by tying his interests to city hall.[34] "Laissez-faire plus the constable" is an apt summary of the combination of mediations and repressions that characterized the liberal state of that era.

It is also scarcely necessary to note that these traditions played a larger role in twentieth century America than their counterparts played in Britain, not to mention the more statist regimes of the Continent. Under the tenets of liberalism, citizenship belonged to individuals not groups. When state legislatures got up the nerve to restrict the hours of labor for men or when Congress grew so bold as to outlaw child labor, the Supreme Court was ready with the Fourteenth Amendment to strike down these infractions upon the individual's freedom of contract.[35] Only a handful of states had dared intrude upon personal thrift and private charity to do something about welfare needs.

But as nineteenth century republican ideology argued, to be a citizen of the republic did not make the worker a citizen of industrial society. That contradiction, which made Debs a socialist[36] and launched numerous campaigns for "industrial democracy," ultimately proved too strong for liberalism to handle within the existing machinery of government. During the ascendancy of Progressivism, the preferred method of harmonizing the conflict of labor and capital was the government commission of inquiry. Beginning with Teddy Roosevelt's Coal Commission in the 1902 anthracite strike, there followed the Industrial Relations Commission on violent disputes like the Ludlow massacre, the President's Mediation Commission on the 1917 copper strike, and Woodrow Wilson's ill-fated Industrial Commissions of 1919–1920.[37] Along with new government bureaucracies like the Labor Department and the various state bureaus of labor, these represented the first gropings toward a recognition of the corporate existence of the working class that eventually came to a head in the New Deal.

However, two observations are in order. First, these new structures themselves became vectors in the rearranged force field. Of the thousands of cases handled by such agencies as the President's Mediation Board, the Railway Labor Board, or the War Labor Board, none (so far as I know) ended with an award of union recognition.[38] As if this was not enough, the repressive forces of the state grew apace. Newly created state police, the Bureau of Investigation, and Military Intelligence took their place beside old-fashioned police and militia. Notwithstanding the Clayton Act's supposed exemption of trade unions, injunctions rained down against strikers. Especially in the period of intense immigrant labor upheaval 1919–1922, the federal government used its full civil and military powers against strikers, while orchestrating the Red Scare against all manner of discontent.[39] In Pennsylvania steel towns, it was said that Jesus Christ would have been run out of town on a rail if he came to talk about the union.

A second point is that, given intensifying native-immigrant conflict, it is impossible to speak of the "cultural hegemony" of the white Anglo-Saxon

Protestant. Such consensus as developed between Yankee-Protestants, on the one side, and Irish or German Catholics, and even Slavs, Italians, or Jews, on the other, assuredly did not develop around universal agreement on what was quaintly said to be "the superiority of Anglo-Saxon institutions." It is true that the commercial culture of advertising, sports, and the department store embodied a cultural bias toward middle-class native whites. But up and down the scale from eastern bluestockings to southern rednecks, they felt their privileges giving way and increasingly turned to the state to shore up their threatened position. Much of the impetus for "good-government," prohibition, Americanization, and of course, immigration restriction came from the irresistible impulse to put the coercive power of the state behind the Yankee-Protestant value system.[40]

It should be noted that this struggle for "consent" took place not only between ethnic groups but also *within* them. For example, tension between privileged Anglo-Saxons and underprivileged Italians was underlain by contests within each group between (for the Italians) middle-class *prominenti* and trade union or anarchist leaders like Sacco and Vanzetti.[41] Given deportation of alien radicals and the Red Scare, state intervention in these family quarrels was anything but neutral.[42] The result was not voluntary consensus so much as "enforced consent."

The Absence Fallacy

From the point of view of labor and the Left, the aftermath of World War I saw a series of crushing defeats from which they never entirely recovered. Now, this fueled many fallacies about American history. The notion of the "absence of socialism" is a case in point. Unfortunately, any effort to explain what did *not* happen, especially with reference to absent causes, is doomed to a logician's perdition we shall call the *absence fallacy*. The premiere example of the absence fallacy is a nonsensical effort to explain the absence of socialism in America by the absence of a feudal tradition. It hardly needs pointing out that the American working class has been a honey pot to the bees of the absence fallacy, who are forever buzzing about the failure to form a British-style Labour party, a German-style Socialist party, a truly class-conscious movement, or what have you.[43] This is not to disparage sound comparative history. On the contrary, significant insight is packed into Jurgen Kocka's *White Collar Workers in America*, an effort to explain why Germany's lower-middle classes went Fascist out of status panic, while America's amorphous occupational boundaries actually militated against authoritarianism.[44] In general, then, what needs explanation is what happened, in terms of real historical alternatives and logical comparison, not what did not happen in terms of absent causes.

We should be dealing with how big business gained hegemony by the

1920s and seemed free to lead the country without having to bargain with industrial workers, whose productivity was the main source of the society's wealth and whose social weight made them the major segment of the American population. The place to seek the reasons for the path actually taken is with the real historical alternatives. To discover these alternatives, it is not necessary to concoct "counterfactual" scenarios or dream of what might have been. It is only necessary to perform a little experiment in time. Take two points in time—1916 and 1926. Separated by less than half a generation, it is hard to object that these points are very close together on the continuum of time, so close that from a distant perspective they appear as one moment. Within this single "moment," then, we have captured our seemingly elusive *real* alternatives in the actual events of the time. The major alternatives must have been Progressivism and the New Era. Subject to more or less the same structural determinants, these were alternative alignments of the same social forces or, again, different ways of resolving the same contradictions. Besides these leading alternatives, often forgotten alternatives come to light if we peer a little deeper beneath the surface: for one, the ultra-nationalism of the patriotic societies on the Republican right wing; for another, the Farmer-Labor parties.

Putting this procedure to the test of events, we see in Progressivism an alignment in which big businessmen did not succeed in translating their manifest economic power into accepted social and political leadership. In the years before World War I, the National Association of Manufacturers (NAM), public relations men like ("Poison") Ivy Lee, and other organs of big business, along with close allies like the YMCA, campaigned vigorously to bring other strata and groups around to their general point of view. But, there was too much resistance from antimonopoly farmers, industrial unionists, and various middle-class strata like social workers, teachers, and reform-minded intellectuals for this campaign to succeed in creating a ruling consensus. Even some technocrats believed with Veblen in a conflict between "engineers and the price system," whereas socialists and other leftists raised a vehement dissenting voice.[45] Although American entry into the Great War all but destroyed the fledgling Left, it seemed to strengthen unionism, promote labor reforms like the eight-hour workday, and generally speaking, increase the power of the state at the expense of private enterprise.

That this alignment so swiftly turned into its opposite in the immediate aftermath of the war offers a study in the way the state reinforced social hierarchy. As class conflict intensified in the biggest-ever wave of strikes and lockouts, intermediate groups tended to gravitate toward opposite poles of the worker-capital field of force. Professional management societies and other technocrats submitted themselves fully to the control of corporate executives. With NAM orchestrating the open shop drive, small businessmen swallowed their fear of big capital to join it in battle against labor.

Government suppression of the Left in the war and the Red Scare frightened many Progressives away from the propertyless masses. And finally, forced to choose between striking workers and the captains of industry holding out against either union recognition or meaningful bargaining in steel, coal, and rails, the Wilson administration, including many "friends of labor" within it, bowed to management intransigence and intervened with injunctions and troops to preserve "order." Along with the rising middle-class fear of militant immigrant workers, state action appears decisive in tipping the balance of power toward business.

The Reign of Big Business

The consequence of enforced consent and state intervention on the side of law and order was to usher in the reign of big business in the New Era. The labor movement was in no position to act as a countervailing force. In many industries by 1930, trade unionism was but a fading memory. Shop floor struggles continued but without benefit of national union organization of the sort that only a decade earlier seemed well on the way to establishing itself in steel, meatpacking, textiles, and elsewhere. Gone was the "new unionism" that sought recognition from the masters of mass production, as well as the syndicalism of the Industrial Workers of the World. Without influence were the Socialist party, once able to command the respect of millions, and the assorted Labor and Farmer parties that had sprung up after World War I. What Mary Beard had called "a titanic force akin to the forces in the natural world" seemed all but spent.[46]

Thus, virtually unimpeded by organized labor or the state, capitalist investors put their record profits into excess capacity, investment trusts, and speculation. For a time, there were only record results; that is, until the reckoning of 1929 hoisted speculators on their own petard. The roots of the Depression, then, are to be found in the consequence of hidden contradictions of the New Era between unrestrained private enterprise and socialized production, between niggardly consumption and abundant productivity, between speculative investment and the unmet needs of the poor; in short, between state and society. Call it a crisis of overproduction, or underconsumption, or "creative destruction," or the "tendency to stagnation," but let us recognize, with the heirs of Marx, the price for excluding the exploited from a place in the sun.

THE GREAT COMPROMISE, 1930–1970

What characterizes the period from the Great Depression to the Vietnam War is a social compromise between industrial workers and big business in which each side recognized certain needs and prerogatives of the other. A protracted, if uneasy, truce supervised by the Democratic party, the federal bureaucracy, and other arms of the state brought an end to the endemic violence of American industrial warfare; and for the first time, the industrial working class entered upon a corporate existence as a more or less officially recognized and somewhat privileged segment of society.

This shift in emphasis of government strategy from repression to mediation at long last marked a positive state response to the egalitarian forces of mass consumption, workers self-organization, and cultural tolerance. At the same time, the promotion of mass production workers to a position of greater privilege than the skilled trades had ever enjoyed in the previous period did not overthrow the dominant corporate-managerial interests. Therefore, this transformation in social hierarchy shifted burdens to other sectors of the working class and to other subordinate groups—working women, blacks, Hispanics, and the overseas employees of transnational corporations.

To identify the causes of this new state of affairs, we must first identify the real alternatives to continuing on an outlaw basis. Franklin Roosevelt has sometimes been portrayed as the savior of capitalist democracy, rescuing it from the perils of both communism and fascism. As astute a critic as John Dewey wrote in 1932: "We have permitted business and financial autocracy to reach such a point that its logical political counterpart is a Mussolini, unless a violent revolution brings forth a Lenin."[47] Perhaps in world-historical perspective, Roosevelt, Mussolini (or Hitler), and Stalin embody comparable alternatives. No doubt, the questions, Why no socialism? and Why no fascism? implicit in Dewey's remark make some sense for the United States. However, from the perspective of the chain of actual causation, these are not real alternatives. No matter how much the American Legion, the Ku Klux Klan, and the Liberty League are stretched, it is impossible to imagine any plausible resorting of events to produce a fascist America in the 1930s, or a soviet one, for that matter.

To get at the real alternatives, let us repeat our experiment in time, collapsing 1926 and 1936 into a single moment, in order to contrast the New Era with the New Deal. The question is, What rebalancing of social forces undid the big business bloc and created the conditions for social compromise between big business and industrial workers? Given that structural determinants remained more or less constant, what released the latent possibilities for something like the New Deal? And, how might things have gone differently?

With the coming of the Depression, the hidden contradictions of the New Era finally burst into the open in the form of mass unemployment, bread lines, and Hoovervilles—all of which tore the mask from "people's capitalism" to reveal the system's more grotesque face. It is important to recognize that militant class consciousness was not an automatic reflex of this massive social distress—the level of strikes in the 1930s never approached that of 1919–1920.[48] Thus, the revival of worker militancy, renewed social reform, and the Communist party's resurgence are all facts that need to be explained, not assumed. But certainly, the Great Depression prepared the way for a new political equilibrium. We concentrate here only on what was probably the most important factor in that transition, the intensification of labor struggles. It is necessary to consider both the "internal" mobilization of working class forces and "external" liaisons among workers and other groups.

Family Welfare and Workers Organization

To begin inside the "world of the worker," the Depression complicated, to say the least, the problems of daily life, forcing housewives to make do with less coming into the family kitty. Since women's labor force participation did not exceed a quarter of the adult female population before World War II and since relatively few married women worked outside the home, what took precedence was concern about housing, feeding, and otherwise caring for the family. Given this structural context, plus the press of Depression, it is not surprising to find that even wage-earning women put family values ahead of feminist ones[49] or that the crying need for social security engendered more women's protest than the issue of equal pay. Once historians link women's role in the reproduction of daily life with the sects, panaceas, and sober reform movements around such figures as Father Divine, Huey Long, and Eleanor Roosevelt, a new chapter in social history will be written.

With respect to women workers, despite certain advances in mass production, especially where the Packinghouse Workers, the Ladies Garment Workers, and other industrial unions gained strength, it would appear that their position relative to men remained virtually unchanged. Neither the decline of low-paid domestic service nor the rise of clerical occupations moved women higher on the scale of pay and power. Although the industrial unions accepted the permanence of women in the labor market, the reins of power within the labor movement remained in men's hands. So, even though patriarchal structures had withered, male privilege persisted in the new setting.

Needless to say, no understanding of the internal organization of the working class is possible without accounts of *The CIO Challenge to the AFL, Labor's Giant Step*, the *Sit-Down* strike, and specific industries like *The Electrical Workers*. Since the 1930s truly were *The Turbulent Years*, they provide the raw material for some of the most dramatic narratives in the field.[50] And make no mistake about it, an inability to narrate a gripping story will doom historians to a game of intellectual ping-pong, batting words back and forth among themselves.

At the same time, the craving to understand *why* pushes beyond simple narrative. In assessing why this internal rallying took place, many accounts emphasize the role of a resurgent labor movement encouraged by the New Deal, led by the experienced and newly emboldened John L. Lewis, driving inexorably toward the industrial unionism embodied in the CIO. Other accounts emphasize the role of workplace conflict in energizing rank-and-file revolt against industrial autocracy, to which overtaxed and somewhat tardy trade unions and political parties attached themselves. Understandably, these different emphases provide grist for the political mills of social democrats and neosyndicalists, respectively.[51] But considered in terms of historical causation, far from being mutually exclusive, these are complementary points of analysis. No rank-and-file upsurge, no labor movement. No industrial unions, no internal organization of class strata. The fact that both *movement* and *organization* were happening at the same time accounts for success in auto, steel, rubber, meatpacking, and other mass production industries (and incidently, discloses a common ground between the "new" labor history and the "old").

Outside this heartland of blue-collar organizing, the terrain is rather poorly mapped. To what extent did industrial workers, rapidly making up for lost time, carry white-collar workers along? Obviously, for the labor movement to conform to the objective existence of the working class, it had to unite this historically nonunion and increasingly female component.[52] That rates of union membership for blue-collar men attained much higher levels (as much as 70 percent in manufacturing) when the union wave crested in the late 1940s at around 35 percent of the entire work force highlights the fact that the breakthrough was much less successful among white-collar workers. Who can say whether women workers' family values, men workers' prejudices, or some white-collar conceit played the major cultural role?

When it comes to the impact of the larger community, the picture gets even more fuzzy. Conventional wisdom has it that the ethnic divisions that had once precluded class conscious organization diminished sufficiently to permit, at least, industrial unions to flourish as never before. Maybe so, but was that because the "melting pot" finally worked or because workers in Polonia, Little Italy, and Irishtown finally found a basis for mutual trust? If so, did "cultural pluralism" or "working class culture" bridge the gap? Was it tolerant acceptance of different customs or customs in common? Certainly, for the Steelworkers Organizing Committee to make any headway, Slavic and Italian steelworkers had to develop mutual respect, as did white ethnics and blacks in the case of the United Auto Workers.[53] At the very least, it would appear that acceptance of cultural diversity was the precondition for America's polyglot work force to develop cross-cultural class loyalties. Whatever the answer, it awaits the kind of cultural studies that have illuminated the world of nineteenth century workers.

With regard to "external" liaisons, not since the heyday of muckraking journalism had so many intellectuals identified the cause of humanity with the worker. From the reform pages of the *Nation* to the proletarian literature of the *New Masses*, a parade of luminaries like Theodore Dreiser, Upton Sinclair, and Richard Wright lined up with labor. Social workers, welfare administrators, and other professionals (though precious few professors) promoted the workers' welfare agenda through such national figures as Frances Perkins and Harry Hopkins. Even many small businessmen, disabused of their faith in big business, listened attentively to the populist ideas of Huey Long and Father Coughlin.[54] Moreover, these neighborhood shopkeepers and professionals were a pivotal force in the struggle for leadership within ethnic communities. Obviously, the presence of such groups, with their own small-property and nationalist agendas, tended to dilute the working-class content of reform demands, but given the complex structures of mass democracies, it is hard to see how workers could have gone it alone.

The New Governing System

It remains to consider how this realignment of social forces came to constitute a new political equilibrium. Since the imbalance between state and society had brought on the crisis in the first place, only state action could transcend it. Contrary to elite theories, top businessmen were tied too tightly to their own balance sheets to take the lead in restoring stability through state intervention; and until they learned to live symbiotically with government regulation during World War II, they were left to wallow in their own loathing for the New Deal.[55]

As for the Republican party, it paid the price of drawing too close to outmoded WASP values. The party of Americanization, immigration restriction, Prohibition, sexual purity, and Calvin Coolidge suffered a loss of confidence as immigrant clannishness, the speak-easy, and the flapper deviously subverted the "enforced consent" of the 1920s. For the same reasons, the party of immigrant machines, wets, and Al Smith picked up new support. The "new" political historians are not incorrect in drawing attention to such cultural factors underlying party politics, but too often they forget to relate these to economic matters. In repealing Prohibition, political leaders not only struck a blow for cultural pluralism, but also gave the immigrant workers who had been its main victims new cultural breathing space. Moreover, although it goes without saying that the main parties were both "capitalist," the Republicans under Hoover could never hope to convince the bulk of depression-scarred working people that do-little economics worked for them. Democratic experimentation, on the other hand, opened the door for the working poor to enter the New Deal Coalition. Thus for both cultural and economic reasons, the era of Republican dominance (1896–1932) gave way to Democratic dominance (1933–1968), a shift which, in turn, cleared away one obstacle to a new equilibrium.[56]

With respect to class interests, it should not be supposed that because big business languished in temporary isolation, the state neglected its interests. More fundamental processes were at work than class hatred of the National Association of Manufacturers for "that man" in the White House. It is true that, in its more "historic" acts, the state gave recognition to the social weight of the working class—Norris-La Guardia (1932) and the Wagner Act (1935) thrust the Bill of Rights inside the factory gate for the first time. Along with the Fair Labor Standards Act (1938), these recognized that socialized production demanded collective not individual bargaining and social not individual contracts for minimum wages and maximum hours. In addition, social security legislation recognized that the combined resources of family economy, ethnic benefit societies, and private charity could not meet the needs of mass poverty and mass unemployment. In such fashion, workers acquired certain privileges under law ("entitlements") and, therefore, entered a corporate existence. With "Ma" Perkins, the National Labor Relations Board, and the Supreme Court all siding with independent unions under the Wagner Act as against Employee Representation Plans, these privileges acquired secure legal footing.[57]

But, it is an open question whether they would have survived in the workplace, given management intransigence in "Little Steel," Ford, and elsewhere, had not World War II come along. The requirement for worker cooperation in the second total war of the century translated into decisions from the War Labor Board and other government bodies favorable to "union security."[58] In contrast to World War I, the federal government did not merely mediate disputes but forced recalcitrant employers to bargain with a union. A grateful CIO drew closer to the New Deal Coalition, setting up its Political Action Committee (later Committee on Political Education) to help elect Roosevelt in 1944 and then to support every Democrat until George McGovern. Thus, the labor movement came to rely on all aspects of the state—law, bureaucracy, party—to gain new rights and privileges. Since the new governing arrangement both recognized the legitimacy of workers' needs and organizations for the first time yet set the limits of legitimacy within fairly narrow confines of collective bargaining and minimal welfare, state intervention was, in the words of David Montgomery, "simultaneously liberating and co-optive."[59]

Thus, the New Deal should not be mistaken for a shift from a "capitalistic" to a "laboristic" equilibrium.[60] If such a term must be applied, then *corporatist* fits best. First and foremost, neither the New Deal nor the wartime command economy assaulted the main citadel of private enterprise, the property right to private profit. By forestalling more radical moves toward investment controls, nationalization, or wartime confiscation of plants and profits ("conscription of wealth"), the state was actually bestowing vital (if unwritten) exemptions on business.[61] Just as General Motors, U.S. Steel, and other corporate converts to realism in labor relations now accepted certain union powers in the labor market, so most labor leaders conceded the quid pro quo of "managerial prerogative" and "fair profit" as preconditions for "civilized" collective bargaining.[62] This was the key to the long truce that lasted through thick and thin until the second Nixon administration. Thus did the emergence of a new governing bloc, which included workers as junior partners, preserve the corporate property right and managerial authority that were fundamental to the twentieth century social hierarchy. Change preserved continuity.

No doubt, others would describe this period quite differently. In the conventional (pluralist) wisdom, the pendulum of reform swung backward in what the AFL liked to call the Taft-Hartley "Slave-Labor Act," which "fundamentally altered relations among labor, management, and government." Alternatively, structuralists argue that organized labor's incorporation in the state caused the movement to ossify in bureaucratic paralysis.[63] It is true that after the war, state action spelled out the limits of organization by promoting the scab's "right to work," including a McCarthy-style purge of Communist unions, and tying militant hands in the coils of legalistic grievance procedures and contract enforcement. Certainly, these tamed a once-bellicose movement, bringing more conservative ideas to the fore, as in the Catholic corporatism of Phil Murray and James Carey or the social democratic corporatism of Walter Reuther.[64] Indeed, many of these increasingly self-satisfied "new men of power" waxed eloquent in defense of the system that had accorded them unexpected prominence. George Meany declared, "When [the Soviets] say I am an agent of Wall Street—if they mean . . . that I am an agent of the American system—as far as I am concerned, I accept that."[65] But, when all is said and done, the basic terms of the truce—peaceful collective bargaining and mutual support for both the welfare state and U.S. expansion—survived intact through Eisenhower, got reinvigorated in the Great Society, and even found an advocate in Nixon's various tripartite Pay Boards and Labor-Management Committees. That this corporatist compromise opened new paths to capital accumulation by rationalizing a wasteful, unstable economy is vouchsafed by the postwar boom, the longest period of prosperity in U.S. history.[66]

If the advance of industrial workers later seemed to be co-optive, so it was. But given the real alternative of leaving things as they had been in the preceding period, these changes must be regarded as progressive. Might things have gone still further toward empowering workers? No doubt, they could have, given a unified labor movement, a larger paternalist wing of the business community, a stronger Left, and so on. But, before long, we will be sliding down the slippery slope of the absence fallacy.

Hidden Contradictions

Who could have forseen at the height of Pax Americana and the domestic Pax Corporata that the new balance of forces contained the seeds of its own undoing? Who could know that by according a measure of recognition to one subordinate group, the system was all the while shifting the burden of subordination to other social groups, such as working women, Afro-Americans, and Hispanic and Asian immigrants? With the state guaranteeing a share of imperial tribute and domestic prosperity to working people, a generation of children grew up beyond the clutches of the terrible insecurity their parents and grandparents had always known. Federal Trade Commission regulations and National Labor Relations Board decisions made it possible for unions to negotiate unprecedented benefits packages like the United Mine Workers' pace-setting medical plan and the United Auto Worker's supplemental unemployment benefits, plus widespread vacation and holiday fringes. Meanwhile, unemployment compensation, Aid to Families with Dependent Children, and federal retirement pensions provided a modicum of paternalist provision for the poor. Although gangsters and "tuxedo unionists" siphoned off an unseemly share of these benefits, such a large segment of the working class received these well-deserved fruits that for the first time, the family economy could orient itself toward the acquisition of consumer goods, not just survival, and ethnic benefit societies could (and did) go out of business.[67]

How jarring it is, then, to confront the truth that these industrial workers were, in some sense, privileged members of society. Bowing to employer pressure in agriculture, service, and certain other sectors, Congress had excluded perhaps one-third of the wage-earning population from the protections of the Wagner Act, and in addition, Taft-Hartley's section 14B raised a major obstacle to union organization, especially in low-wage, "right to work" regions of the South and West.[68] In consequence, the proportion of workers enjoying union work rules, shop floor rights, and high pay scales (roughly a 20 percent differential) steadily declined with the shift from an industrial to a service economy, dropping below 20 percent in the 1970s.[69] Economists have located these poorer workers in a "secondary labor market" akin to the casual labor markets of the nineteenth century—low pay, high turnover, frequent unemployment, plus lots of part-time hiring to escape paying the benefits that normally kick in at a 40 hour week. At the bottom end, things shade over into the underground economy of hustling, petty crime, and prostitution. Although millions of poverty-stricken people

were a standing contradiction to the more secure workers, not to mention
the affluent middle classes, and whereas the War on Poverty began to rectify
this imbalance, business saw no bottom-line advantage in eradicating poverty and organized labor lacked the will.

It is no accident that a large proportion of the workers caught in this
maelstrom of poverty were women or minorities. Already on the down side
of male privilege and racism, these groups were destined to place dispropor-
tionate numbers on the lower rungs of the occupational ladder,[70] which, in
turn, could not fail to disturb both gender relations and the ladder of cultural prestige.

At long last, the gradual quantitative rise in women's labor force participation from 20 percent in 1900 to more than 50 percent in 1980 became
a qualitative change in the status of women in society at large. Pulled by
the attraction of white-collar jobs, pushed by the desire to get on the consumer gravy train, and released from some child-rearing by the return to
low birth rates after the postwar baby-boom, women made a historic leap
free from motherhood as their overriding, lifelong task.[71] The idea (derived
from nineteenth century socialists) that paid work was the precondition for
women's emancipation proved to be only one side of the coin. The other
side was the restructuring of reproduction, which permitted most women
to enter directly into the network of property relations, unmediated by family economy, a move that undermined antiquated patriarchal rationaliza-
tions for women's subordination ("a woman's place is in the home,"
etc.).

To the extent that women shifted their priorities from housework to paid
work, they ran up against contradictions not only in their continued double
burden of housework, but in unequal pay, discrimination, and sexual
harrassment. Although middle-class feminists like Betty Friedan sparked the
revival of the women's movement in the late 1960s, these structural contradictions forced the movement to address such issues as equal pay, which
women in the labor movement had been talking about for a century and
more.[72] The preconditions for a thorough challenge to male privilege had
finally been met.

A similar destabilization affected the ladder of cultural prestige. At first,
despite A. Philip Randolph, the Scotsboro Defense, and interracial CIO organizing, the parties to the Great Compromise deferred to that earlier racial
settlement of the 1890s that had produced North-South concurrence on Jim
Crow. However, it proved impossible to permit segregationists to remain
within the Great Compromise for two reasons: maintaining segregation was
no way to win over newly emerging African nations to the "free world";
and black migration to northern cities plus the industrialization of the South
raised the Afro-American proportion of the working class to more than one-
fifth. It became necessary to modify, if not repeal, the laws making blacks

second-class citizens. Recognizing that the black middle class had a vital stake in the civil rights struggles epitomized by Martin Luther King, the black working class played a role, too often overlooked, in making unions like the Amalgamated Clothing Workers and the UAW the most important rallying ground outside the black churches and civil rights organizations themselves.[73]

However, the fact was that the color line, in the main, ran outside the more privileged sectors of the working class, and many white workers intended to keep it that way. All the while de jure segregation was crumbling under the blows of the "second Reconstruction," de facto segregation among workers was increasing; Irish and other building tradesmen were restricting access; second-generation Slavs and Italians were rising to political influence by race-baiting; and white "ethnics" among the police too often appeared as an occupying army in the black ghetto.[74] Had corporatist compromise contained more room for public employment where private enterprise refused to go (as in inner-city housing), or had it launched a frontal attack on racism from the beginning (not a reluctantly tendered sheaf of civil rights laws), then the contradiction between white supremacy and black pride might not have climaxed in the riots of the 1960s.

International Relations

International relations, too, produced unforeseen contradictions in the postwar settlement. It is hard to overstate the impact of the U.S. rise to world power on the social order. Imperial tribute underwrote industrial truce in the form of both excess profits and cheap oil and other resource imports. Cold War McCarthyism set the outer limits for negotiation, not only by outlawing communism but by stigmatizing progressive ideas from whatever source. And as time went on, transnational corporations played a major role in creating the "Rust Belt," with all its dire consequences. That a subject of this significance should receive so little attention is the prime scandal of labor historiography. In place of scrupulous investigation, we are treated to ideological ax-grinding represented at opposite poles of the spectrum by Philip Taft's *Defending Freedom* and Ronald Radosh's *American Labor and U.S. Foreign Policy*. Three lines of analysis stand out in the literature on workers' role in international affairs—the ideology of anticommunism, nationalism, and imperialism.

The Ideology of Anticommunism

Just as a small cadre of "national security managers" conducted U.S. foreign relations, so a small AFL-CIO International Affairs Department, run out of Jay Lovestone's vest pocket, conducted the foreign policy of American workers. From the days of Gompers' battles with Debs at home and

Lenin abroad, anticommunism has contributed a cohesive world view and unswerving moral purpose. Anyone who so much as "temporizes with Bolshevism," said Gompers in 1919, committed "an unspeakable crime against civilization." Whether seen as "pure-and-simple union" federation or sophisticated "transnational institution," the AFL (later joined by the CIO) had no greater purpose than stopping communism.[75] In defense of this interpretation, not only was it easy to demonstrate that George Meany, at least, stood somewhere to the right of John Foster Dulles, but most of the key people making foreign policy had fought hard battles with Communists in their own unions, including David Dubinsky (Lovestone's political godfather), James Carey, and Walter Reuther. What is significant is not only that they (perhaps excepting Reuther) viewed the Soviet Union as a vast open shop employer and international communism as a monolithic conspiracy, but that this view justified subversion and deceit in the form of covert operations against leftist unions overseas, often in collusion with the CIA.[76]

Nationalism

Realists argue that just as balance-of-power politics determines overall U.S. foreign policy, so trade union leadership and prolabor politicians act on what they view as the national security interest of American workers. For people like Reuther and Hubert Humphrey, this was identical with the national interest. Although anticommunism was a potent force, national interest overrode anticommunist ideology; for example, during World War II, when CIO leaders embraced the Soviet ally, and during the late stages of the Vietnam War, if only for the Reuther brothers and a handful of other breakaway members of the AFL-CIO Executive Council. The significance of the Reuthers' stand is not only the rebuke to knee-jerk anticommunism but the presumption that mere citizens, and workers at that, should dare defy the state in defining the national interest.[77] In any case, world events such as the failure of U.S. intervention in Vietnam and Nixon's trip to China did much to undermine anticommunism as a world view among the rank and file.

Imperialism

Theories of imperialism contend that just as the contours of U.S. foreign policy follow to one degree or another the penetration of U.S. capital overseas, American workers hitched their interests to U.S. economic expansion. As the Marshall Plan was moved up to the CIO's #1 legislative priority in 1947, top officials were proclaiming labor's stake in international trade "because the United States is such a large exporter of the products of American labor and because our standard of living is, in part, dependent upon importing many commodities from countries abroad."[78] Responding to Soviet charges that the Marshall Plan was a cover for U.S. imperialism, the head of the Free Trade Union Committee, Matthew Woll, contended that U.S. policy "seeks to continue American prosperity and prevent an economic depression at home by promoting reconstruction and popular welfare abroad. This is not imperialism."[79]

Says who? The fact that western Europe, Canada, and Japan undoubtedly benefited from U.S. trade and aid does not mean that for a generation after World War II the United States did not benefit much more. Meanwhile, U.S. investments were piling up in Latin America and elsewhere in the Third World, doing more to divide the world between North and South than any other single influence. Just as political and economic historians have been forced to come to grips with imperialism, whether the "informal empire" of the Open Door or the "core-periphery" dichotomy of the "world system," so organized labor will have to address this question.[80]

Not to discount either anticommunism or nationalism, imperialism suggests answers to many puzzles. Why did U.S. labor leaders support British and French conservatives against the Soviets in Europe, while opposing these same conservatives in Asia, Suez, and Africa? Why did the CIO quit the World Federation of Trade Unions in a dispute with the Soviets over the Marshall Plan? Why did isolationists like Lewis lose influence to interventionists like Carey and Meany? And ultimately, why did the great bulk of ordinary workers give their support to U.S. interventions from Korea to Vietnam? The fact that American workers received an indirect material bounty from the rise of American capitalism to world supremacy is one piece of the puzzle. The attempt of "labor statesmen" to use the rapidly expanding imperial apparatus for their own power advantage is another.[81]

What specific chain of causation brought American workers into junior partnership with overseas expansion? Again, our method for determining causes is to identify the real historical alternatives by compressing time into a single "moment." Thus, to discover the alternative to anticommunism, we take 1941–1963 as a moment of contrast between the Grand Alliance and the Cold War. Just as the perpetuation of the Grand Alliance under United Nations auspices was the lost path of postwar relations, so international labor cooperation appears to have been a real alternative. Sidney Hillman, in particular, shared Roosevelt's vision of Big Three cooperation and bent every effort to bring U.S. unions into the World Federation of Trade Unions.[82] It bears asking to what extent the CIO was drawing on alternative working-class beliefs, such as a favorable attitude toward the Soviet Union's apparent success in escaping the ravages of the Depression. Indeed, were there echoes of pre-World War I pacifism in the neutrality laws, peace campaigns, and Good Neighbor policies of the 1930s?[83] It is necessary to explore such alternatives before assuming that the voice of Meany and Lovestone was the last word on the subject.

In summary, the story of organized labor's foreign policy is a tale of ironies full of tragic consequences. What does one make of AFL "voluntarism," given its record going back to World War I of open collaboration and secret collusion with the federal government? What became of the adversarial relationship with business when Meany sat down with corporate heads like W. R. Grace to promote capital investment in Latin America, Asia, and Africa through the American Institute for Free Labor Development (AIFLD) and its sister organizations? The sad truth is not only that multinational companies fared far better under Pax Americana than either American or foreign workers, but that AIFLD and the other ostensible representatives of workers' interests helped establish dictatorial and military regimes in Guatemala, Brazil, the Dominican Republic, to name a few, that became safe havens for runaway U.S. corporations.[84] Thus, by the 1970s it finally became clear that the consequences of job loss and deindustrialization were contradicting the very premise of AFL-CIO foreign policy that U.S. economic expansion underwrote jobs and prosperity for American workers. Imperial chickens were coming home to roost.

The Public Sector

As both a consequence and counterforce of the Great Compromise, the expanding public sector seemed to presage a new field of force characterized by public ownership and civil service bureaucrats as opposed to corporate ownership and profit-seeking managers. By 1970 total government purchases and transfer payments accounted for upwards of 35 percent of GNP, and federal military outlays alone amounted to 8 percent.[85] To be sure, in many cases private profit merely wore the mask of public interest, as in the military-industrial complex and government bonded indebtedness; so, too, were highways, airports, and other social overhead capital at the disposal of private enterprise. Nonetheless, the means of socialized production and reproduction did not march to the direct commands of the profit motive. In fact, they increasingly contradicted the very purpose of rationalizing the economy for which, in most cases, they had been created in the first place.

Military spending is a case in point. Pumping billions of dollars into the capital-intensive aerospace industry produced economic waste, while creating far fewer jobs than social services or other alternative outlets.[86] A second case is public employment itself; originally, the public sector sopped up the potential pool of workers unemployed by rising productivity in private manufacturing. But the higher employment levels rose for public school teachers and social security clerks, the fewer opportunities for investors to turn a profit on workers' labor. No wonder avid enterprisers, armed with reams of tax breaks, began competing with the post office, social security, medicare, child care, and so on.

A further contradiction between state intervention and big business issued from the very success of the welfare state in raising the "social wage." Not only was this expensive (taxes rose to around two-fifths of national income), but in reducing unemployment and setting high standards of living, the effect was to tilt market forces toward wage earners (or at least those fortunate enough to be in the "primary" labor market). From two sides, then, rising taxes and wages, business profits felt a squeeze from state intervention.[87] By the 1970s, the snake was swallowing its own tail.

THE COMPROMISE ABROGATED

By the 1970s the old equilibrium was so wracked by inner conflict that dominant groups began to question the governing system they had sustained over the past four decades. A multitude of destabilizing forces had arisen from below: the rising cost of both the "social wage" and negotiated wage and benefit packages; environmental, safety, and health regulations that restricted business; rising demands for nondiscriminatory treatment; and frustration in Cuba, Vietnam, and other Third World nations. In response, dominant interests resorted to concession bargaining, decertification elections, breaking the Professional Air Traffic Controllers Organization, industrial deregulation, capital flight, and similar measures that added up to an abrogation of the Great Compromise. At the same time, they moved to rescind affirmative action and reduce welfare as a means to check demands of women, blacks, and the poor for equal treatment. All this prompted once-comfortable labor leaders like Douglas Fraser of the UAW to talk of "class warfare" and inspired the National Organization for Women and the Urban League to join AFL-CIO head Lane Kirkland to mobilize Solidarity Day in September 1981, the largest mass demonstration of workers in American history.

Since this crisis of political will and ideas is still upon us, it is impossible to gauge the outcome. It is unclear whether the destiny of twentieth century American history lies along the path of progressive New Deal reform ("liberalism," to its friends, "corporate liberalism," to its enemies), or instead, in the hegemony of big business, with America's more affluent consumers occupying a privileged position at home and in the world at large.[88] Or, is there some as yet unrevealed model of state and society still to emerge from the contemporary crisis? Ten or twenty years down the road, it should be possible to discern clearly the real alternatives. Today, it is not.

In the meantime, there are some ominous suggestions in the arrival of the new conservatism in Washington of what, at least, one possibility would look like. First of all, a new class relation became apparent in the restructuring of capital around the transnational corporation and the redivision of labor on a global scale to create exotic hybrids like GM-Toyota and invidious competition between American and foreign workers. On one level, this would seem to render obsolete the nation-state, which nuclear weapons have already done on another. But, in fact, transnational corporations, the International Monetary Fund, and other international capitalist institutions have made good use of labor-repressive regimes around the world, and to a lesser degree, the accession of neoconservative Republicans marked a tilt toward repression in the United States.

Certainly, Reaganism (along with its counterparts in Britain and elsewhere) represented the first sign of a major breakthrough since the New Deal. Everything else along the way, including both the Great Society and Nixonomics, appear in retrospect to have been mere adjustments one way or the other in the terms of compromise. The New Right, ideological shock troops of the conservative movement, seemed intent not only on rescinding the New Deal but on repealing the gains won by the 1960s liberation movements, as well.[89] It would use the power of the state to enforce consent to its "family values" of women's subordination, sexual repression, and self-reliance. It not only resurrected the same values of the WASP minority of the 1920s but also the same methods once used to impose Americanization and Prohibition on European ethnics. The so-called Family Protection Act, school prayer, and the antiabortion amendments were not just political counterpunches to the Equal Rights Amendment, but an effort to restore the crumbling gender supports of the capitalist economy. Jessie Helms knew as well as any feminist-socialist scholar that as long as women's first duty was to husband and hearth, their social resources would be too meager to overcome their second-class status in the labor market.[90] Similarly, gutting affirmative action did not merely rekindle the fires of white prejudice but resharpened the competitive edge racism provided against blacks and Hispanics. Thus, the political logic of the New Right's cultural agenda harmonized at many points with the interests of U.S. corporations, particularly in the increasingly important service sector.

The same can be said of the culture of consumerism. Although the capital-intensive industrial corporations still turned a larger volume of profit than service firms, the latter employed a larger number of people, as we have seen, and tended to be more labor-intensive. Thus, twentieth century trends in restructuring capital and redividing labor made the struggles of telephone, hospital, retail, and similar workers of primary importance.[91] Given that profit remained the name of the game where everything from heart transplants to *est* weekends was a commodity, employers have often found in the culture of consumerism a powerful legitimating ideology, wherein employees were seen as "special interests" in conflict with the general interests of the consumer. Finally, the return to bellicose Cold War posturing vis-à-vis the Soviets and imperial bluster toward the Third World marked the effort to reestablish American world hegemony with a swaggering, macho style of militarized diplomacy.

To date, no alliance of subordinate groups has emerged to contest this emerging governing system. The reasons have to do not only with the evident disarray of popular forces but also with compromises forged in the earlier period. First of all, so long as organized labor lives off past attachments to the Cold War mentality, U.S. overseas investment, and the CIA, it will be unable to break through to a new conception of its political role. Notwithstanding the fact that the American worker, on balance, has long since lost an economic stake in spread-eagle expansionism, many top AFL-CIO leaders, nonetheless, continue to act as if making Central America safe for the United Fruit Company promoted well-being at home. This has become an albatross on the neck of the labor movement, particularly after "stagflation" and deindustrialization reduced once-powerful industrial unions to proverbial shadows of their former selves. At the same time, the 1960s liberation movements lost their momentum in the 1970s, as affirmative action got bogged down in bureaucratic red tape and the Equal Rights Amendment stalled in state legislatures. The inability of Civil Rights, Black Power, or Women's Liberation to maintain their momentum, let alone create a political alliance capable of governing, proves that without the workers movement, no significant realignment is possible.

It may be that instead of evolving toward a new, higher form of life, the body politic will merely get rigor mortis. However, a more egalitarian realignment cannot be ruled out. The very rise of Reaganism demonstrates the social weight of its opponents. The cuts in "entitlements" go to show that the "social wage" won by three generations of popular struggle had raised living standards significantly. The need to discipline workers at the point of production points to the importance of rights won in the workplace. Likewise, the backlash against women measures the importance of the historic step they took to leave the household.

When all is said and done, there is no escaping the question of struggle between hierarchal and egalitarian forces that drives the process of social transformation forward. Given that the twentieth century is socializing reproduction in the mass marketing of leisure activity, collectivized education, and state welfare, it is essential to emphasize the rise of service occupations, and especially the new women workers who made the transition from serving food, child rearing, and nursing in the home to performing these tasks under the auspices of a capitalist employer. The intersection of trade union traditions and women's preferred modes of organization will have a major bearing on whether the "new working class" is able to organize itself as well as (or better than) industrial workers did in the 1930s and 1940s. It also seems likely that a significant mobilization will not take place unless the new workers find a way of linking workplace issues to the aspirations of the poor and ethnic minorities for a better way of life. In the past that meant they drew on socialist, Jewish and Christian, and humanistic values, and no doubt, so it will be in the future.

A RETROSPECT ON SOCIETY AND THE STATE

Toward Equality

It is remarkable how well social hierarchy survived in the twentieth century in the face of egalitarian challenges and massive social change. The tides loosed against privilege in the democratic revolutions of the eighteenth century continued to rise in the twentieth. Not only did successive popular movements for higher living standards, women's rights, and civil rights beat upon private fortunes, male privilege, and white supremacy, but these were only the conscious expression of deeper trends pointing toward a more egalitarian social order. Interlocking changes in property and the family undermined inherited structures of authority. With the exception of rails, textiles, and banking, nineteenth century property ownership had been so deeply lodged in the family it makes sense to think in terms of family capitalism, where ownership of the firm or farm and authority within it converged on the paterfamilias. However, with the twentieth century, ownership of the major means of production shifted from private families to publically owned corporate securities. Similarly, control within the firm shifted from the family proprietor to top management. Indeed, in the Ford Motor Company and a few other cases, corporate boards fought to remove the family heir apparent so they could get on with their business.

These changes in property relations weakened a key structural underpinning of women's subordination; namely, the need of propertied families to control the sexuality of daughters and wives so as to ensure clarity of inheritance. And further, just as this basis for women's subordination was crumbling at the top of the social pyramid, so working-class families at the base were losing their patriarchal underpinnings as women bore and raised fewer children, and as a majority by 1980 went *Out to Work*.[92] Twentieth century demographics continued the nineteenth century trend toward fewer births (falling from over 30 per 1000 population in 1900 to less than 15 per 1000 in 1980) and smaller households (from 4.76 persons in 1900 to 3.14 in 1970).[93]

What was more, the period also witnessed the cession of so many family functions to schools, social agencies, and fast-food chains that it makes sense to speak of the "socialization of *re*production" as a long range consequence of the socialization of production in the Industrial Revolution. The relentless increase of adult women's labor force participation brought the proportion of working women to well over half the adult female population, confounding the old stereotypes of male breadwinner–female homemaker. Similarly, the separation of sexuality from procreation by means of birth control technology and, to a lesser extent, cultural acceptance of extramarital sex and homosexuality challenged the received double standard.[94] The sum of these complex forces was a challenge to women's status as the domestic servant of her husband. Thus, women's domesticity, which had once rested on family ownership in the propertied classes and a functional division of labor in the laboring classes, no longer corresponded to the main lines of social reality.

As Joan Kelly pointed out in "The Social Relation of the Sexes," these changes also confounded established categories of social analysis.[95] Domestic life, socialization of the young, and "women's sphere" were once thought to cohabit the same social space but were increasingly torn asunder as socialization and even procreation took place in schools and hospitals, and as women took up paid positions in the "men's sphere" of production and public affairs. Although Kelly's proposed dichotomy of public-private to supplant production-reproduction is subject to criticism, her insistence upon linking changes in gender to changes in class relations and upon locating analysis of social hierarchy firmly within the stream of history is well taken.

Alongside these earthshaking changes in property and family were equally seismic changes in productive technology and the division of labor. In this regard, nothing is more significant than the mass production technology and complex division of labor that sent productivity soaring. Between 1900 and 1950, the Gross National Product per capita rose almost two and a half times. Productivity in manufacturing could increase by as much as 72 percent in the single decade of the 1920s. Gains in agriculture were even more staggering—four farmers grew enough at the start of the century to feed themselves and six others; by 1980 it took only *four-tenths* of a farmer to feed the same number![96] Surely, these figures display the potential for mass abundance.

Such remarkable feats were made possible by the high-speed technology and fast-paced labor epitomized by the automobile assembly line, accompanied by a new social division of labor that saw service jobs come to dominate the occupational structure. Using the broadest occupational categories, in 1900 agriculture accounted for 38 percent of the gainfully employed, "industry" 37 percent (including mining, manufacturing, construction, transportation, and utilities), and 25 percent were in "service" (including service, retailing, and government). Moving like subterranean tectonic plates, agriculture dropped down to 4 percent by 1980, industry to 33 percent, and service rose to an astounding 63 percent.[97]

Intertwined with the occupational shift away from agriculture and the

decline of the man cum protector, racial segregation (at least de jure) lost
its hold as blacks left the patriarchal culture of southern sharecropping for
the more individualist culture of northern industry. Thus, some of the most
powerful forces of the twentieth century pointed toward a flattening of the
social pyramid.

Securing Hierarchy

However, it is abundantly clear that egalitarian trends did not dominate
twentieth century development. Statistical measures of inequality show remarkable stability throughout the century. For example, the share of national wealth and income going to the top decile appears to have declined
only slightly in the middle decades from the plateau reached well before the
1920s, only to increase slightly again in the 1970s.[98] Women's income as
a share of men's varied within a range of half to two-thirds, while rates of
poverty, unemployment, and other indices of economic misery stood stub-
bornly twice as high for blacks as for whites.

Although it is true that a new social hierarchy was a necessary precondition for new directions in capitalist development, we should be careful in
speaking about it as a "social structure of accumulation," in the phrase pro-
ferred by the authors of Segmented Work, Divided Workers.[99] The causal
links between the profit motive and a given social order are not reduceable,
one to the other. Obviously, capitalists find ways to make money in open,
democratic regimes as well as in repressive, authoritarian ones. What is
needed is a sense of dialectical causation in which family organization, the
mode of reproduction, race relations, and other elements of the social order
shape the path of accumulation even as they, in turn, are shaped by it.

Probing for new markets, merchandisers found shrinking nuclear families, status ambiguity, and the individualist ethos decidedly vulnerable to
commercial blandishment. As they moved in on family life, leisure, and recreation to sell the new commodities of fast food, packaged entertainment,
and sports events, eventually, Sears, AT&T, and McDonalds took their
places beside Exxon, U.S. Steel, and Mellon Bank among the superstars in
the Fortune 500 galaxy of giant enterprise.[100]

Barring ruthless enforcement of the antitrust statutes or some yet more
fundamental political resistance, it seems inevitable that productive wealth
would become ever more concentrated in oligopolistic corporations. By the
1920s, a majority of manufacturing employees worked in firms worth over
$1 million; the share of manufacturing output controlled by the 200 largest
firms rose steadily to 43 percent by 1970.[101] Whatever tendency toward
equality existed in socialized production and reproduction, the emergence
of Croesuslike corporations saw to it that the distribution of wealth would
remain decidedly uneven. Studies by Lampmann and others show that

whereas homes and other consumer durables may have become distributed more widely in the twentieth century than ever before, the richest 1 percent hold upward of three-quarters of corporate stock and similar forms of capital.[102] Works as different as Chandler's *The Visible Hand* and Baran and Sweezy's *Monopoly Capital* make clear that nothing is more important to the creation of the new nexus of inequality than accumulation of productive property in the hands of private corporations.[103]

Closely tied to the corporate form of ownership, managerial authority constituted another segment of the new nexus. As David Montgomery's studies on *Workers' Control* make clear, it is a mistake to take management control over production for granted, since it had to be imposed against workers' resistance. Contrary to the notion that corporate bureaucracy grew in direct response to the expanding scale of production, Harry Braverman's *Labor and Monopoly Capital* shows it grew in order to take control of the labor process away from the shop floor. What was more, the legions of mostly women workers who came into the front office themselves became the object of a new round of management control.[104] In assessing the implications of these changes for class relations, it is clear that the paternalist management styles of nineteenth century bosses would not do in the world of personnel relations, the Hawthorne effect, or the time-study man. But it remains for historians to clarify how class relations at the workplace evolved new mechanisms of time, work-discipline, and resistance, particularly in the rising service industries.

With respect to gender inequality, analysis of social transformation offers escape from certain theoretical straight jackets. The concept of patriarchy as a timeless set of gender relations is a case in point. In the writing that followed in the wake of Kate Millett's *Sexual Politics*, patriarchy appears as an almost immutable fact of human nature, changeless over the centuries from Athena's birth out of Zeus' head to D.H. Lawrence's phallic worship. Although French poststructuralist philosophy rarely percolates through to American history, it, too, offers a view of patriarchy as deeply ingrained from birth. Indeed, followers of Jacques Lacan seem to argue that language is destiny, or at least that the language of sexual identity structures female subordination into the deepest recesses of the mind.[105] It scarcely needs saying that these notions of "cultural feminism" and structural linguistics are methods for analyzing changeless genetic replication not social transformation. Lacking a sense of historical dialectics, they are the means to negate not write history.

Theories of capitalist patriarchy are not entirely successful in attempting to break this impasse. To be sure, fruitful results have emerged from studies of job segregation by sex, and certainly, the consignment of women to jobs low on the scale of pay and power provides a vital clue to the persistence of all types of inequality, not just gender. Job segregation, the "feminization of poverty," and the "double burden" on working wives all help explain why neither the vast increase in white-collar jobs nor the entrance of women into paid labor proved as liberating as expected for either workers or women.[106] All the same, the capitalism-patriarchy framework, like other dual-systems analysis (Gemeinschaft-Gesellschaft; traditional-modern) fails to grasp the dialectical unity of the whole social process. (The same is true, incidentally, of mechanical applications of the trichotomy sex-class-ethnicity.) If patriarchy is to have any meaning, it must have a history, no less than capitalism. Just as the twentieth century has seen a shift from the capitalism of the competitive family firm to the oligopolistic corporation, so, too, has the rule of the father through the family lineage given way to other forms of male privilege. Indeed, it might do for the twentieth century to substitute the term *andrarchy*; that is, a generalized male privilege, for the concept of patriarchy.

To summarize, we have seen the evolution of a new field of force in which corporate accumulation and managerial authority supplanted family capitalism, while "andrarchy" supplanted patriarchy, and new forms of racial and cultural rank arose. We do not suppose, however, that the transformation in social hierarchy proceeded automatically without the influence of the state. Given the contradictions built into the process of social transformation between dominant and subordinate groups, in one aspect, and old and new hierarchies, in another, it was necessary for the state, a seemingly "outside" force, to arbitrate these disputes.

Theories of the State

It is important to recognize that the state itself was changing. Where the nineteenth century liberal state had relied on parties and police for mediation and repression, twentieth century politics generated new bureaucratic mediations (regulatory agencies, Women's Bureau, National Labor Relations Board, etc.) and new forms of coercion (Federal Bureau of Investigation, Red Scare, Taft-Hartley Act, etc.). As a result of these accretions, government at all levels came to employ almost one-fifth of the work force by 1980 and, in addition, through military purchases and transfer payments, accounted for upwards of 35 percent of GNP.[107] A system of this magnitude (which, incidentally, compares with European states) could not fail to affect the balance of social forces in profound ways. What is needed, then, is a theory that approaches the state as both the product of social forces and the enforcer of an uneven balance among them.

Probably the greatest influence on (certainly the "old") labor history was the pluralist view of politics as a Madisonian battleground in which rival interest groups—labor, capital, small business, farmers, and so on—competed for the favor of what was essentially a neutral coercive apparatus representing the public interest. Through the towering influence of John Commons and Selig Perlman's *Theory of the Labor Movement*, or more distantly, through pluralist analysis like Grant McConnell's *Private Power and American Democracy*, two generations of labor historians learned to think of labor as an interest group that had spurned socialists and other intellectual suitors to go in for pure-and-simple collective bargaining, supplemented by Gompers's nonpartisan politics of "reward your friends and punish your enemies."[108]

However, where Commons and Perlman had been concerned with the role of labor in society at large, their followers increasingly narrowed the range of concern to a catalogue of unions, strikes, parties, and elections. With David Brody as the only major exception, increasingly absent was serious investigation of the position of workers in the balance of forces in society at large and in the international arena. This was probably true for two reasons: first, the existing balance had come to be accepted as permanent; and second, a series of substitutions took place, in which the AFL-CIO substituted for the working class, and Gompers or Meany substituted for organized labor. By the late 1960s, "Whig" historians of the labor movement had led their subject into an intellectual cul de sac.[109]

In a head-on challenge to pluralist assumptions, "corporate liberal" writers denied that organized labor had ever so much as served as an adversary of business. Heavily influenced by the elite theory of C. Wright Mills, and more distantly by Veblen, they saw most unions as willing collaborators of the liberal wing of the corporate establishment in setting up a tripartite system of business-labor-government corporation, which, in the end, directly served capitalist interests. Gabriel Kolko propounded the concept of "political capitalism" and went so far as to regard workers and their organizations as essentially irrelevant to the making of American history. Little wonder that apart from James Weinstein's *Decline of Socialism in America*, as well as Ronald Radosh's *American Labor and United States Foreign Policy*, this group produced little in the way of labor history. Expressing a parallel current in the Marxist tradition, Ralph Miliband's *State in Capitalist Society* took pluralism to task for failing to credit the hierarchical character of society in which groups struggle for power and instead argued that the dominant economic class was also the political ruling class.[110]

Veering away from these ideas of the state as the willing instrument of big business interests, theorists of "corporatism" emphasized the role of the state itself in constituting ruling institutions out of the more or less organized producer groups in society; notably, labor and capital. A concept that changes color quicker than a chameleon, corporatism has been used to describe everything from Mussolini's Italy to Roosevelt's America, with Social Democratic Sweden and Labourist Britain in between. In all fairness, certain theorists have imparted coherence to the corporatist idea by identifying different paths by which nation-states have integrated their main socio-economic groups in a ruling system that accedes to the welfare needs of working classes, while preserving the dominance of capitalist classes. Particularly as the old ghost of "American exceptionalism" fades into the night, it can be expected that corporatist theory, adjusted for the liberal democratic context of American politics, will begin to make its influence felt.[111]

Meanwhile, the combined effect of the elite and Marxist assaults on pluralism knocked the pins from under the "old" labor history, with the result that historians who took the field in the 1970s wrote in varying degrees of revolt against Commons's labor economics and consensus historiography. Since this "new" labor history prided itself on the study of working people, not just their organizations, the focus of attention shifted, not surprisingly, from labor leaders to rank-and-file movements. The anarcho-syndicalist bent of Jeremy Brecher's *Strike!* and the preference for rank-and-file insurgency over established bargaining rituals in James Green's *World of the Worker* probably owed more to the activism of the 1960s than the ideas of Rosa Luxembourg or C. L. R. James, but there is no doubt about the inspiration of Thompson's *Making of the English Working Class*.[112] In the American context, Thompson's socialist humanism (or cultural Marxism) usually became "history from the bottom up," long on the recovery of forgotten stirrings of social protest but short on analysis of how that is translated into real power. It was as if working people were forever consigned to be political outcasts, sporadically and spontaneously revolting against their oppression but unable to change it. In these accounts the state often loomed as a Janus-faced coercive-cooptive apparatus that broke strikes and jailed dissenters, while handing over pallid reform imitations of radical ideas. (It should be noted in passing that neither liberal pluralism nor the New Left is politically neutral; a self-satisfied apology for the status quo like Ozanne's *Century of Industrial Relations* has no greater claim on truth than an impatient condemnation like Brecher's *Strike!*)

This antiauthoritarian inclination eventually attached itself to structuralist theory and surfaced with the appropriate invocation of Poulantzas in *Labor's War At Home*, by Nelson Lichtenstein.[113] In the direct opposite of Joel Seidman's *American Labor from Defense to Reconversion*, a paen to post-Wagner Act unionism, the structuralist state as rendered by Lichtenstein is a Mephistopheles enticing CIO leaders into a wartime "no-strike pact" that enhanced their power at the expense of emerging rank-and-file militancy. Also influenced by structuralism, Fred Block argues in "The Ruling Class Does Not Rule" that the state can intervene to transform capitalism, even over the obstreperous protests of at least some of the capitalist elite who would vainly try to keep things as they are. This convenient division of labor between capitalists and state managers makes possible economic rationalization via state reform.[114]

Indeed, by structuralist lights, the federal government did extremely well in performing one of its main functions, which is to thwart the development of a revolutionary working class by ameliorating its condition and dividing its ranks. Its other main function is to assist in the process of capital accumulation both by underwriting the preconditions of capitalist social relations and, as outlined in James O'Conner's *Fiscal Crisis of the State*, performing those tasks of business regulation, business-cycle modulation, education, research and development, and so on that monopoly capital requires but refuses to undertake itself.[115] In other words, since the state is an expression of the logic of capital, there is no room for social struggle within it. If so, what is the point of studying (or practicing) real politics?

Criticizing these functionalist assumptions, realists argue that the state is not merely "autonomous" from the influence of the dominant class, it is in a sphere unto itself. In a world of Hobbesian Leviathans, the highest law is not to serve the interests of the dominant class, but self-preservation of the nation-state. Training realist guns upon neo-Marxist theories of the state in the context of the New Deal, Theda Skocpol blasts corporate liberalism for overestimating the enlightened class consciousness of rather selfish big businessmen under the NRA, while underestimating the prolabor content of the Wagner Act. At the same time, she targets structuralism for overlooking New Deal failures in restoring economic growth and unexpected successes in helping to organize the working class. In the end, she attempts to bridge realist and neo-Marxist ideas by locating power politics in concrete historical circumstances and social systems, as she did for France, Russia, and China in *States and Social Revolutions*.[116] It should be pointed out that this marriage is not normally sanctioned in realist circles, which tend to view statecraft as the embodiment of order and reason, not social oppression or even social forces of any kind.[117] So, apart from mavericks like Skocpol and Barrington Moore, the realist mainstream has a very limited amount to contribute to our project.

If our goal is a comprehensive understanding of workers, capital, and the state in the twentieth century no one is more relevant than Antonio Gramsci. Adapting historical materialism to the modern democratic state, Gramsci portrays social groups engaged in a "war of position," as opposed to the "war of movement" for quick seizure of power that characterizes authoritarian systems. The life of the state is seen as "a continuous process of formation and superseding of unstable equilibria . . . between the interests of the fundamental group and those of subordinate groups—equilibria in which the interests of the dominant group prevail, but only up to a certain point, i.e. stopping short of narrowly corporate economic interests."[118]

However, if Gramsci's analysis of "relations of force" is to be employed, care must be taken not to reduce it to notions of "ideological hegemony" or "cultural hegemony." To be sure, he emphasized the "educative" role of the state in winning legitimacy for a given social order, but he never forgot either the covert coercions of economic compulsion or the overt coercion of military force, "which from time to time is directly decisive."[119]

What the foregoing points amount to, then, is a series of rejoinders—to pluralists, who see politics as social warfare in disguise, but do not recognize the disguise as that of a hierarchical system of class and other privileges; to elitists and structuralists, who see politics as a contest that is over before it starts and do not recognize that state structures are also a terrain of class and other struggles whose outcome is determined, but not predetermined; to realists, who see politics as a more or less self-enclosed game of strategy and will, but who are reluctant to recognize that the stakes ultimately come down to not just which politicians but which social groups and systems win or lose. At least, so it seems to be in twentieth century America.

CONCLUSION

This essay has argued the following points. First, the maturation of industrial capitalism in the early part of the century created an industrial working class of preponderant social weight among the American people, and so long as it remained a political pariah, there remained an unresolved tension in American politics that could be overridden only by force, whether *force majeure* (strike breaking, vigilantism, injunctions) or "enforced consent" (suppression of radicals, Red Scare, KKK-style intimidation, Prohibition), and that, furthermore, allowed economic contradictions to ripen fully, making the New Era an unintended victim of its own excess.

Second, in the ensuing rebalancing of social forces, that same industrial working class moved toward internal solidarity while simultaneously attracting fragments of other lower-class groups and numerous middle-class elements to its general point of view, which in the context of big business' temporary loss of esteem made it expedient for pragmatic political leaders like Roosevelt and Wagner to improvise new institutional arrangements, such as banking reform, NLRB, and the social security system that recognized the corporate existence and needs of the working class (i.e., gave it privileged status), while at the same time, benefited other popular groups and finally rationalized capitalism along countercyclical lines. This was the basis for a long-term political settlement that lasted until the period of the Vietnam War, whereupon hidden problems broke to the surface in ghetto rebellions, antiwar protest, women's liberation, deindustrialization, and the painful consequences of corporate investment overseas.

Three, finally, the essay has argued that in the inevitable breakdown of corporatist compromise, new balances became possible—either "enforced consent" to the repressive moral code of a cultural minority, plus military force abroad to ensure that the United States and the economic interests that dominate its economy will "prevail" against friend and foe alike; or a coalition of popular forces in which the new working class with its large service and female components would play the leading role and would seek a more rational balance in international affairs, guided by the overriding self-interest of peace in the nuclear age; or some other as yet undetermined arrangement of forces. Intellect requires a pessimistic assessment of the outcome; will, on the other hand, inclines toward the optimism of Joe Hill as he faced the firing-squad: "Don't mourn. Organize!"

NOTES

Acknowledgments: I wish to thank Fred Block, David Brody, Alice Kessler-Harris, and the participants in the Northern Illinois University Symposium "The Future of American Labor History," especially Eric Hobsbawm, for their helpful criticism.

1. Recent works that take the crisis of contemporary labor as a point of departure include Stanley Aronowitz, *Working Class Hero* (New York, 1983); and Marianne Debouzy, *Travail et travailleurs aux Etats-Unis* (Paris, 1984). A comparable perspective for England is offered by Eric Hobsbawm, *The Forward March of Labour Halted?* (London, 1981).

2. Gerald Feldman, *Army, Industry, and Labor in Germany, 1914–1918* (Princeton, NJ, 1966); David Abraham, *The Collapse of the Weimar Republic* (Princeton, NJ, 1981); Charles Maier, *Recasting Bourgeois Europe* (Princeton, NJ, 1975); Keith Middlemas, *Politics in Industrial Society* (London, 1979).

3. E. H. Carr, *What Is History?* rev. ed. (New York, 1967), pp. 34–35.

4. E. P. Thompson, "Eighteenth-Century English Society; Class Struggle without Class?" *Social History* 3, no. 2: 151–52. Since Thompson employed the *field of force* metaphor strictly in regard to eighteenth century English society, I hereby absolve him of any blame that may attach itself to the use of the notion for twentieth century America.

5. The leading work on this period is David Montgomery, *The Fall of the House of Labor: The Workplace, the State, and American Labor Activism, 1865–1925* (New York, 1987); employment figures are based on the author's calculations from *Historical Statistics of the United States, Colonial Times to 1957* (Washington, DC, 1960), pp. 74–78; Harry N. Scheiber et al., *American Economic History* (New York, 1976), pp. 448–49; Stanley Lebergott, *Manpower in Economic Growth* (New York, 1964), p. 510.

6. David Brody, *Steelworkers in America: The Nonunion Era* [1960] (New York, 1969); David Montgomery, *Workers' Control in America* (Cambridge, 1979).

7. Martin Sklar, *The Corporate Reconstruction of American Capitalism, 1890–1916* (Cambridge, 1988); James Holt, "Trade Unionism in the British and U.S. Steel Industries, 1890–1914: A Comparative Study," *Labor History* 18 (Winter 1977): 5–35.

8. Stuart Ewen, *Captains of Consciousness* (New York, 1976).

9. Steve Meyer, *The Five Dollar Day: Labor, Management and Social Control in the Ford Motor Company* (Albany, NY, 1981); Robert Hoxie, *Scientific Management and Labor* [1915] (New York, 1966), pp. 15–17.

10. Brody, *Steelworkers*, p. 48.

11. Peter Shergold, *Working Class Life: The "American Standard" in Comparative Perspective, 1899–1913* (Pittsburgh, 1982), pp. 207–30, demonstrates through careful statistical procedures that common laborers in Pittsburgh were no better off than their counterparts in Birmingham, England, although at the top of the pay scale more Americans partook of Sombart's "shoals of roast beef and apple pie."

12. Alexander Keyssar, *Out of Work: The First Century of Unemployment in Massachusetts* (Cambridge, 1986); Michael Nash, *Conflict and Accommodation: Coal Miners, Steel Workers, and Socialism, 1890–1920* (Westport, CT, 1982), p. 106.

13. Robert Hunter, *Poverty* (New York, 1904); Crystal Eastman, *Work Accidents and the Law* (New York, 1960). Saposs conducted two sets of interviews probing the Americanization of immigrant workers: (1) rank and file industrial workers, (2) trade union leaders. They are what is probably the best single source on immigrant workers' mood 1919–1921. The theme of poverty too often slides into the background in the (no longer) "new" social history.

14. *Muller* vs. *Oregon* (1908); Josephine Goldmark, *Fatigue and Efficiency* (New York, 1913).

15. Stuart Brandes, *American Welfare Capitalism, 1880–1940* (Chicago, 1976).

16. Margaret Byington, *Homestead* (New York, 1910); Edith Abbott, *Women in Industry* (New York, 1910).

17. Tamara Hareven, *Family Time: Industrial Time* (Cambridge, MA, 1982); the quote is from Stacia Treski interview, John Bodner, *Worker's World* (Baltimore, 1982), p. 22.

18. Charlotte Perkins Gilman, *Women and Economics* (Boston, 1898); among the several works that emphasize family values is Virginia Yans-McLaughlin, *Family and Community: Italian Immigrants in Buffalo, 1880–1930* (Urbana, IL, 1982).

19. Maureen Greenwald, *Women, War, and Work* (Westport, CT, 1980); Leslie Tentler, *Wage Earning Women* (New York, 1979); David Katzman, *Seven Days a Week: Women and Domestic Service in Industrializing America* (New York, 1978).

20. Alice Kessler-Harris, *Out to Work: A History of Wage-Earning Women in the United States* (New York, 1982), Chapter 7; Heidi Hartmann, "Capitalism, Patriarchy, and Job Segregation by Sex," *Signs* 1, no. 3, part 2 (Spring 1976): 137–69.

21. Rosalyn Baxandall et al., *America's Working Women* (New York, 1976), p. 405, table.

22. The classic study is W. I. Thomas and F. Znaniecki, *The Polish Peasant in Europe and America*, 2 vols. (New York, 1918).

23. Hareven, *Family Time*; Carol Stack, *All Our Kin* (New York, 1979).

24. Generally speaking, the framework of mobility analysis has obscured the question of ethnic cultural adaptation to the material environment, for example, in Josef Barton, *Peasants and Strangers* (Cambridge, MA, 1975). By contrast, the framework of immigrant adaptation to industry illuminates such studies as John Bodnar, *Immigration and Industrialization* (Pittsburgh, 1977), and Victor Greene, *The Slavic Community on Strike* (Notre Dame, IN, 1968).

25. Stephan Steinberg, *The Ethnic Myth* (New York, 1974); John Higham, *Strangers in the Land* (New York, 1963).

26. Rudolph Vecoli, "Anthony Capraro and the Lawrence Strike of 1919," in G. E. Pozzetta, ed., *Pane E Lavoro* (Ontario, 1980); John Bukowcyzk, "The Transformation of Working Class Ethnicity: Corporate Control, Americanization, and the Polish Immigrant Middle Class in Bayonne, 1915–25," *Labor History* 25 (Winter 1984): 53–82.

27. Gerd Korman, *Industrialization, Immigrants, and Americanization* (Madison, WI, 1967); William Tuttle, *Race Riot: Chicago in the Red Summer of 1919* (New York, 1970). Because of their sensitive treatment of the complexities of class and ethnic factors, these works attain significance beyond their subject matter proper.

28. The percentage is from William Miller, ed., *Men in Business* (New York, 1952), p. 199, table.

29. This period cries out for a new synthetic monograph; in the meantime, understanding can be gleaned from Robert Zeiger, *Republicans and Labor 1919–29* (Lexington, KY, 1969); William Preston, *Aliens and Dissenters* (Cambridge, MA, 1963); David Montgomery, "Liberty and Union: Workers and Government in America 1900–1940," in *Essays from the Lowell Conference on Industrial History 1980 and 1981* (Lowell, MA, 1981); Montgomery, *Workers Control*; Edwin Witte, *The Government in Labor Disputes* (New York, 1932); Interchurch World Movement, *Report on the Steel Strike of 1919* (New York, 1920).

30. Samuel Gompers, *Seventy Years of Life and Labor* (New York, 1925).

31. Selig Perlman, *A Theory of the Labor Movement* (New York, 1928).

32. Higham, *Strangers*, pp. 305–306, 321–22; Brody, *Steelworkers*, pp. 251–61; Kessler-Harris, *Out to Work*, pp. 201–205; Martha May, "The Historical Problem of the Family Wage: The Ford Motor Company and the Five Dollar Day," *Feminist Studies* 8 (Summer 1982): 399–424.

33. An innovative approach to socialism is Mari Jo Buhle, *Women and American Socialism, 1870–1920* (Urbana, IL, 1983); the leading work on the Wobblies is Melvyn Dubofsky, *We Shall Be All: A History of the I.W.W.* (New York, 1969); Nathan Fine, *Farmer and Labor Parties in the U.S.* (New York, 1928).

34. An example of the large literature on ethnic politics is John Allswang, *A House for All Peoples* (New York, 1978).

35. *Lochner* vs. *New York* (1905); *Hammer* vs. *Dagenhart* (1918).

36. Nick Salvatore, *Eugene V. Debs: Citizen and Socialist* (Urbana, IL, 1982).

37. Graham Adams, *The Age of Industrial Violence 1910–15* (New York, 1966), examines the Industrial Relations Commission.

38. Not even the most famous labor victory through mediation, Judge Alschuler's award of the eight-hour wage scale to packinghouse workers, included bargaining rights. The Supreme Court upheld the "yellow-dog" contract in *Hitchman Coal Company* vs. *Mitchell* (1917). No wonder labor law loomed so large among "liberal" labor historians; since liberalism had historically been used against them, it was important to carve out a place for collective bargaining in American jurisprudence.

39. Preston, *Aliens,* passim; Robert K. Murray, *Red Scare: A Study in National Hysteria* (New York, 1955).

40. For an intellectual history of Protestant crusaders, see Paul Boyer, *Urban Masses and Moral Order in America, 1820–1920* (Cambridge, MA, 1978).

41. Documentary material can be found at the Immigration History Research Center and the Balch Institute; useful secondary literature includes Edwin Fenton, "Immigrants and Unions" (diss., Harvard University, 1957) for Italians; Irving Howe, *World of Our Fathers* (New York, 1976) for Jews; and Carl Ross, *The Finn Factor* (New York Mills, MN, 1977) for Finns.

42. Important primary material bearing on state action includes the voluminous files of the FBI and Military Intelligence at the National Archives; Kate Claghorn, *The Immigrant's Day in Court* (New York, 1969; orig. 1923); Constantine Panunzio, *The Deportation Cases of 1919–1920* (New York, 1921).

43. Louis Hartz, *The Liberal Tradition in America* (New York, 1955), is the prime example. To list all the works keyed to the concept of "absences" in American working-class historiography would be a major bibliographical task in itself; suffice it to say that exits from the absence fallacy are identified in Jean Heffer and Jeanine Rovet, eds., *Why Is There No Socialism in the United States?* (Paris, 1988). At the same time, little is to be gained by trying to squeeze republican producer ideology into the mold of European class consciousness, as attempted by Sean Wilentz, "Against Exceptionalism," *International Labor and Working Class History* (Spring 1984).

44. Jurgen Kocka, *White Collar Workers in America* (London, 1980), trans. Maura Kealey.

45. Among the best treatments of working-class socialism in this period is J. H. M. Laslett, *Labor and the Left* (New York, 1970).

46. Stanley Mathewson, *Restriction of Output among Unorganized Workers* (New York, 1931); J. M. Budish and George Soule, *The New Unionism in the Clothing Industry* (New York, 1920); James Weinstein, *The Decline of Socialism in America* (New York, 1967); given the remarkable fact that no major treatment of third party efforts 1919–1924 has appeared in over half a century, Nathan Fine, *Labor and Farmer Parties in the United States, 1828–1928* (New York, 1928) stands up rather well; Mary Beard, *The American Labor Movement* [1920] (New York, 1931), p. 9.

47. John Dewey, *The Nation* (July 27, 1932).

48. Melvyn Dubofsky has cautioned against easy assumptions of 1930s militancy in "Not So 'Turbulent Years': Another Look at the American 1930s" *Amerikastudian* 24 (1980).

49. Lois Scharf, *To Work and to Wed: Female Employment, Feminism, and the Great Depression* (Westport, CT, 1980); Winifred Wandersee, *Women's Work and Family Values: 1920–1940* (Cambridge, MA, 1981); women reformers regained influence lost in the 1920s, as shown by Susan Ware, *Beyond Suffrage: Women in the New Deal* (Cambridge, MA, 1981).

50. Walter Galenson, *The CIO Challenge to the AFL* (Cambridge, MA, 1960); Art Preis, *Labor's Giant Step* (New York, 1972); Sidney Fine, *Sit-Down* (New York, 1969); Ronald Schatz, *The Electrical Workers* (Urbana, IL, 1983); Irving Bernstein, *The Turbulent Years* (New York, 1970).

51. Contrast Bernstein, *Turbulent Years*, with James Green, *World of the Worker* (New York, 1980), Chapter 5.

52. See Kocka, *White Collar Workers*.

53. August Meier and Elliott Rudwick, *Black Detroit and the Rise of the UAW* (Oxford, 1979). See Bodnar, *Worker's World* for an emphasis on conservative family values and Peter Freidlander, *The Emergence of a UAW Local* (Pittsburgh, 1975) for an emphasis on second-generation radicalism.

54. A recent addition to the large literature on these subjects is Alan Brinkley, *Voices of Protest: Huey Long, Father Coughlin, and the Great Depression* (New York, 1982). The role of Communists, Socialists, and others on the Left was absolutely essential, not only in helping launch the CIO but in creating a political climate in which workers' needs became paramount, a fact that torrents of anticommunist writing has not been able to wash out. See Schatz, *Electrical Workers*; Alice Lynd and Staughton Lynd, *Rank and File* (Boston, 1973); Maurice Isserman, *Which Side Were You On?* (Middletown, CT, 1982); Roger Keeran, *The Communist Party and the Auto Workers Unions* (Bloomington, IN, 1980).

55. Howell Harris, *The Right to Manage* (Madison, WI, 1982), makes a convincing case that the preponderance of business opinion did not run in "corporate liberal" channels but in those of "realists" or "brass hat" militant managers.

56. Walter Dean Burnham, *Critical Elections and the Mainsprings of American Politics* (New York, 1970).

57. William Leuchtenberg's pluralist rendering of these events, *F.D.R. and the New Deal* (New York, 1963), remains the best narrative on the politics of the 1930s. For two views of the Wagner Act, see Karl Klare, "Judicial Deradicalization of the Wagner Act," *Minnesota Law Review* 62 (March 1978): 265–41; Christopher Tomlins, *The State and the Unions: Labor Relations, Law, and the Organized Labor Movement in America, 1880–1960* (Cambridge, 1985), pp. 132–47; 230–43. Although Klare and Tomlins disagree on the original character of the act itself, they concur that it became the basis for a legalistic taming of collective bargaining.

58. Nelson Lichtenstein, *Labor's War at Home: The CIO in World War II* (Cambridge, 1982).

59. Montgomery, *Workers' Control*, p. 165.

60. The suggestion was made by Summer Slichter, "Are We Becoming a

'Laboristic' State?" *New York Times Magazine* (May 16, 1948), quoted in David Brody, *Workers in Industrial America*, p. 211.

61. Paul O. Koistinen, *The Military Industrial Complex: A Historical Perspective* (New York, 1980).

62. For example, William Serrin, *The Company and the Union* (New York, 1973).

63. Seidman, *American Labor*, p. vii; see also R. Alton Lee, *Truman and Taft-Hartley* (Lexington, 1966); Lichtenstein, *Labor's War at Home* emphasizes ossification.

64. Schatz, *Electrical Workers*, contains a valuable discussion of Catholic corporatism derived from Leo XIII's *Rerum Novarum*. For a clear contemporary statement of social democratic corporatism, see Clint Golden and Harold Ruttenberg, *The Dynamics of Industrial Democracy* (New York, 1942).

65. C. W. Mills, *New Men of Power*; Meany, speech to Bond Club, New York, March 19, 1964, quoted in A. Robinson, *George Meany and His Times* (New York, 1981).

66. Irving Siegel and Edgar Weinberg, *Labor-Management Cooperation* (Kalamazoo, MI, 1982); Gordon et al., *Segmented Work, Divided Workers* (Cambridge, 1982), pp. 22–26.

67. For the period after about 1948, the typewriters of labor historians have fallen mysteriously silent, forcing one to scrounge among economists, sociologists, and journalists. A notable exception is David Brody, *Workers in Industrial America* (New York, 1982).

68. Lee, *Truman and Taft-Hartley*.

69. Much pertinent data on recent trends in trade unionism can be found in Richard Freeman and James Medoff, *What Do Unions Do?* (New York, 1977).

70. Frances Piven and Richard Cloward, *Poor People's Movements* (New York, 1977); Gordon et al., *Segmented Work*, pp. 204–15.

71. Carl Degler, *At Odds* (New York, 1980).

72. Barbara Wertheimer, *We Were There: The Story of Working Women in America* (New York, 1977).

73. Often overlooked is the fact that nonwhite workers show a higher percentage of union membership than white workers. See Freeman and Medoff, *What Do Unions Do?*, p. 27; William L. Harris, *Keeping the Faith: A. Philip Randolph, Milton P. Webster, and the Brotherhood of Sleeping Car Porters* (Urbana, IL, 1977); Jervis Anderson, *A. Philip Randolph* (New York, 1973).

74. See William Kornblum, *Blue Collar Community* (Chicago, 1974); John Leggett, *Class, Race, and Labor: Working Class Consciousness in Detroit* (New York, 1968).

75. Gompers quoted in Philip Taft, *Defending Freedom* (Los Angeles, 1973), p. 3; Roy Godson, *American Labor and European Politics: The AFL as a Transnational Force* (New York, 1976).

76. On the AFL-CIO and the CIA see Philip Agee, *Inside the Company: CIA Diary* (New York, 1975). For a view of AFL-CIO foreign policy as anticommunist, see, in addition to Taft, *Defending Freedom*, Carl Gershman, *The Foreign Policy of American Labor* (Beverly Hills, CA, 1975).

77. On the Reuthers, see Victor Reuther, *The Brothers Reuther* (Boston, 1976). On the CIO, see John P. Windmuller, *American Labor and the International Labor Movement* (Ithaca, NY, 1954).

78. CIO education director Ruttenberg, quoted in LeRoy Lenburg, "The CIO and American Foreign Policy, 1935–1955," (Ph.D. diss., Pennsylvania State University, 1973).

79. Woll quoted in Taft, *Defending Freedom*, p. 125.

80. William Appleman Williams, *Tragedy of American Diplomacy* (New York, 1959) and *Empire as a Way of Life* (New York, 1980); Immanuel Wallerstein, *The Modern World System* (New York, 1980).

81. For helpful hints, see Henry Berger, "Unions and Empire: Organized Labor and American Corporations Abroad," *Peace and Change* 3 (Spring 1976): 34–48; Carolyn Eisenberg "Working Class Politics and the Cold War," *Diplomatic History* 7 (Fall 1983): 203–306; Peter Weiler, "The United States, International Labor, and the Cold War," *Diplomatic History* 5 (Winter 1981): 1–22.

82. Relevant archival material includes the Brophy Papers, Catholic University; Carey's main files are in the CIO International Affairs Department Papers, Reuther Archives; on the AFL, see the papers of Serafino Romualdi, New York State School of Industrial and Labor Relations. According to Philip Mason, no researcher has yet received permission to see the Lovestone collection; however, the Deverall Papers, Catholic University, and Florence Thorne Papers, State Historical Society of Wisconsin, contain much in-coming Lovestone correspondence.

83. Simeon Larson, *Labor and Foreign Policy: Gompers, the AFL, and the First World War, 1914–1918* (Rutherford, NJ, 1975).

84. Keenan Papers, Catholic University; George Morris, *CIA and American Labor: The Subversion of the AFL-CIO's Foreign Policy* (New York, 1967); Serafino Romualdi, *Presidents and Peons: Recollections of a Labor Ambassador in Latin America* (New York, 1967); Agee, *Inside the Company*, pp. 244–45.

85. Scheiber et al., *American Economic History*, pp. 422–25.

86. Seymour Melman has argued this case in many works including *The Permanent War Economy* (New York, 1974).

87. James O'Conner, *The Fiscal Crisis of the State* (New York, 1973).

88. The scope of liberal disenchantment is measured by the emergence of neoconservative thinkers, and by liberal self-criticism like Theodore Lowi, *The End of Liberalism* (New York, 1969), which calls for a realist-style system of "juridical democracy"; the resurgence of the once-discredited, free-market philosophy is evident in such works as George Gilder, *Wealth and Poverty* (New York, 1981) and Charles Murray, *Losing Ground: American Social Policy, 1950–1980* (New York, 1984).

89. On the New Right, see "Facing Reaction," a special issue of *Radical America* 15 (Spring 1981).

90. Zillah Eienstein, *Feminism and Sexual Equality* (New York, 1983).

91. Harry Braverman, *Labor and Monopoly Capital* (New York, 1974).

92. Leslie W. Tentler, *Wage Earning Women*; Kessler-Harris, *Out to Work*.

93. U.S. Bureau of the Census, *Historical Statistics of the U.S., Colonial Times to 1970* (Washington, 1975), pp. 49, 41; U.S. Bureau of the Census, *Statistical Abstract of the United States: 1982* (Washington, 1982), p. 60.

94. Ann Snitow et al., eds., *Powers of Desire* (New York, 1983), emphasizes the larger consequences of the separation of sexuality from procreation, as does Linda Gordon, *Women's Body/Women's Right* (New York, 1976); Susan Strasser, *Never Done: A History of American Housework* (New York, 1982) deals with the links between the housewife and corporate capitalism.

95. Joan Kelly, *Women, History and Theory* (Chicago, 1984), pp. 1–18; a similar perspective is found in Gita Sen, "The Sexual Division of Labor and the Working Class Family," *Review of Radical Political Economics* 12 (1980): 76–86.

96. GNP and occupational structure from U.S. Census, *Historical Statistics of the U.S. . . . to 1970*, pp. 139–145. Productivity from Stanley Lebergott, *The Americans: An Economic Record* (New York, 1984), p. 435, Table 33.3.

97. Author's calculations from the following sources: *Historical Statistics U.S.; Economic Report of the President* (Washington, DC, January 1976); Scheiber et al., *American Economic History; Dollars and Sense* (July–August, 1982): 7.

98. Several studies are collated in Peter H. Lindert, *Fertility and Scarcity in America* (Princeton, NJ, 1978); Gabriel Kolko, *Wealth and Power in America* (New York, 1962).

99. David Gordon, et al., *Segmented Work, Divided Workers*, pp. 9–10.

100. *Fortune Magazine* (June 11, 1984), pp. 153–202.

101. Scheiber, *American Economic History*, p. 232, Table 15–3; *Historical Statistics of the U.S. . . . to 1970*, pp. 177–80.

102. Robert Lampmann, *The Share of Top Wealth Holders in National Wealth, 1922–56* (Princeton, 1962), p. 209.

103. Alfred Chandler, *The Visible Hand* (Cambridge, MA, 1977); Paul Baran and Paul Sweezy, *Monopoly Capital* (New York, 1966).

104. To note only a few of the large number of studies of modern management, Braverman, *Labor and Monopoly Capital*; Alfred Chandler, *Visible Hand*; Richard Edwards, *Contested Terrain* (New York, 1979); Montgomery, *Workers Control*; Daniel Nelson, *Managers and Workers* (Madison, WI, 1975). In addition, the main writings of the prophets of scientific management are easily available and other texts have been reprinted by Alfred Chandler, ed., *Application of Modern Systematic Management* and *Pioneers in Modern Factory Management* (both New York, 1980).

105. Kate Millett, *Sexual Politics* (Garden City, NY, 1970); cf. article by Annette Kuhn in Kuhn and Ann Marie Wolpe, eds., *Feminism and Materialism* (London, 1978); Juliet Mitchell, "Freud and Lacan," *Women: The Longest Revolution* (New York, 1984); Catherine McKinnon, "Feminism, Marxism, Method and the State," *The Signs Reader* (New York, 1983).

106. Heidi Hartmann, "Capitalism, Patriarchy, and Job Segregation by Sex," *Signs* 1, no. 3, part 2 (Spring 1976). Recent works sensitive to this gender-class tension include Nancy Schrom Dye, *As Equals and as Sisters* (Columbia, MO, 1980);

Ruth Rosen, *The Last Sisterhood* (Baltimore, 1982); the best account of the suffrage campaign remains Eleanor Flexner, *Century of Struggle* (Boston, 1959); see also Nancy Cott, *The Grounding of Modern Feminism* (New Haven, 1987).

107. Scheiber et al., *American Economic History*, discusses the trend of government growth and provides the statistics; for this and other reasons, this revision of Harold U. Faulkner's original text stands up better than several close competitors, including Stanley Lebergott, *The Americans: An Economic Record* (New York, 1984).

108. After the Wagner Act, it became possible to believe that a certain equality of bargaining power had at long last been achieved. Many works appeared in the postwar period aimed at explaining, in the title of one important study by Clint Golden and Virginia Parker, *The Causes of Industrial Peace* (New York, 1955). These included Robert Ozanne's account of the shift from a barbaric to a civilized relationship during *A Century of Labor Management Relations at McCormick* (New York, 1967); Clark Kerr, et al., *Industrialism and Industrial Man* (Cambridge, MA, 1960); and the enduring narratives of Irving Bernstein, *The Lean Years* (Boston, 1960) and *The Turbulent Years*.

109. One of the best critiques of the "old" labor history is Paul Faler, "Working Class Historiography," *Radical America* 3 (1969): 56–58.

110. Kolko's works include *Triumph of Conservatism* (New York, 1963) and *Main Currents in Modern American History* (New York, 1976); James Weinstein, *Decline of Socialism;* Ronald Radosh, *American Labor and U.S. Foreign Policy* (New York, 1969); Ralph Miliband, *State in Capitalist Society* (London, 1969).

111. An especially lucid exposition is Leo Panitch, "The Development of Corporatism in Liberal Democracies," *Comparative Political Studies* 10, no. 1 (April 1977): 61–90; see also the more abstract Philipp Schnitter, "Still the Century of Corporatism?" *Review of Politics* 36, no. 1 (January 1974): 85–131; Keith Middlemas, *Politics in Industrial Society* (London, 1979). For an interpretation of the New Deal as social democracy, see Maurizio Vaudagna, "The New Deal and European Social Democracy in Comparative Perspective," in Heffer and Rovet, *Why Is There No Socialism in the United States?*

112. Jeremy Brecher, *Strike!* (Boston, 1972); Green, *World of the Worker;* Thompson, *Making of the English Working Class* (London, 1963); Green goes a long way toward integrating the narrative themes of class, sex, and race.

113. Lichtenstein, *Labor's War at Home.*

114. Fred Block, "The Ruling Class Does Not Rule," *Socialist Revolution* 33 (1977): 6–28; cf. also Block, "Beyond Corporate Liberalism," *Social Problems* 24 (1977): 352–61.

115. James O'Conner, *Fiscal Crisis of the State* (New York, 1973); see also Alan Wolfe, *The Limits of Legitimacy* (New York, 1977).

116. Theda Skocpol, "Political Response to Capitalist Crisis: Neo-Marxist Theories of the State and the Case of the New Deal," *Politics and Society* 10 (1980): 155–201; Skocpol, *States and Social Revolutions* (Cambridge, MA, 1979).

117. See, for example, the presentation of statecraft as the embodiment of reason by Gertrude Himmelfarb, *Harpers* 268 (April 1984), pp. 84–92.

118. Antonio Gramsci, *Selections from the Prison Notebooks*, ed. and trans. Quinton Hoare and G. Nowell-Smith (New York, 1971), p. 243.

119. On ideological hegemony, see Aileen Kraditor, "American Radical Historians," *Past and Present*, no. 56 (August 1972): 136–53; on cultural hegemony, see Genovese, *Roll, Jordan, Roll*; and T. Jackson Lears, "The Concept of Cultural Hegemony: Problems and Possibilities," *American Historical Review* 90 (June 1985): 567–93.

· A ·
NEW
SYNTHESIS
Problems and Prospects

· D A V I D   B R O D Y ·

On Creating a New Synthesis
of American Labor History

A Comment

*I*n her essay in this volume, Mary Jo Buhle refers to a paper of mine entitled "The Old Labor History and the New," which was read at the meetings of the Organization of American Historians in 1978. That early paper was symptomatic, I think, of a growing disquiet among labor historians that the immense achievements of recent years were somehow not crystallizing into a new synthesis. How, I asked, did we intend to rewrite American labor history so that it reflected the new scholarship, given "the narrow focus of our research, our devotion to intensive, local study of workers" and given also "our acute sense of the complexity and variety of working-class experience, in which all lines of inquiry—family, ethnicity, mobility, technology, and so on—converge into an intricate web of connections"?[1] Buhle's own essay is likewise expressive of that same disquiet, although perhaps at an appropriately more discerning and sophisticated level of historiographical argument. The parallels she draws between labor and women's history certainly yield a subtler discussion of the influences under which both have flowered since the 1960s and, if anything, intensify her sense of urgency about the need for synthesis. Buhle's feminist perspective, indeed, leads her to demand a grander conception that would unite gender and class analysis.[2] The essays in this book, if they do not reach quite so high, are certainly responsive to the felt need for a rethinking of American labor history. It would seem to be poetic justice that, as one of the instigators of the debate, I should be called upon to discuss the implications of these essays for a new labor-history synthesis.

Let me start by specifying what I have in mind by the term *synthesis*.

Social scientists, and historians of a more theoretical bent, doubtless would take a more elevated approach. For myself, I find it useful to think in terms of that commonplace artifact of the historical trade—the survey. I do not mean comprehensive works of original research and fresh interpretative thrust such as John R. Commons's pioneering *History of Labor in the U.S.* (1918–1935) or Philip Foner's *History of the Labor Movement in the U.S.* (1947–), but texts based on the secondary literature and with no pretense to originality; that is to say, works that serve as an index of the current state of scholarly thinking. For American labor history, the liveliest and certainly the most successful is Foster Rhea Dulles's *Labor in America*, which first appeared in 1949 and remains in print in a version revised by Melvyn Dubofsky. Consider the table of contents for the 1966 edition:

1. Colonial America
2. The First Unions
3. The Workingmen's Parties
4. Labor Strength in the 1830's
5. The Impact of Industrialism
6. Toward National Organization
7. An Era of Upheaval
8. Rise and Decline of the Knights of Labor
9. The American Federation of Labor
10. Homestead and Pullman
11. The Progressive Era
12. Thunder on the Left
13. The First World War—and After
14. Labor in Retreat
15. The New Deal
16. Rise of the C.I.O.
17. Labor and Politics
18. The Second World War
19. Taft-Hartley to the A.F.L.-C.I.O.
20. Disappointed Hopes
21. The Challenge of the 1960s

The elements of a viable synthesis shine through Dulles's chapter headings. There is, first of all, a firm hold on the central subject: it is the American labor movement. There is, second, a clear sense of narrative development— beginnings, an exploratory period that ends with the Knights of Labor; a first era of growth associated with the AFL; a more triumphant second, CIO phase; and then a postwar age of maturity and incipient decline.

Embedded within this periodization, finally, is a substantial explanatory thrust. This by no means reveals the certitude suggested by Michael Reich's notion that "the old labor history involved an articulated theoretical framework of industrial and labor development" and, indeed, an assumption of "iron laws of macro-economic or political development as the primary generating factors." It is true that John R. Commons relied on market structure to explain class differentiation in early American industrialism, as did Lloyd Ulman to analyze the dominance of national trade unions.[3] But, beyond such specific developments, the old labor history never in fact managed to generate a unifying theory, notwithstanding Selig Perlman's *A Theory of the Labor Movement* (1928).[4] Dulles invokes a multiplicity of discrete explanations—industrial, social, political, legal—at various junctures of his account, reflecting the imperfect theoretical state of the old labor history even in its final stages. A fully realized synthesis doubtless would require a unified theory, but a synthesis serves well enough if the other elements— the definition of the central subject and the shape of its narrative development—enable the historian to incorporate causation into the narrative. And this, clearly, the old labor history enabled Foster Dulles to do.

But if his synthesis satisfies as a construct, it scarcely any longer does so as a reflection of the current state of labor-history scholarship. Is the old synthesis still capable of incorporating the new labor history? This to some degree is the operating assumption of Leon Fink's essay in this book. He offers a thoughtful assessment of nineteenth-century workers' culture, stressing its "residualist perspective" and transnational character. But both of these quite original points are made in relation to the development of labor movements, and it is precisely this linkage that structures the essay and gives it its sharp analytical edge. Some of that edge is lost toward the end when, confronted by a thinning out of the culturalist vein in the modern era, Fink drifts away from the movement framework and, insofar as he relates his speculations about the prospects for a modern culturalist analysis to twentieth-century collective activity, does so more vaguely with reference to class conflict.

For the nineteenth century, certainly, Fink's essay suggests the continuing utility of the old synthesis, not only for ordering what we know about workers' culture, but also by opening up the comparative analysis that might enable us to deal more effectively with the stubborn issue of American exceptionalism.[5] Nor, it might be added, does reliance on the movement synthesis require that it be done on the old terms—that is, in which organizational developments in themselves constitute the central story. The balance can be shifted so that instead organizations can be taken as institutional manifestations of the consciousness of workers, which is indeed what Fink intends when he speaks of "the subjectivity of worker movements." The "conceptual dilemmas" that his essay probes relate to the problems of applying nineteenth-century culturalist analysis to the twentieth century. It would certainly be worth thinking further about how we might make the transition to the twentieth century with the labor movement still at the center but not on the old institutional terms. What place does the culturalist strain play in twentieth-century trade-union history? And how would that be balanced against the political/collective-bargaining functions that take on increasing importance. Alan Dawley's essay, discussed later, is quite suggestive about how power relationships (and hence collective activity) might serve as the center of a twentieth-century synthesis. What might most usefully be done in this regard is to explore the transitional period, the 1880s and 1890s, for the ways by which the labor movement (more broadly defined than the AFL) passed into its modern, twentieth-century forms. This approach might even be reconciled with a class analysis, at least if one followed Ira Katznelson and Aristide R. Zolberg's argument in *Working-Class Formation: Nineteenth-Century Patterns in Western Europe and the United States* (1986) that collective activity be defined as the final level of class formation.

The other contributors to this book, however, do not seem inclined to make so modest an attack on the problem of synthesis. E. P. Thompson's *The Making of the English Working Class* (1963), of course, had established class as the central paradigm of the new labor history. But Thompson's class analysis took a very particular direction. He argued that class was "a cultural as much as an economic formation," and, although acknowledging the determining impact of the productive relations on class experiences, Thompson's own concern was mainly with "the way these experiences are handled in cultural terms: embodied in traditions, value-systems, ideas, and institutional forms." The central subject of his great book was English working-class consciousness. American labor historians have been immensely influenced by Thompson—by the unknown terrain of working-class life he mapped out; by his imaginative capacity for rekindling that world; and, perhaps most of all, by his insistence on human agency in the history of working people. But it is important also to see where his American followers parted company—by no means willingly—from Thompson. If they have sought the manifestations of workers' consciousness that Thompson first uncovered, they have not necessarily done so within an explicit class framework.[6] And it seems that, if a class analysis is to be pursued, it cannot be done by replicating the particular unifying cultural formulation that distinguished *The Making of the English Working Class*. The essays by Michael Reich, Sean Wilentz, and Alan Dawley in this book are explorations of alternate routes to making class the framework for American labor history.

Of the three, Reich's essay contains to the greatest extent the elements of a fully realized synthesis. (It should be noted that his essay is an elaboration on *Segmented Work, Divided Workers: The Historical Transformation of Labor in the U.S.* [1982], which he coauthored with David M. Gordon and Richard Edwards.) There is, first of all, a well-defined central subject, denoted in the book's subtitle as the "transformation of labor." This involves three overlapping phenomena—the shift from independent to wage labor, or *initial proletarianization*; an increasing degree of uniformity in the labor process under the drive system, or *homogenization*; and, finally, a division between primary (internal) and secondary (casual) labor markets, or *segmentation*. The central subject of labor history thus becomes work, with the labor movement now a subordinated topic treated from within the new work-related perspective. There is, second, a clearly asserted periodization, which connects initial proletarianization, homogenization, and segmentation to three particular stages of labor development, each of which is then further refined into phases of exploration, consolidation, and decay. Most powerful—far exceeding that of the old institutional synthesis—is the third ingredient, causation, for Reich offers us nothing less than a full-dress theory of labor transformation. Each stage is associated with a long swing of the business cycle, itself the consequence of crisis and response between capitalist accumulation and what Reich calls the *social structure of accumulation*. "Labor history, we propose, should be embedded in a larger account of the dynamics of capitalist development and class conflict"; and this, Reich asserts, they achieve through their "political-economic theory of macroeconomic development."

The problems posed by this theory are formidable indeed. At first blush, the capital accumulation–social structure of accumulation formulation seems no more than an elaboration on Marxist analysis. In Marx, however, there is a precise rendering of how the relations of production eventuate in capital accumulation. Here economic base and political-social superstructure are subsumed in a social structure of accumulation whose inner dynamics have yet to be charted. In *Segmented Work, Divided Workers*, this did not seem an especially consequential matter since in practice the social structure of accumulation translated into work relations, and the book was actually about how specific phases in work relations advanced or retarded capital accumulation. In this essay, however, Reich ventures out into the farther reaches of the social structure of accumulation for the period 1890–1920, including politics. Reich tells us, for example, that the 1896 election constituted a major turning point for American capitalism—the resolution of a crisis that opened the way for a new social structure of accumulation. So sweeping and unexamined a conclusion does not, in truth, inspire confidence that Reich and his co-authors have truly worked out a "political-economic theory of macroeconomic development." It is like being given a handsome clock, but with the clockwork missing. But for the historian, if not the political economist, theory is not the crucial thing. The historian normally moves from the empirical to the explanatory. First, what happened? Then, why did it happen? If Reich can get us started with the first, we can take our chances with the second. And we can, in any case, mine *Segmented Work, Divided Workers* for what has explanatory utility for labor history without worrying about the fate of its theory of macroeconomic development.

So let us turn to empirical matters. The reader will note that Reich makes his essay the occasion for answering certain criticisms I had raised in a review of *Segmented Work, Divided Workers*.[7] One had to do with the statistical evidence for the long swings, in particular, for the designation of the second half of the period 1839–1899 as one of "stagnation." In the realm of statistical analysis, of course, one is predisposed to defer to the technically expert economist. In his paper, Reich suggests a failure on my part (and Frank Wilkinson's) to separate cyclical from the trend movements indicative of long swings. He must be referring to my observation that, had he shifted his breaking point at 1874 either forward or backward by five years (Gallman's statistics, Reich's source, are given quinquenially), the small decline Reich finds in rates of industrial output would have disappeared. By choosing 1874, in fact, Reich has violated his own rule of separating cyclical from trend movements. His stagnant phase (1874–1899) does not begin and end at comparable cyclical points but, on the contrary, at opposing ones— the first (1874) on the downswing, the second (1899) on the upswing—so that both the depressions of the 1870s and 1890s are included in his calculations on industrial output. In any case, Reich says he now has further supporting evidence, the most important being the industrial statistics from W. Arthur Lewis, *Growth and Fluctuations, 1870–1913* (1974). It is puzzling why Reich should think that his Table 3 indicates "a consistent slowdown in industrial growth from the 1870s to the 1890s." An inspection of his five-year moving averages for industrial production does not clearly show this (and does not seem a particularly useful way of exploiting Lewis's series), whereas Lewis's own calculations (which Reich disregards) indicate precisely the opposite; namely, that the period 1870–1913 was exceptional for the "constant rates" at which industrial production grew in the United States as well as in the United Kingdom, Germany, and France. More important for Reich's purposes is "a falling profit rate" that Reich reports from Lewis's book. Unfortunately, that is not exactly what Lewis says. His Chart 4.1 does show a sharp drop in the 1880s; but Lewis considers this "anomalous," and concludes that it resulted from a sample of stock earnings that was "unrepresentatively low" (p. 101). Finally, Reich ignores the finding that one might have thought would have most interested him, that is, industrial productivity. Output per person increased, according to Lewis, by 2.0 percent per year from 1872 to 1882, 1.9 percent 1882–1892, 1.85 percent 1892–1906, a rate of change so slight as to be "presumably constant, except for some small reflection of shorter hours" (p. 98). If W. Arthur Lewis's book is Reich's notion of supporting evidence, he has a long way indeed to go to demonstrate the long–swing stagnation that he acknowledges "is crucial for our account."

The other empirical issue I raised involved the characterization of the stages of labor. Under initial proletarianization (1820s–1890s), for example, wage labor is established, but work itself is "untransformed." The precise meaning of that last term proves to be highly elusive but is centrally linked to Reich's notion "that there was little technological innovation during this period and that capitalists adapted existing techniques to their new wage-labor system" (*Segmented Work, Divided Workers*, p. 81). In the limited sense of mechanization—that is, the substitution of machine for hand labor—Reich is partially right, but clearly that defines the changes affecting the way men and women worked in the nineteenth century too narrowly. It is hard to think of labor as being untransformed in the face of widespread division of labor, the subcontracting system in the garment trades, the new technologies of production (not necessarily involving the mechanization of work) in metal processing, fabrication, and a host of other industries. One is not persuaded by Reich's response that I am invoking individual cases whereas he is dealing with "central tendencies."

If the empirical groundings are uncertain, however, the implications of Reich's work for rewriting American labor history are very bold. In this new synthesis, work relations become the central subject. It would be up to historians to modify or refine Reich's particular characterizations of initial proletarianization, homogenization, and segmentation so that they square with what we know (or will discover) about the history of work in America. Reich's periodization will likewise need much further study to determine the moments at which one labor stage gives way to the next, and whether these coincide with the moments of economic crisis. We should be clear, however, about the nature of this synthesis. Notwithstanding Reich's assurances to the contrary, it will subordinate culture and community (no less than the labor movement) to work relations. And, if we follow Reich's analysis, not much scope will remain for human agency, at least not for workers. For the transformations of labor he describes arise out of crises of capitalism and occur at the initiative of management. He is dealing with the side of class formation that E. P. Thompson has defined as "largely determined by the productive relations into which men are born—or enter involuntarily."

In Sean Wilentz's essay on the period 1776–1877, we are confronted with a grander conception of working-class formation. "If we are to understand anything about this process," Wilentz asserts at the outset, "we must discard the normal assumption that labor history is simply about wage earners, or about relations between workers and employers on the shop floor. Class formation was a political and cultural, as well as an 'economic' process; it touched every aspect of American life. Interpreting the history of the

American working class thus requires a thorough rethinking of all of American history." That last statement, echoing a plea first made by Herbert Gutman,[8] immediately carries Wilentz beyond even E. P. Thompson's frontiers, and out into "all of American history." Wilentz's essay should be read sympathetically as a first exploratory foray into fresh terrain. But it should also be read—tested is perhaps the better word—against the requirements of a coherent synthesis.

Wilentz's essay proceeds on two levels. One might be termed immediate working-class history, and follows the economic-cultural dichotomy of recent Marxist provenance. Like E. P. Thompson, Wilentz is not especially engaged by the economic side of the equation. The distinction he draws between merchant and industrial capitalism, while important in other contexts, is not an especially useful way of capturing the effect of the evolving productive relations of American capitalism on workers. In practice, Wilentz takes intensifying exploitation and alienation as givens in the process of working-class formation. His active concern is with the resultant growth of class consciousness, which leads him into a highly textured and informed discussion of ethnicity, community, gender and family, leisure, ideology, and collective labor activity. At every juncture, he carefully assesses what was unifying, what divisive, in this complex history. It was, he acknowledges, "never a smooth and even development. At almost every point before the mid-1870s, the growing numbers of American wage earners were divided by ethnicity, skill, region, religion, race, and sex"; and, while they had some local success, they "failed to build a unified presence in national politics." Nevertheless, "a certain logic united the history of American workers in the nation's first century." This was, of course, republicanism, which derived from the Revolutionary era and inculcated American workers, whatever their origins, with deeply held convictions about equality and independence. The central dynamic for Wilentz arises from "the disparities between the 'wages' system and America's professed political and social ideals." From these felt disparities, more acute with each generation of workers, solidarity grew "in a cyclical pattern of ever increasing intensity" and climaxed after the crisis of the 1870s in "the first national rising of the American working class."

Thus far, what we have is the new labor history as currently understood, although given a distinctive edge by Wilentz's championing of republicanism as a central force in nineteenth century working-class experience. Where Wilentz breaks new ground is in what might be called labor's national history. Insofar as Wilentz actually "rethinks" American history, he does so through the prism of class. Thus in the South: "class formation among whites pitted slaveholders . . . against propertied, mostly nonslaveholding whites—the yeomanry." But class formation, although much invoked, is not used systematically or with much conviction. Wilentz's instincts here are entirely understandable—what would be more logical in a study of working-class formation than to interpret the larger society in terms of class formation?—but so ambitious an undertaking clearly exceeds his present grasp. Let the task of "rethinking all of American history" be put down on the agenda for the future.

In the meantime, there are more modest uses to be made of American history. Out of this capacious subject, Wilentz chooses to write mainly about the emergence of the middle class, the politics of party and section, and about the South. The criteria for selection, since he does not make them explicit, have to be interpolated from what Wilentz finds of importance in these choices. The middle class is of interest primarily for the values it imposes on the working class; the major parties, for their success at capturing labor's loyalty; the rise of the Republican party, for its espousal of free-labor ideology. All of these effects relate directly to the cultural-political emphasis Wilentz has given to working-class history. In essence, American history becomes a resource to be mined for what amplifies an already defined central subject.

Only Wilentz's concern for southern history cannot be explained in this instrumental way. Why, in an essay devoted to the rise of the working class, should Wilentz choose to devote so much attention to a region distant physically (and in many other ways) from the lives of wage workers? Part of it is a palpable unwillingness to exclude slaves and poor southern whites from working-class history. A view championed by Herbert Gutman, among others, it must have seemed especially compelling to Wilentz, given his determination to write labor history on a broad canvas.[9] A formidable analytical problem is thereby created, however. How are slavery and wage labor to be united in a single analysis? One possibility is to deny that the working class is limited to wage workers, which Wilentz tries out, but in practice finds unworkable. In the end, his definition of the working class is clearly limited to wage workers, prior to 1848 "dominated by native Yankee men and women and British immigrants" in the Northeast, then after 1848 consisting "mainly of Irish and German immigrants (and their children) and free blacks." A second possibility is to note, as Wilentz indeed does, that slaves eventually become wage workers, but they do not in fact do so during the nineteenth century. Nothing was more consequential for the shaping of either the American working class or of Afro-American history, than the imprisonment of the freedmen in the southern share-cropping system during the crucial half century of America's industrial transformation.

So prominent a southern presence in Wilentz's essay derives from a larger claim he is advancing, namely, that the crisis of the Union itself constitutes the central event of nineteenth century working-class history. It was "an irrepressible national conflict over labor, liberty, and the nation's destiny," and its outcome forever resolved the struggle between free and slave labor systems. This is not a rethinking of American history. Wilentz does not see the sectional crisis in new terms. Rather, his originality is in asserting its relevance to labor history. It is the latter that Wilentz has rethought and expanded. A national crisis has become labor's crisis as well.

Wilentz has thus begun to chip away at the boundaries confining American labor history. This is a major advance, but also, it should be recognized, one that complicates the search for a new synthesis. Consider, for example, the matter of periodization. For Wilentz, 1848 marks the break between two great phases of working-class formation. This makes sense for labor's national history, which takes the sectional crisis as the central nineteenth-century event. But 1848 (or thereabouts) is much more problematic a breaking point in the history of working-class consciousness. Wilentz does his best to align things. Thus, he speaks of the "midcentury crisis" as a "conjuncture" of changes. But one of these—the period of sustained economic growth—in fact, started at least ten years earlier.[10] And the second—the surge of immigration from the mid-1840s onward—constitutes an important but highly ambiguous factor in Wilentz's treatment of class consciousness. Both are more confidently asserted as factors in the intensifying sectional crisis. More interesting is Wilentz's effort to link his two levels through Lincoln's free-labor ideology. This "would unite the North in the wake of secession" and—note the shift in Wilentz's tone—"also help create a context for fresh struggles within the North over the proper form of American labor relations." One catches the reference to David Montgomery's *Beyond Equality: Labor and the Radical Republicans* (1967), but it remains unclear that, in the rising curve of working-class militancy as Wilentz has described it, a distinct second phase begins with the "midcentury crisis." Wilentz has not managed to find a periodization that works for both levels of his essay. Nor does his duality permit him to keep his central subject steadily in focus or enable him to develop the full explanatory force his account demands. In these ways, his expansive approach to labor history works somewhat at cross purposes with the coherence that is the essence of synthesis.

Leon Fink's observation about the great chasm in labor historiography, noted earlier, is amply borne out in the contrasting essays on the nineteenth and twentieth centuries in this book. Whereas Sean Wilentz seeks to recapture a lost working-class world, Alan Dawley deals in the commerce of political power and organized struggle. Wilentz is evocative and historically concrete, sensitive to human agency, even literary in his analysis, so that, indeed, his two main sections end with invocations of Melville and Whitman. Dawley's approach is much more clinical, and his essay has an air of the laboratory about it. ("Take two points in time. . . . Within this single 'moment', then, we have captured our seemingly elusive *real* alternatives.

. . . Putting this procedure to the test of events" and so on). If Dawley's essay is somewhat flawed by the normal standards of historical argument and exposition, it nevertheless constitutes the most ambitious rethinking of twentieth-century American labor history we currently have. The essay repays close reading for what it suggests about the prospects for a new synthesis of the modern period.

Dawley's starting point is his insistence that this is a history of "systemic conflict." The core ingredients are in themselves familiar. Dawley focuses on the industrial work force, big business, and the state, and takes as the main issues unionization and social policy. About all this, an ample historical literature exists, and only after 1948, as Dawley puts it, is he forced "to scrounge among economists, sociologists, and journalists." What Dawley adds to this familiar history is, first of all, a determined effort at expanding its boundary lines, so that race, ethnicity, and, most important, gender and family are incorporated, and the range of issues broadens out to include international affairs. Then, Dawley reorients labor history in two critical ways. First, he directs our attention away from its inner processes (i.e., away from the perspective of institutional history) outward toward its links to the corporate and political orders. And the labor-corporate-public relationship so identified becomes the central theme of twentieth-century American history. Labor history is, so to speak, no longer a side show but part of the main event.

This main event, finally, Dawley places within an elaborate theoretical framework. He posits "fields of force" as a kind of magnetic field within which capital and labor are forever "bound together in polar opposition." The function of the state is to hold the field of force in equilibrium. This is, however, inherently unstable, always subject to internal "contradictions," and destined to give way to a new field of force. From one angle, disequilibrium seems to arise from conflicting "hierarchical" and "egalitarian" pressures; from another, from shifting agglomerations of potential power. Thus, the source of instability in the field of force of the early twentieth century is the growing "social weight" of industrial labor—"its size, its key role in creating wealth, its manifest welfare needs, its cultural estrangement, its conscious struggle for power." With the onset of economic depression in 1929, the state (the New Deal) draws capital into a Great Compromise with industrial labor, and a new field of force ensues that after thirty years duration is now breaking up in favor of a capital-dominated field of force of yet uncertain dimensions.

The utility of Dawley's formulation in certain ways is very striking. It offers, for one thing, a highly articulated periodization and conveys powerfully a sense of historical development. With equal force it defines power as the central subject of modern labor history, and this generates under Dawley's hand a strong integrative capability. Dawley manages to handle even gender and family in ways that draw these themes into the orbit of systemic conflict (although still on subordinate terms unsatisfactory from Mary Jo Buhle's perspective). The result is not a synthesis productive of historical explanation, however. On the contrary, Dawley's absorbed concern with his theoretical construct seems to be positively destructive on that score.

What begins as a "metaphor"—the word that initially introduces the "field of force"—takes on the weight of historical reality.[11] Dawley would surely deny that he is speaking other than metaphorically in describing the new public agencies of the Progressive and war eras as "vectors in the rearranged force field," or in saying that after World War I "intermediate groups tended to gravitate toward opposite poles of the worker-capital field of force." But the second statement does in fact misconstrue the role of smaller business. The National Association of Manufacturers and its small-business satellites were not in some kind of middle ground and then drawn by the polarities of the field of force onto the side of corporate business; on the contrary, they led the battle for the open shop after World War I and, in city after city, much exceeded the representatives of national corporations in their zeal for the American Plan. (Dawley is wrong also on the facts of the first point—the wartime labor agencies went far beyond mediation of industrial disputes—but not I think because of his fields-of-force concept.) Or consider how Dawley explains the impact of the Great Compromise on those on the outside:

> The promotion of mass production workers . . . did not overthrow the dominant corporate-managerial interests. Therefore, this transformation in social hierarchy shifted burdens of oppression to other sectors of the working class and to other subordinate groups.

The formulation becomes the explanation, where, in fact, it can do no more than point to the problem—"a shift in the burden of oppression"—that calls for explanation. Equally troublesome, the fields of force become a kind of closed system for Dawley. Thus, the possibility is excluded that the Great Depression, which set in motion the forces leading to the Great Compromise, could have derived from other than the power imbalance between labor and capital. The limitations on Dawley's scope for explanation have a more striking effect on his discussion of the breakdown of the Great Compromise. With no place for the structural changes and competitive pressures that have built up since the 1960s, Dawley offers a nearly unrecognizable account of why corporate business has turned on the labor movement.

In his introduction, Dawley remarks that he has "relied on methods that derive ultimately from Marx." Is there some kind of alchemy in Marx's name that reduces the gravitational pull of historical reality? Dawley, Reich, and

Wilentz are operating on a grand scale, true, but not on so grand a scale as Marx himself; and Marx did not omit fixing invented theory in an empirically demonstrated labor process and, in *The Eighteenth Brumaire*, class struggle. If American labor history is to be rewritten along class lines, it will surely take a similarly tough-minded linking of theory and event. Dawley's "field-of-force" will only work if it is accompanied by and tested against empirical analysis of the systemic conflict it purports to describe, and the same applies to Michael Reich's "social structure of accumulation." Sean Wilentz's chapter does not rely on such formalistic constructs. But class formation as a concept would have served him better had he subjected it to the kind of definition and rigorous usage shown, for example, in Katznelson and Zolberg's *Working-Class Formation*. One is put in mind of Eric Hobsbawm's reminiscences about his early years as a Marxist labor historian in England.

> The atmosphere . . . turned sharply anti-Marxist in '48. After that, we were isolated. This was not without its advantages. The disadvantage, of course, is obvious. The advantage was that we couldn't get away with bullshit. We didn't have a homemade public that expected to read and approve of anything that called itself Marxist. On the contrary, we had to fight our way. . . . And I think as a matter of intellectual discipline this wasn't all bad.[12]

Life is not so hard today. Does it have to follow that the intellectual discipline that reshaped English labor history cannot be summoned up to reshape American labor history?

NOTES

1. *Labor History* 20 (Winter 1979): 122.
2. This is probably the place to say that, regretfully, I will not be commenting further on Buhle's fine historiographical chapter because I have taken as my task an assessment of the chapters in this book as substantive contributions to a new synthesis of American labor history.
3. John R. Commons, "The American Shoemakers, 1648–1895," *Labor and Administration* (New York, 1913), Chapter 14; Lloyd Ulman, *Rise of the National Trade Union* (Cambridge, MA, 1955).
4. On Perlman's theoretical problems, see especially Charles A. Gulick and Melvin K. Bers, "Insight and Illusion in Perlman's Theory of the Labor Movement," *Industrial and Labor Relations Review* 6 (1953): 510–31.
5. For a provocative opening foray, see Sean Wilentz, "Against Exceptionalism: Class Consciousness and the American Labor Movement, 1790–1920," *International Labor and Working Class History*, no. 26 (Fall 1984): 1–24, and responses by Nick Salvatore and Michael Hanagan, pp. 25–36.

6. See, for example, the pioneering essay by Herbert G. Gutman, "Work, Culture and Society in Industrializing America, 1820–1920," *American Historical Review* 78 (1973): 531–87.

7. *Journal of Interdisciplinary History* 14 (Winter 1984): 701–705.

8. Herbert G. Gutman, "Whatever Happened to History?" *The Nation* (November 21, 1981), pp. 553–54.

9. Gutman himself is ambiguous on the relationship between slavery and wage labor as class phenomena; that is, as to whether these should be treated as parallel processes of class formation or as parts of a single working-class history. In his thoughtful introduction to Gutman's posthumous essays, Ira Berlin suggests the latter, but, given Gutman's absorption in the interior dynamics of class-cultural formation, it seems more likely that he never fully faced up to the problem. Note, for example, his subsequent comments on *The Black Family in Slavery and Freedom* (New York, 1976): "What I uncovered, in other words, were the passageways through which the experiences and beliefs of these people traveled. . . . Suddenly, therefore, the very same kind of historical questions can be asked of slaves that historians ask about any other exploited population. . . . On the first page of *The Black Family* I noted that it was about a *special aspect of working-class history.* . . . The answers, of course, would be different because the exploitative relationships differed, but the questions were similar because a *similar historical interaction* had been uncovered" (my italics). Herbert G. Gutman, *Power and Culture: Essays on the American Working Class*, ed. Ira Berlin (New York, 1987), pp. 45–46 (Berlin), 349. The other leading class analyst of slavery, Eugene Genovese, emphatically does separate the slave system from working-classs history. See especially "The Legacy of Slavery and the Roots of Black Nationalism," in Eugene Genovese, *In Red and Black: Marxian Explorations in Southern and Afro-American History* (New York, 1971), Chapter 6.

10. Robert Gallman, "Commodity Output, 1839–1899," in National Bureau of Economic Research, *Trends in the American Economy in the Nineteenth Century* (Princeton, NJ, 1960), especially pp. 16 and 24, Tables 1 and 3.

11. It is instructive to compare E. P. Thompson's cautious use of the metaphor (Dawley credits Thompson with giving him the field-of-force notion) in attempting to grapple with the complexities of systemic struggle and reciprocity in eighteenth-century England. Aware of the objections that might be raised, Thompson noted that in *Grundrisse* Marx himself turned metaphorical to amplify his argument that "it is a determinate production and its relations which assign every other production and its relations their rank and influence." And then Thompson draws our attention to the dangers of a more formalistic usage: "What Marx describes in metaphors of 'rank and influence', 'general illumination' and 'tonalities' would today be offered in more systematic structuralist language; terms sometimes so hard and objective-seeming (as with Althusser's 'repressive' and 'ideological state apparatuses') that they disguise the fact that they are still metaphors which offer to congeal a fluent social process." E. P. Thompson, "Class Struggle without Class: Eighteenth-Century English Society," *Social History* 3 (May 1978): 151–52.

12. MARHO, eds., *Visions of History* (New York, 1983), p. 30.

· A L I C E   K E S S L E R - H A R R I S ·

A New Agenda for American Labor History

A Gendered Analysis and the Question of Class

*T*he question of how social history relates to and alters more traditional perspectives on American history has troubled historians since the field reached maturity in the mid-1970s. As a body of data, social history has successfully pointed up the rich diversity of American society and the enormous complexity of human motives that drive it. But, it has not yet developed a way of understanding the past that might replace the easy and probably false coherence suggested by interpretations that posit a unified set of values. It poses then the question of what understanding can emerge from a study of the lives of ordinary people.

No group of historians has, I think, taken this task more seriously than historians of labor. As the conference from which these papers are drawn demonstrates, it has been easier to identify the problem than to offer a way of thinking about the past that embodies a solution. Nevertheless, the meeting, as much as the papers presented, stirred such rich controversy, that the ideas it generated, as well as those it repeated, deserve exploration. I want in this essay to use the conference to suggest what might be some of the difficulties of achieving a synthesis, or an interpretive framework, and then to propose a way of thinking about the past, through gender, that might cast some new light on American history as a whole.

On the face of it, a conference to debate new directions in labor history seemed not merely timely but ripe. It had been nearly twenty years since labor history had begun to edge its way into the canons of historical scholarship. Perhaps fifteen years had passed since historians had begun to talk about a "new" labor history rooted in the work of E. P. Thompson and exemplified by the pathbreaking essays of Herbert Gutman. And it had been more than a decade since labor historians had called a national meeting to define their enterprise. In the meantime, what had begun as a tentative exploration, peripheral to the dominant concerns of most American historians had been catapulted, perhaps by force of circumstance, to the leading edge of social history. Labor history had benefited from the expanded vision of social history that emerged from the 1960s; and at the same time, the search for a history of the working class had stimulated new research of unprecedented depth and range.

The meeting began with every good omen. A small grant, a limited assembly (restricted at the cost of some hard feelings in order to enhance possibilities for discussion), papers in advance, and plenty of space for informal conversation—all these augured a fruitful outcome. Among the participants were the revered and those hoping to be so; a small but respectable representation of women and minority groups, and even a few social historians invited to provide distance and critical perspective. But, after two days of discussion, no synthesis had emerged; no vision of a future agenda had materialized. Instead, many participants, as one of them noted, came away with negative feelings. Michael Frisch described them as "frustrated at best, disappointed on average, and cynical at worst."[1] The conference had not only been unable to achieve a synthesis, it seemed to have fostered dissension and confusion about what might be the agenda of labor history. In its aftermath, Eric Foner provided one version of the results. It remained unclear, he suggested, "how to reformulate labor history without simply incorporating race and gender into preexisting paradigms, abandoning class as a category of analysis, or creating an endless jigsaw puzzle of separate experiences lacking a coherent overview."[2]

What accounts for the disappointment? How, in light of the tremendous richness of our empirical research, do we explain the failure to move toward a new paradigm? Part of the answer is rooted in the limits of our emerging research.

By the mid-1970s, most practitioners in the field had tacitly agreed that the history of organized labor was insufficient to explain the history of the working class. Following the lead of Herbert Gutman, they had redefined the history of workers to include every element of wage work and the family that supported it; and they had redefined the terrain to extend from unions to the factory floor, the neighborhood, and the tavern. Redefinition had opened the field to questions about the experience of a preindustrial labor force, which preceded formal organization, and to issues of working class formation. To answer these questions, labor historians focused heavily on local history and adopted new quantitative and anthropological methods that attempted to reconstruct the lives and self-experiences of workers in their communities. In this "culturalist" approach, power was intrinsic in the capacity of workers to retain customs, values, language, and traditions in the face of a destructive capitalism. Workers' power resided in their capacity to use these indigenous attributes of their lives to confront, even to stave off, the initiatives of a dominant industrial elite and to shape the future of an industrial society.[3] The search for workers' resistance, wherever and however it appeared and whether in formal or informal institutions, replaced the history of structures.

But the process of exploring what David Montgomery called "the friction that comes out of everyday life" had fragmented the history of workers, producing, in practice, an eclectic pattern of behavior and belief that defied any attempt to identify a coherent vision or purpose among working people. In the absence of an identifiable working class, researchers focused on the unique rather than the shared qualities of workers. Implicitly, as much as explicitly, they replaced the Marxian notion that consciousness came from the social relations of production with a broader concept of culture, in which identity derived from an amalgam of factors such as race, skill, community, religion, and ethnicity. Increasingly, the particularism of the field undermined attempts to speak of common class interests.

Despite the efforts of Gutman and others to see power in the resistance embodied in working-class behavior, questions remained about the capacity of labor historians to explain larger political developments. The new techniques, after all, were rooted in data that affirmed the depth and strength of an empirically ascertained culture. For most of the assembled group, working-class experience mattered primarily because it offered alternative visions and challenges to a dominant bourgeois ethos. Rejecting interpretations of labor history that resided in such notions as American exceptionalism, the new historians saw in workers' culture a concern for values of community, equality, and justice that transcended particular and narrow interests and suggested the possibilities for alternative directions to capitalism. Whether they resisted or adapted to industrial and postindustrial culture, workers projected values of cooperation and democracy, of independence, virtue, and citizenship that were obscured by the dominant ideology as it appeared in government bureaucracy, court decisions, and the public press.

Identifying these indigenous values was important—the more so because they had for so long been perceived as romantic ideology or written out of history altogether. Yet, a troubling question remained, Why, then, had the working class been so successfully incorporated? Within a framework of opposition, how did we account for the emergence and widespread acceptance of competitive individualism? How do we account for the undiminished, hostile, role of the state in repressing the collective visions of workers? What could we say of the apparent support of most twentieth century working people for a successful capitalism? The new labor history did not speak to the structures of power nor did it lend itself to questions about the relationship of an ideology that sustained power to cultures of resistance. Labor historians thus faced the question of what their enterprise contributed to explaining the dynamic of American history.

As the culturalist approach floundered, an emerging body of literature emphasized the relationship between larger social and economic structures and political change. Challenges came from two directions: from economists and economic historians who sought explanations of macroeconomic trends (represented in this book by the chapter by Michael Reich); and from labor historians concerned with the expanding role of the state. Instead of placing workers and their struggles at the center of historical change, these scholars urged us to rely more heavily on analyses of economic trends and structural changes to explain the behavior and consciousness of working people. And yet, such approaches threatened to drown out visions of working-class resistance altogether. Culturalist approaches might beg questions of the relationship of workers to the exercise of power. But alternative structural approaches tended to subsume the culture of workers into larger patterns, making grass-roots activities largely peripheral as explanations for social change.[4] Though we recognized the tension, we could not and would not abandon our work of the past decade.[5]

Resolution seemed to require an explanation of how resistance functioned in relation to capitalism; or to put it the way it was so often put by us, an explanation of class relations in which the development of capitalism was rooted in the history of workers as they confronted the power of capital. Was such an explanation possible? Our answers defused into discrete illustrations from which we could draw no general conclusion. Hindsight suggests that what divided conferees, disturbed a sense of equilibrium, and inhibited consensus among us was our failure to move the discussion of workers' culture to a different level. We did not want to abandon the notion. Far from it; most of us took its existence for granted. But, as eager as we were to acknowledge the various forms of worker resistance, we were reluctant to ask why resistance, in the long run, had failed to alter the structure of power. The tapes that recorded the conference suggest how and why we skirted that question. And they, therefore, provide clues as to how we might move the level of debate to a new agenda.

A piece of the answer lay in our own experience. The early excitement generated by the field of labor history had emanated from its overtly political purpose and vision. Reacting negatively to the liberal ideology of the 1950s, young scholars were drawn to the history of labor in part as an explicit rejection of the consensus history it spawned. Unlike the accepted version of the 1950s, which saw the United State moving harmoniously, if slowly, toward agreed-upon principles of equality and justice, the radicalism of the New Left sought explanations for conflict and diversity. It found them in the treatment of blacks, Indians, and other ethnic minorities, and it looked to people's movements (among them the labor movement) as agents of change. As one participant put it, "Many of us ventured into labor history for political reasons . . . it was part of the whole project of changing something in the sixties." But labor historians who looked to the labor movement as a vehicle of change were frequently disappointed. Seeking there the innovative ideas and the political energy to redirect American society and redefine American democracy, they found only limited confirmation. To be sure, the crowd activity of preindustrial Americans and the workingmen's associations and cooperative societies of the early industrial period carried the seeds of change, as did the Knights of Labor in a later period. But the efforts of these groups were translated into ephemeral action and undermined by a self-definition that could not withstand capture by the prevailing ethic of power.[6] And the picture in the modern period is even bleaker.

Despite the general lack of social vision among most union leaders, a briefly revitalized labor movement, reminiscent of the 1930s, gave credence to the project. In the 1960s, a few unions joined with the civil rights movement. A few took active stands against the war in Vietnam. Others began to organize the unskilled and women.[7] Membership, in decline since the mid-1950s, stabilized only briefly. A decade and a half later, membership in trade unions had sunk to 18 percent of the labor force, and a conservative spirit ruled the land. Along with the decline of the labor movement went the sense of moral purpose associated with its revival. Increasingly, the instrumental orientations of the working people of America undermined whatever latent social vision remained in the movement, pointing up its bureaucratic flaws and its inability to represent the interests of all workers.

Though they hung, like stagnant air, over the conference, we never directly confronted the questions raised by a pessimistic view of the contemporary working class and organized labor's possibilities. As the political arm of workers, the labor movement represented whatever was left of a millennial vision. And despite our disenchantment with unionism as a sufficient explanation of historical change, labor historians had not stopped seeing trade unions as vehicles for conveying workers' aspirations and as the embodiments of their bravest achievements. Did labor's metamorphosis into an institution that represented particular rather than broader interests indicate that a history with workers at its center had romanticized working-class aspirations? An economy in which the labor movement played out its cyclical role relegated workers to the periphery rather than the center of social change. How, given these perceptions, would our enterprise change?

The marginalization of the labor movement implicit in culturalist approaches and the effort to seek change at the level of individual behavior, ideas, and values as well as in political activity have posed a set of intellectual challenges that remain hanging. In part, these questions had turned labor historians toward culturalism to begin with. For, as unions were seen as increasingly preoccupied with the material advancement of their members, they generated questions about their capacity to carry the banners of social justice and democracy for all. Where, then, did such ideas reside? We had found them in the heroism of ordinary lives as well as in everyday resistance to capital. But, if we continued to look for them on the shop floor and in the working class communities where we believed them to be nurtured, we would sooner or later confront the traditionalism of the working class. We would face a devastating uncertainty as to whether the evident conservatism of workers in the 1980s did not negate the hypotheses of the 1960s. Our sense of loss was so profound that Jesse Lemisch asked at one point if we were not merely saying Kaddish for the sixties.

Although we sidestepped these issues at our meeting, the fundamental questions they raised created unease about the explanatory possibilities of a workers' culture. In some ways we wanted to rest on our laurels. A decade of scholarship in this arena had opened the door to an inclusive conception of what constituted the labor force. Culture served as an umbrella that incorporated race and gender, region and ethnicity, as well as skill. It had invigorated research into the preindustrial labor force and brought us closer to European forms of analysis. Stimulated by the work of E. P. Thompson, and sustained by a romance with anthropology, it had taken firm root among historians of the U. S. working class. Explorations of customs and ritual as they existed among different ethnic groups had produced rich troves of material detailing the lives of specific worker communities. Quantitative and anthropological techniques (including most especially the capacity for "thick description" popularized by Clifford Geertz) satisfied a thirst to know what happened on the shop floor, as well as at the family hearth, and they told us something of the connection between the two.

But, in the end, we never struggled with the meaning of culture.[8] We simply abandoned abstract Marxian conceptions of class and shifted to more comfortable Thompsonian versions without asking what, as a result, we had lost. In contrast to most interpretations of the 1960s (which defined *class* in terms of such abstractions as the relationship to the means of production and the consciousness that emerged therefrom), Thompson insisted on paying attention to social reality. Class, he asserted, was "a social and cultural formation, arising from processes which can only be studied as they work themselves out over a considerable historical period."[9] The definition extended a breathtaking invitation to explore class formation in historical context, but it carried the temptation of reifying the processes—of romanticizing the agency of working people and divorcing them from the power relations that created tension and change. Absent a way of understanding the class relations that inhered in culture, a cultural approach seemed merely to fragment our vision, instead of providing a mosaic on which to build. It failed to provide clues to the dynamic forces that sustained and resisted capitalism or to offer possibilities of a new direction.

Reluctance either to shape and focus the conception of culture or to abandon it encouraged a hovering question about whether we were not succumbing to nostalgia. Like the "workerism" of the 1960s, which held that a political program was implicit in the self-identification of an individual as a worker, the labor history of the 1970s and 1980s seemed dangerously close to romanticizing workers past.[10] Every lost or broken tool could be interpreted as an act of sabotage, every stolen cigar or day off as an act of resistance. Sabotage and resistance were seen less as elements that shaped class relations, than as attempts to preserve self, family, and community in the face of structural economic change. They did not so much actively resist capital, as they provided an unstable (and readily destroyed) bulwark against it.

Culture seemed to have become a way of evading class rather than of enhancing our understanding of the relationships among production, consumption, and politics. It had all the trappings of an exploration of consciousness. As historians developed the notion, it did not neglect social action; yet, because it remained resolutely empirical, it was not connected to larger questions of social order. As a result, although it avoided the deadendedness of fights over abstractions, it did not increase our understanding of how the whole functioned. It carried none of the political vision or the abrasiveness of Marxian class. In the hands of historians, preserving tradition seemed to be the central interest of most workers, ethnic roots their most powerful loyalty.

Yet, despite our evident discomfort with the use of Marxian notions of class as explanatory categories, we neither abandoned them nor replaced them with a more coherent conception of culture as an active phenomenon. Instead, we tried to use class in a way that incorporated culture but without fully integrating the concept. One after the other, speakers pointed out that their ethnic group or region had been forgotten or not appropriately accounted for. Sometimes we did this humorously. Worcester, Massachusetts, the setting of Roy Rosenzweig's perceptive exploration of working-class leisure, became a playful code that symbolized both the new capacity to illuminate and the limits of the space illuminated. What emerged at the meeting was the question of whether, in engaging in extended explorations of process, we had not diffused the meaning of class, denuding it of teeth, without simultaneously offering another model of social change.

The result was that the history of the working class had become curiously vapid and unthreatening; our enterprise contributed little to understanding how culture was connected to ideology or shaped the distribution of power. Rather, the method lent itself to exploring how workers used democratic forms instead of shaping them, how they adapted republican ideas to their own purposes, instead of departing from them. Ironically, in revealing the enormous inadequacy of traditional views of class, we seemed to have shaped a new consensus—to have written a history of how workers colluded in the development of liberal capitalism rather than one of how they constrained or structured it.

The core of discontent at the conference surfaced around these issues. At one extreme, we heard David Noble insisting angrily that we had been betrayed, offered a culture without content, left intellectually impoverished. At the other, were those who still believed that uncovering the texture of American diversity lay at the heart of our enterprise and could not be abandoned lightly. But, in the center, there was groping. For some, these extremes came together in a common understanding that we had outgrown the reification of culture. Being a worker was not, as Eric Hobsbawm put it, the equivalent of "having a culture." Insofar as we agreed that culture was not simply a passive phenomenon but an active agent in the formation of behavior and values, we knew we had to struggle to understand the connection of culture to theory.

The problem lay in the perception of many that culturalist approaches had not simply led us astray, but that, in emphasizing differences among workers, they had revealed the curiously empty meaning of class. Although enhancing our capacity to describe, research into working-class culture had undermined our capacity for understanding working-class transformation. Our work revealed a Marxian paradigm that was neither rich enough nor complex enough to incorporate the cultural diversity we had uncovered. Eric Foner put it this way: "the 'culturalist' approach now appears inadequate as either a definition of class or a substitute for it. Producing a patchwork of local studies illuminating the diverse values and identities among working people, it has failed to provide a coherent overview of labor's historical development." And yet it did not solve the dilemma merely to articulate it. For, as Foner pointed out, "Nor does a return to a purely economic understanding of class, or to such time-honored paradigms as base and superstructure or 'false consciousness' seem likely to explain either the history or behavior of today's working class."[11]

The tension between the richness of description and the need for analytic categories to explain change proved insurmountable at the conference. Unwilling to abandon our own contributions and unable to substitute alternative analytic frameworks, the group broke up dissatisfied.

Yet, we could have moved in a more fruitful direction had we listened more carefully to those who advocated race, ethnicity, and gender as analytic categories. These notions, suggested by the culturalist approach, have theoretical meaning that, accommodated to each other and to class, offer to illuminate class relations and to suggest ways of bridging the gap between culture and power. I can best illustrate the opportunity that was missed in failing to merge these conceptions to that of class by looking at gender.

Tensions in the group rose high whenever the issue of gender entered the conversation. Identified by Eric Hobsbawm (along with the decade of the 1960s, Edward Thompson, and Karl Marx) as one of the four ghosts haunting the conference, gender became a symbol of things forgotten, of items for which we could not account. Wrongly, I think, even sympathetic conferees used it as a symbol of the culturalist approach—an anachronism with which they knew they had to deal but that refused to speak to more pressing questions of power and authority. In so doing, the group failed to distinguish between gender as a theoretical construct and its empirical manifestations as reflected in the history of women. A discussion of the practical implications of the idea of gender turned into a conversation about particular women and their particular forms of resistance.

Repeatedly raised by the female participants, gender was just as repeatedly passed over. In his summation, Eric Hobsbawm dismissed it saying that he was not sure that "there was any very clear idea of what is meant by this." He then took pains to reject patriarchy as a useful historical category and turned to women, as consumers, tertiary workers, and members of public sector labor unions. Moving from questions of gender to the specifics of what women did changed the terms of the debate, repeating once again an emphasis on the fragmented nature of the working class at the cost of exploring the issue of how a system of ideas functioned to shape class relations in the work force.[12]

Yet a discussion of gender (or race or ethnicity) could have enriched our understanding of the key issues into which we had become locked. Just as the history of blacks in the United States is both separate from and a part of the history of racism, so the history of women workers, which describes an aspect of cultural diversity, must be distinguished from that of gender. Gender functions as an analytic framework that is about women only insofar as they are its active subjects. Instead of focusing on women, or on men per se, a gendered exploration of the past explores how the social relations of men and women create and inhibit expectations and aspirations and ultimately help to structure institutions as well. Thus, a gendered exploration rests on an empirical base that can open the door to a system of ideas out of which reality is constructed.

I want to suggest that the concept of gender offers access to possibilities for understanding working-class culture, both as a material construct (in so far as we understand culture as consisting of behavior and traditions) and as a meaning system (the root of values and orientations that provide the basis on which people will act).[13] In this latter form, gender may provide a special service: first in demonstrating how notions of culture might participate in conceiving, shaping, implementing, and resisting state policy; and second, in providing insight into the maintenance of internal divisions among workers, and between workers and middle-class and elite groups, that help to unpack some of the ways in which an accommodation occurs between workers and the industrial process. I suggest, then, that fully integrating a cultural concept such as gender into labor history can illuminate both class formation and class relations.

In offering an analytic category for looking at the culture of working people that transcends class divisions, gender provides a way of enriching notions of class. A gendered analysis functions in a way analogous to class, although not independent of it. Like class, gender is ideational and normative—a creator of consciousness that can be expected to tell us something about an individual's world view, and a part of any individual's perspective of what is right or wrong, acceptable or not. Though one might ask whether gender has shared meanings that transcend cultural and class lines, it is fairly easy to describe its manifestations under specific historcal circumstances. And yet, gender, like class, is a process. Paraphrasing Thompson's definition of *class*, one could argue that gender is a "historical phenomenon" not a "structure" or a "category" but something that happens in human relationships.[14]

Unlike class, which is said to be rooted in the material reality and social relations of the workplace, gender is rooted in the material reality and social relations of the household (which is sometimes also a workplace and, in any event, never unrelated to the workplace). But since neither household nor wage work is independent of the other, gender participates in class formation just as wage work participates in gender formation. Recent scholarship illustrates the point. We learn from Mary Blewett that gender influenced the "form and context of work" among preindustrial and industrial shoemakers, shaping the way men and women divided jobs and related to the workplace. At the same time, the particular manner with which gender affected workplace struggle varied. Divisions between indoor and outdoor women shoe workers, for example, reflected differential family situations that conditioned the issues around which women would struggle and their perceptions of the importance of male alliances.[15] Together class and gender help us understand how the particular forms of labor struggle between male and female workers and their employers are influenced by the different needs and expectations of the men and women who are workers.

In a gendered approach, women are not merely introduced into labor history. Rather we begin to understand (more clearly at certain moments than at others), how ideology about male and female roles orders the behavior and expectations of work and family, influences the policies adopted by government and industry, and shapes perceptions of equity and justice. Because gender, like class, helps to construct consciousness, it operates at all levels—

in the process of household production, on the shop floor, within the family, in the neighborhood, and in the community—to shape the ideas that form the core orientations on which working people will act. The historian's task must include an analysis of how gendered perceptions contributed to certain kinds of decisions and actions.[16] It is not enough to argue that men and women experience a social transformation in different ways. By demystifying seemingly natural roles, a gendered interpretation contributes to understanding how work (waged and unwaged) is organized, and it enables us to see how the larger political values and purposes of the society have been developed.

Many of the crucial concepts around which labor historians have organized their work have clear gendered content but are neither utilized nor understood that way. Compare, for example, the content of republicanism as it appears in the work of Sean Wilentz and the same word as it is used by Linda Kerber.[17] In the former it describes direct participation in the polis and incorporates ideas of citizenship and virtue that, by dint of their public content, exclude women. The ideal of "possessive individualism" is legitimated as a way of achieving the respect required for participation in the polis, and the search for the common good becomes a by-product of enhanced self-esteem. In Kerber's analysis the public end or good of the commonweal predominates. The content of republicanism is defined by women's attempts to find a voice in a revolutionary, preindustrial society, and the idea is defined with respect to gendered conceptions of order, hierarchy, household, work, and education. In the one case, the emerging content of republicanism is defined by pride in craft and the possibilities for independence and equality embedded in the rewards of skilled work. In the other, its content reflects the constraints of the household as well as the pivotal place of community norms in the search for the common good. Tensions within republicanism reflected these dual meanings and shaped how men acted in the public arena.

Gendered ideas help to explain transformations in other key ideas as well. The idea of free labor rested on the notion that ownership of productive property yielded the independence necessary to participation in the public realm. Citizenship, like skilled work, were both incontestably male. In the post-Civil War battle that transformed this conception into the doctrine of liberty of contract, or the right to sell one's own labor, workers' capacity to defend their right to independence and dignity in the courts vanished. Not accidentally, however, these ideas find their way into arguments for the dignity of women, who, as wards of the state, are permitted even encouraged to retain vestiges of the social conceptions of independence and equality that characterized free labor. The doctrine of equal rights is modified by notions of domesticity and in turn modifies them. Susan Levine effectively demonstrates the capacity of domestic ideals to transform a doctrine of equal rights into collective action.[18] And gendered ideas are apparent in descriptions of manliness at work—a key element in working-class resistance at the end of the nineteenth century.[19] But if notions of manliness helped to maintain the unity of the artisan class, they could also, as Pat Cooper has shown, foster an exclusivity that helped to destroy the unifying organization.[20]

Gendered ideas tell us something about both sides of the power equation. They reveal how custom, expectations, and ideology with regard to sex roles affect the choices men and women make, as well as their willingness to undertake certain kinds of waged and unwaged work. And they tell us something about how the structures of power (religious and educational institutions, corporate bureaucracy, and government agencies) touch ordinary people in ways that create and affirm acceptable behavior and condition expectations. The social and economic policies adopted by the United States during World War II spring immediately to mind. Their explicit messages about the propriety of wage work for certain women and implicit support for the sexual division of labor reflected a general (though not universal) consensus about the roles of men and women.[21] Wartime needs notwithstanding, they protected the positions of men. Thus, gendered ideas can tell us something about the collusion of men across class lines in the interest of affirming a meaning system that transcends class itself.

At the same time, how gendered systems are preserved in different class contexts tell us something about how class divisions are maintained and how the process of class formation occurs out of the indivisible reality of home and workplace. We have begun to understand, for example, how the changing system of production in antebellum United States produced a shared understanding of "women's proper place," or an ideology of "true womanhood," that played a powerful part in perpetuating traditional roles for women while they simultaneously pushed men into commerce and manufacturing and, thus, toward a more rapid acceptance of the modern world. At the same time, the capacity of wage-earning women to resist that ideology was to some extent undermined by working men, who not only had a stake in keeping their wives at home but who had an overriding interest in legitimating and protecting their work-force positions. As Christine Stansell's *City of Women* demonstrates, an oppositional ideology flourished among women outside the workplace and was sustained by community and neighborhood norms.[22] We know that the sexual and work behavior of women quickly became an important indication of class position and a factor in shaping class identification and control mechanisms.

Within the framework of gender analysis, the language of sexuality (in both its literal sense and its symbolic usages) emerges as a code for family structure, class division, and notions of respectability that bind working-class women from certain ethnic and racial groups to particular kinds of home roles and that can serve as a metaphor for such middle-class values as thrift and self-discipline. How far was the capacity of the elite to identify workers as "other" and to brutally suppress resistance derived from perceived differences between their own home lives and those of workers?[23] One could go on. We need to know more, empirically, about where and how ideas of the family wage are rooted in the development of a self-reinforcing ideological syndrome that had controversial effects on the structure of male-female wages and on the development of social policies that enshrined them. These illustrations suggest that class is not merely conditioned by gender, but that gender (like ethnic allegiance or race in the United States) constitutes the bricks and mortar out of which class is constructed.

At another level, the values revealed by a theoretical construction of gender challenge the dominant ethos of liberal capitalism. One example should suffice. Central to capitalism's legitimacy in the United States in the late nineteenth and twentieth centuries has been the possibility of upward economic mobility. The constellation of qualities surrounded by the success ethic and an aggressive individualism is rooted in and reinforces notions of the free labor market on which it is built. The material and political equality for which Americans sacrifice so much and that they defend in war and peace is rationalized by a meritocratic ethic that holds that everyone has the chance to move up toward wealth, status, and fame. But women's historical experience (more clearly than that of people of color, because women share the class position of their male kin) calls into question the existence of a free market for labor and thus raises questions about the legitimacy of the egalitarian ethic. In so doing, it challenges some of the fundamental ideas by which we live. Describing the occupational structure of the labor force, then, requires paying attention to the issue of the effect of women's presence in the labor market on the idea that equality of opportunity is generally available. The practical effect of this understanding appears in the political campaigns for demands such as protective labor legislation for women, but not for men, in the early twentieth century and contemporary demands such as government subsidized child care, comparable worth, and affirmative action.

Issues of gender encourage us to think about the unity of home and work and explore the values on which people act and at what level of consciousness. Interdisciplinary perspectives and an analysis of gender difference raise questions about the commonality of interests among men of all classes transcending, at least at certain times, the class interests of working men and women. Heidi Hartmann suggested many years ago that the shared manliness of employer and employee contributed to occupational segregation and to the inability of trade unions to organize and represent women effectively.[24] But, trade unions that fail to represent the interests of a large segment of workers, undermine class cohesion and response.[24] Theories of gender difference offer a mechanism that explains why, although it made little economic sense to exclude women from certain forms of production, employers and women workers themselves have at times colluded in doing so in obedience to a shared understanding of culture. The resulting labor market segregation affirmed women's dependence while contributing to arguments for men's power in the family and workplace.

The use of concepts like gender to translate culture from neighborhood to nation, to distinguish between discrete behavior and ideological overlay, moves culture from a passive, descriptive position to active agency. It illuminates how ideas about the social roles of men and women helped shape particular historical processes like proletarianization and class formation. It joins issues around a new series of questions. How does a gendered ideology (as opposed to women's behavior) alter the consciousness and expectations of male and female workers in ways that make it more or less likely that they will identify with other workers in sustaining and opposing dominant values and interests? How do gendered expectations around work and family lives create or inhibit structures of work for both men and women? How do they participate in conceiving forms of resistance and accommodation? How do they manifest themselves in divisions and alliances among workers? On the other side of the equation, how do institutions accommodate and utilize gendered perspectives to create privilege, to act as models of exclusion, or to promote competition?

Let me speculate about a familiar example in this context. For years, we debated Werner Sombart's famous question "Why is there no socialism in America?" without reference to gender. Yet, when all the arguments are said and done, and we have explored the absence of labor parties, the existence of opportunity, and immigrant ambition to death, we will still have to ask whether the shifting gender relations that were characteristic of late nineteenth and early twentieth century America are not as much part of the answer to that question as anything else. One notes such things as the incentive offered by an egalitarian spirit to cross class alliances of women that provided vents for despair, the immense desire for home ownership as a mechanism of family survival, and normative codes that restricted wage work for women whose families aspired to mobility—all of which played a special role in the United States. And we could argue that the roots of state action to defuse the worst features of industrialism and accommodate working-class protest originated in such female-based and sometimes wrong-headed voluntary organizations as those that fought for urban playgrounds, sanitation, and protective labor legislation in the workplace; for sexual morality, access to birth control information, and child-rearing manuals in the home; and for assimilation in immigrant communities.

How does this help us to think about labor history, to integrate and understand the relationship of workers to the state? Just as we earlier agreed that labor history is not only about the labor movement, so we seem to have come to the conclusion that labor history is not simply about workers, waged and unwaged. It is about class formation and the emergence of class relations, understood as a political and cultural as well as an economic process. But, as such, it must take account of the central organizing principle of human life, the sexual division of labor, and all that that implies for social relations. This principle is not simply subsumed into class once the process of industrialization begins but persists thereafter. We have begun to explore how it is manifested in the dynamics and feelings of workers. We know far less about how it is incorporated into the institutions, laws, and policies that frame the conditions within which workers struggle. Nor do we understand how the pressure of shared gendered assumptions can modify male behavior, inhibit class resistance, invoke sympathy, and so on. Analyses that utilize this central tension will be both richer and more productive.

To omit this tension—to assume a shared set of interests between men and women—is to overlook a key source of dissension and division within the working class, as it evolves and as it attempts to resist the control of capital.[25] And it is also to ignore a key factor in the maintenance of class relations. Acknowledging gendered divisions, in contrast, opens the door to empirical research into how divisions work—who takes advantage of them and when; who benefits; who suffers—as well as into such issues as the meaning of the provider role. These divisions teach us something of the dynamics of working-class life absent when shop-floor relations alone are the subject of empirical research.

The process by which gendered differences emerge and the political role they play is often blurred by virtue of their seemingly "natural" existence. Exposing these differences to examination opens questions of ideological influence within classes and among groups; and the process provides access to methods (like the analysis of symbolic language) that reveal something of the roots of behavior and tradition and thus touch directly on the relationship of culture to power.

I want, then, to suggest that in so far as a labor history embedded in the culture of workers has reached a theoretical stasis, it is in the interests of labor historians to shift the focus from explorations of culture as description to explorations that confront the issue of why power has been so elusive. Not culture itself but the process of transformation becomes the object of our enterprise. To do this in a manner that respects the self-experience of ordinary people requires an analysis of the major components of their cultural meaning systems. Among these, gender stands out. At the same time, since gender is such a crucial part of the meaning system of almost everybody, it behooves us to investigate the role it has played in shaping and regulating institutions of power. If we could do so, we might provide a way of thinking about U.S. history that transcends the working class and that could serve as a model for thinking about race and ethnicity as well.

It is arguable that, had we confronted gender, we would have been pulled into thinking about some of the larger issues of social process. Women historians at the conference were not alone in pressing the claims of their special group. Nor need the central importance of gender undermine the validity of thinking about the nation as a whole as a part of a culture-power nexus. Those who had studied ethnic groups, regions, and race insisted that each group provided access into problems that seemed discrete but were in fact common to all. The point is they were right. An emerging synthesis must be not merely respectful of culture but cognizant of its active role in shaping work-related values, attitudes, and behavior. It must also be fully aware of competing values. The use of gender, race, ethnicity, and region are crucial as analytic categories for demystifying the work force, putting cultural content into class, and clarifying the relationship between class and social action. Gender may be only the clearest and, perhaps, the most persuasive example. Thus, it was especially disappointing when conference participants converted gender into the readily dismissable examples of women and the controversial issue of patriarchy.

However we stood on the issues, tension and disappointment were the inevitable consequences of our failure to resolve the pressing questions of our field. In headier moments, labor historians believed the dynamism of American history could be explained by ordinary people acting in their unions, their communities, and their workplaces. The meeting did not dispell that notion so much as it forced us to construct a framework to support it. The challenge we failed was the challenge to translate the language, symbols, and celebrations that constituted the visible manifestations of what we call culture into viable interpretations of class formation and speculation about the structure and activity of the state.

The struggle to construct theoretical approaches that speak to the richness of our historical data is infused by on-going conflicts within industrial society. Ethnicity, race, religion, and gender are the central features of that debate. They will continue to inform our discussions and to challenge our understanding of the relationship of class to working-class culture, and they will provide us with an opportunity to broaden our perspective. One conferee suggested that writing a history of American labor might, in the end, be nothing less than writing a history of American capitalism. Another noted that there was no possible synthesis of American history without a synthesis of labor history. I suspect that both are right. And I suspect, too, that both the frustration and the contribution of this effort at synthesis was its revelation that labor history, in grappling with the broader questions of social history (power, politics, and the state), has moved from the periphery to the center of the debate.

NOTES

1. Michael Frisch, "Sixty Characters in Search of Authority: The Northern Illinois University NEH Conference," *International Labor and Working Class History* 27 (September 1985): 101.

2. Eric Foner, "Labor Historians Seek Useful Past," *In These Times* (December 12–18, 1984): 11.

3. A good summary of this position can be found in Ira Berlin, "Introduction: Herbert Gutman and the American Working Class," in Herbert G. Gutman, *Power and Culture: Essays on the American Working Class* (New York, 1987), pp. 3–69.

4. See David Gordon, Richard Edwards, and Michael Reich, *Segmented Work, Divided Workers: The Historical Transformation of Labor in the United States* (Cambridge, 1982).

5. Troublesome issues surrounding social history were raised by Herbert Gutman in "The Missing Synthesis: Whatever Happened to History?" *The Nation* 233 (1981), pp. 521, 553–54. For full scale critiques, see Eugene Genovese and Elizabeth Fox-Genovese, "The Political Crisis of Social History: A Marxian Perspective," *Journal of Social History* 10 (Winter 1976): 205–20; Gertrude Himmelfarb, *The New History and the Old* (Cambridge, MA, 1987), especially Chapter 1; and Theodore S. Hamerow, *Reflections on History and Historians* (Madison, WI, 1987).

6. Sean Wilentz, *Chants Democratic: New York City and the Rise of the American Working Class, 1788–1850* (New York, 1984); and see the critique by John Patrick Diggins, "Comrades and Citizens: New Mythologies in American Historiography," *American Historical Review* 90 (June 1985): 614–38; together with Leon Fink, "The New Labor History and the Powers of Historical Pessimism: Consensus, Hegemony, and the Case of the Knights of Labor," *Journal of American History* 75 (June 1988): 115–36, and the roundtable that follows, particularly John P. Diggins, "The Misuses of Gramsci," pp. 141–45.

7. These progressive unions include Local 1199 of the National Health and Hospital Workers Union; the American Federation of State, County and Municipal Employees; and District 65, now a national local of the United Auto Workers.

8. Here, Herbert Gutman's absence from the meeting was crucial. Had he been present, we would not, I think, have been permitted to take the concept for granted.

9. E. P. Thompson, *The Making of the English Working Class* (New York, 1963), p. 11.

10. A point made by Eric Hobsbawm at the meetings.

11. Foner, "Labor Historians Seek Useful Past."

12. For an elaboration of the usefulness of gender analysis, see Joan Scott, "Gender: A Useful Category of Historical Analysis," *American Historical Review* 91 (December 1986): 1053–75; and see as well Sally Alexander, "Women, Class and Sexual Difference," *History Workshop*, no. 17 (Spring 1984): 125–49, and the unpublished essay of Ava Baron, "Gender and Labor History: Notes towards a New Historical Look at Women, Men and Work."

13. I have borrowed the notion of a meaning system from Frank Parkin, *Marxism and Class Theory: a Bourgeois Critique* (New York, 1979), pp. 44–46.

14. Thompson, *Making of the English Working Class*, p. 9.

15. Mary Blewett, *Men, Women and Work: Class, Gender and Protest in the New England Shoe Industry, 1790–1910* (Champaign, IL, 1988), p. 320. Blewett's interpretation should be contrasted with that of Alan Dawley, *Class and Community: The Industrial Revolution in Lynn* (Cambridge, MA, 1974). See also Susan Porter Benson, *Counter Cultures: Saleswomen, Managers, and Customers in American Department Stores, 1890–1940* (Champaign, IL, 1986), and Sallie Westwood, *All Day, Every Day: Factory and Family in the Making of Women's Lives* (Champaign, IL, 1985).

16. For example, I find inadequate the caveat offered by Ira Katznelson and Aristide Zolberg, *Working Class Formation: Nineteenth Century Patterns in Western Europe and the United States* (Princeton, NJ, 1986), p. 4. Although the authors apologize for omitting a discussion of the consequences of industrial transformation for women, they fail to acknowledge that to appreciate the process of transformation requires an understanding of gender.

17. Sean Wilentz, *Chants Democratic*, Chapter 2; Linda Kerber, *Women of the Republic: Intellect and Ideology in Revolutionary America* (Chapel Hill, NC, 1980).

18. Susan Levine, *Labor's True Woman: Carpet Weavers, Industrialization and Labor Reform in the Gilded Age* (Philadelphia, 1984). On the idea of free labor, see especially William E. Forbath, "The Ambiguities of Free Labor: Labor and the Law in the Gilded Age," *Wisconsin Law Review* (1985): 767–817.

19. The idea is best developed in David Montgomery, *Worker's Control in America* (New York, 1979), Chapter 1; but see also Nick Salvatore, *Eugene V. Debs: Citizen and Socialist* (Champaign, IL, 1982).

20. Patricia A. Cooper, *Once a Cigar Maker: Men, Women and Work Culture in American Cigar Factories, 1900–1919* (Champaign, IL, 1987), p. 156.

21. See Ruth Milkman, *Gender at Work: The Dynamics of Job Segregation by Sex during World War II* (Champaign, IL. 1987); Ruth Roach Pierson, *"They're Still Women After All": The Second World War and Canadian Womanhood* (Toronto, 1986).

22. Christine Stansell, *City of Women: Sex and Class in New York, 1789–1860* (New York, 1986).

23. The best illustration here is Rebecca Harding Davis's novel, *Life in the Iron Mills* (Old Westbury, CT, 1972). And see also the animal-like representations of workers reproduced in the film, "The Grand Army of Starvation," produced by the American Social History Project.

24. Heidi Hartmann, "The Unhappy Marriage of Marxism and Feminism: Towards a More Progressive Union," *Capital and Class* (Summer 1979): 1–43.

25. A parallel argument was made for the history of race and racism by Barbara Fields at the meeting. Fields suggested that in addition to looking at the history of race as the history of black people, we also need to ask what it tells us about the development of an economy based on relations between black and white people.

Contributors

DAVID BRODY is a professor of history at the University of California, Davis. He is the author of *Steelworkers in America: the Nonunion Era* (1960), *Workers in Industrial America: Essays on the 20th Century Struggle* (1980), and numerous other articles and books on American labor and social history. He is also coeditor of the Working Class in American History Series at the University of Illinois Press and a board member of *Labor History*.

MARI JO BUHLE currently holds a joint appointment in American civilization and history at Brown University. She is coeditor of *The Concise History of Woman Suffrage* (1978) and author of *Women and the American Left: A Guide to Sources* (1983). She is currently working on an encyclopedia of the American Left, writing sections of a general textbook in U.S. history, and serving as editorial advisor to the University of Illinois Press series on women in American history.

ALAN DAWLEY is distinguished research professor at Trenton State College. He is the author of the Bancroft Prize-winning book *Class and Community: The Industrial Revolution in Lynn* (1976) and articles on American social and labor history. He is currently completing a manuscript, "Struggle for America: The United States, 1889–1936." He is a former senior lecturer in American labor history at the University of Warwick.

LEON FINK is on the faculty at the University of North Carolina at Chapel Hill. He is the author of *Workingmen's Democracy: The Knights of Labor and American Politics* (1983) and co-author with Brian Greenberg of *Upheaval in the Quiet Zone: A History of Hospital Workers' Union, Local 1199* (1989). In 1983–1984, he served as Fulbright guest professor at the America-Institute, University of Munich.

ALICE KESSLER-HARRIS is professor of history at Temple University, where she heads The Center for Studies of Women, Work, and Society. She is the author of *Out to Work: A History of Wage-Earning Women in the United States* (1982), and other books and articles on working women. She is currently engaged in an exploration of the transformation of the ideology of gender difference in twentieth century United States.

J. CARROLL MOODY teaches American labor and economic history at Northern Illinois University. A revised edition of his *The Credit Union*

Movement: Origins and Development, 1850–1980, coauthored with Gilbert C. Fite, was published in 1984. He served with Alfred Young as codirector of the Future of American Labor History conference on which this volume is based.

MICHAEL REICH is a professor of economics at the University of California, Berkeley. His publications include *Segmented Work, Divided Workers: The Historical Transformation of Labor in the United States* (1982), coauthored with David Gordon and Richard Edwards, and many other books and articles examining racial inequality, labor markets, and class structures. He is also co-editor of the journal *Industrial Relations*.

SEAN WILENTZ is professor of history at Princeton University. His prize-winning book, *Chants Democratic: New York City and the Rise of the American Working Class, 1788–1850* was published in 1984.

The Future of American Labor History

Toward a Synthesis
A Conference Held at Northern Illinois University
October 1984

CONFERENCE PARTICIPANTS

James R. Barrett
Susan Porter Benson
Ira Berlin
John Bodnar
Stephen Brier
Joshua Brown
Mari Jo Buhle
Bruno Cartosio
Alan Dawley
Thomas Dublin
Melvyn Dubofsky
Stanley L. Engerman
Paul Faler
Barbara Jeanne Fields
Leon Fink
Eric Foner
Michael Frisch
Gary L. Gerstle
Lawrence Goodwyn
James R. Green
Jacquelyn Dowd Hall
William H. Harris
Susan E. Hirsch
Eric Hobsbawm
Dirk Hoerder
Dolores Janiewski
John B. Jentz
Stuart B. Kaufman
Michael Kazin
Gregory S. Kealey
Alice Kessler-Harris
Bruce Laurie
Daniel J. Leab
Jesse Lemisch

Bruce Levine
Susan Levine
Walter Licht
Nelson Lichtenstein
Stephen Meyer
Ruth Milkman
David Montgomery
J. Carroll Moody
Gary B. Nash
Daniel Nelson
David F. Noble
Richard Ostreicher
Bryan Palmer
Carl Parrini
Richard Price
Jonathan Prude
George P. Rawick
Michael Reich
Roy Rosenzweig
Vicki L. Ruiz
Ronald Schatz
Peter Shergold
Martin J. Sklar
Judith E. Smith
Christine Stansell
Shelton Stromquist
Warren I. Susman
Barbara M. Tucker
Rudolph J. Vecoli
Daniel J. Walkowitz
Sean Wilentz
Alfred F. Young
Olivier Zunz